Supervision in the helping professions

Peter Hawkins and Robin Shohet

Open University Press

Open University Press
McGraw-Hill Education
McGraw-Hill House
Shoppenhangers Road
Maidenhead
Berkshire
England
SL6 2QL

email: enquiries@openup.co.uk
world wide web: www.openup.co.uk

and Two Penn Plaza, New York, NY 10121–2289, USA

First published 2006

A catalogue record of this book is available from the British Library

ISBN 10: 0335 218 172 (pb)   0335 218 180 (hb)
ISBN 13: 978 0 335 218 172 (pb) 978 0 335 218 189 (hb)

Library of Congress Cataloging-in-Publication Data
CIP data applied for

Typeset by YHT Ltd, London
Printed in Great Britain by Bell & Bain Ltd, Glasgow.

The McGraw·Hill Companies

Contents

Preface   ix
Acknowledgements   xii

PART ONE: The supervisee's perspective   1

1   'Good enough' supervision   3
2   Why be a helper?   8
3   Continuing to learn and flourish at work   15
4   Being an effective supervisee   32

PART TWO: Becoming a supervisor and the process of supervision   45

5   Becoming a supervisor   47
6   Maps and models of supervision   56
7   The seven-eyed process model of supervision   80
8   Working with difference – transcultural supervision   104
9   Supervisor training and development   125

PART THREE: Group, team and peer-group supervision   149

10 Group, team and peer-group supervision   151
11 Exploring the dynamics of groups, teams and peer groups   170

PART FOUR: An organizational approach   181

12 Supervising networks   183
13 Towards a learning culture   193
14 Developing supervision policy and practice in organizations   209
15 Conclusion: keeping our hearts and minds open   217

Glossary   222
Appendix 1   227
Resources   230
Bibliography   233
Index   247

To all our supervisors and supervisees, especially those who were with us in our formative years at St Charles House Therapeutic Community of the Richmond Fellowship

'Quis custodiet ipsos custodes?'
(Who will care and protect the carers?)

Juvenal, Satires, vi: 347–8

Preface to third edition

It is now over six years since we wrote the second edition of this book and 17 years since the original edition. As with the first edition we have been amazed and delighted by both the number of copies sold and the letters and responses we have received from people in a great variety of professions from all over the world. In addition, along with our colleagues, Joan Wilmot and Judy Ryde, we have taken supervision training into new settings. In the first edition our focus was predominantly on the fields of psychotherapy, counselling and social work. In the second edition we broadened out, having used the material for training in such settings as marriage guidance, local government, probation, and hospitals. Since the second edition we have been doing more supervision training and work in education, coaching, consultancy organizations, police and complex multi-disciplinary teams. In addition, we have been running trainings in a number of different countries and cultures including work with refugees and asylum seekers. These very rich experiences are reflected in the new material in this edition.

In each new setting, new questions and new issues have emerged. Over time we have come to realize some of the omissions, errors and limitations of our first two editions, and to recognize that both we and the world of supervision have moved on.

Writing a new edition of a book is very akin to having supervision. One has the opportunity to look back at one's previous work from a new perspective. One has the 'ouch' feeling on discovering mistakes made and then the opportunity to turn these failures into new learning for oneself and others. One has the joy of discovering new levels of meaning in what one previously said or did, but only half comprehended at the time, and the opportunity to apply learning from one context to a new time and to new settings.

In particular, we have been struck by how much the importance of supervision has been recognized in the intervening years. This is in part due to the more widespread acceptance of counselling which requires supervision, but also a recognition of the importance of supervision for all the people professions, whether they be educational, caring or developmental. Supervision courses have increased both in number and length. Ethical guidelines, systems of accreditation and professional standards have been established by a number of the professional associations. A number of professional bodies have been established particularly for supervisors, and supervision has started to become a profession in its own right. Research papers and supervision books have gone from famine to flood.

This combination of factors – our continued learning and development, the dramatic increase in interest, research and literature, and the feedback we have received have all led us to write a third edition. A further factor is the change in the social and political context. Local government, health, social work departments face increasing demands made on them often with shrinking resources. In some places their role has changed in emphasis from providing services to commissioning and registering services often provided by others. In the health service there has been constant change. Health trusts and primary care trusts have developed and been reconfigured with the numerous attempts by governments to increase both the quality and efficiency of the health services. Accountability has become increasingly prominent, as our culture moves towards increasing professionalization. This is paralleled in the field of supervision.

In this third edition there is a significant shift from the earlier editions. When we first wrote the original edition our focus was more on the therapeutic professions and the emphasis was on facing and using one's own shadow, including one's mixed motivation for being a helper and using awareness of one's own struggles to engage with others more fully. As our work has spread into the fields of education, organizational change and across many other people professions, we have balanced the above with a more developmental focus. This includes a greater emphasis on learning and building on the positives in order to flourish at work. The title of the conclusion has changed from 'The Wounded Helper' to 'Keeping our Hearts and Minds Open'. It is not that we just learn from our wounds, but that woundedness and learning are two inextricable strands of effectively enabling others. When we stop learning or believe we have finally sorted ourselves out, we become a closed system and, therefore, no longer of service to others.

We have kept the format of the book the same – namely the individual, group and organizational approach. We have inserted an extra chapter – Chapter 3 entitled 'Continuing to learn and flourish at work'. As the demands across all the helping professions grow, it becomes increasingly important to find ways of continually renewing ourselves throughout our working life. In this chapter we share approaches and methods for doing this both individually and collectively.

We have also enlarged Part Two of the book on supervision, taking account of the many developments that have happened in the field in the last 17 years. Chapter 6, 'Maps and models of supervision' includes new models on both the functions of supervision and a process model for understanding the stages of a typical session. There is also additional material working with metaphors and sensory modes as well a section on supervision research. In Chapter 7 we have revisited the 'Seven-eyed model', both refining some aspects and expanding others. We have also engaged with a number of the challenges and suggestions that other writers have made concerning this model, which is now very widely used. In Chapter 8 on 'Working with difference' we have added a new section written by our colleague Judy Ryde on working with refugees and asylum seekers, as well as new elements drawing on her doctoral research on working transculturally.

In Chapter 9 on Training supervisors we have written with our colleague Joan Wilmot a new section on using video and interpersonal recall. Drawing on the pioneering work of Kagan, use of these techniques has become a key aspect of our advanced training of supervisors.

In Part Three on supervising groups, team and networks, additional techniques for working with group supervision have been added as well as new material on understanding effective teams. This theme is picked up in Chapter 11, where we offer more ways of facilitating team reviews.

In Part Four on the organizational context, we develop the theme of learning, this time in the organizational settings. In Chapter 13, 'Towards a learning culture', we describe our more recent work using appreciative inquiry, with a case study of work in a school.

In this book we have aimed to retain our original freshness. We have kept many of the early chapters as they were originally written. We want to honour the continuing validity of our writing in the 1980s while expanding it with our later experience and updating it into the current context. What remains constant for both of us is that supervision and supervision teaching is an important part of our lives, and as long as we continue to work with people it will remain so. We hope the love and passion we feel and the pleasure we get from empowering ourselves and others will transmit itself through the theories, models and stories in this new edition of our book.

Acknowledgements

We would like first to thank the late Brian Wade of Changes bookshop for the initial idea of writing this book.

Much of the material on which this book is based has been developed over the last 30 years or more in the training courses in supervision we have been running through the Centre for Supervision and Team Development. Joan Wilmot made a substantial contribution to both the creation and teaching of these courses and has been a source of inspiration to us both. We would also like to thank others who have taught with us and the many who have attended these courses, both in the UK and internationally, from whom we have also learnt a great deal.

For this third edition we are particularly grateful to Judy Ryde who wrote much of the first draft of Chapter 8 on 'Working with difference' and the new section on working with refugees and asylum seekers, and Joan Wilmot who wrote the new section on the use of video. Both gave valuable help to other parts of this edition.

For the first edition many colleagues were very generous with their own ideas and experience of supervision, especially the late Frank Kevlin, Alix Pirani, Brigid Proctor, Helen Davis, Terry Cooper and Hymie Wyse. Mary Parker and Michael Carroll helped us find our way around the American literature on supervision.

For the second edition we also benefited greatly from those who have written books for our Open University Press series on 'Supervision in Context'; Allan Browne and Iain Bourne; Meg Bond and Stevie Holland; and Maria Gilbert and Ken Evans. Also Elizabeth Capewell who provided specialist advice on supervising those working in traumatic situations.

For the third edition we have also had an important contribution from Nick Smith who has co-authored with Peter Hawkins the new book on *Coaching, Mentoring and Organizational Consultancy: Their Supervision and Development*.

In preparing the text we have had enormous support from the administrative staff at Bath Consultancy Group, especially Lesley Bees.

Finally, we would once more like to thank our partners Judy Ryde and Joan Wilmot for their patience, colleagueship and support, as well as their important contributions to the writing of this edition of the book.

PART ONE
The supervisee's perspective

1 'Good enough' supervision

The late Donald Winnicott, paediatrician and psychoanalyst, introduced the concept of the 'good enough mother' – the mother who, when her child throws the food back at her, does not overreact to this event as a personal attack, or sink under feelings of inadequacy and guilt, but can hear this event as the child's expressing its temporary inability to cope with the external world. Winnicott points out that it is very hard for any mother to be 'good enough' unless she herself is also held and supported, either by the child's father, or another supportive adult. This provides the 'nursing triad', which means that the child can be held even when it needs to express his or her negativity or murderous rage.

This concept provides a very useful analogy for supervision, where the 'good enough' counsellor, psychotherapist or other helping professional can survive the negative attacks of the client through the strength of being held within and by the supervisory relationship. We have often seen very competent workers reduced to severe doubts about themselves and their abilities to function in their work through absorbing disturbance from clients. The supervisor's role is not just to reassure the worker, but to allow the emotional disturbance to be felt within the safer setting of the supervisory relationship, where it can be survived, reflected upon and learnt from. Supervision thus provides a container that holds the helping relationship within the 'therapeutic triad'.

In choosing to help, where our role is to pay attention to someone else's needs, we are entering into a relationship that is different from the normal and everyday. There are times when it seems barely worth while, perhaps because we are battling against the odds, or because the client is ungrateful, or because we feel drained and have seemingly nothing left to give. In times of stress it is sometimes easy to keep one's head down, to 'get on with it' and not take time to reflect. Organizations, teams and individuals can collude with this attitude for a variety of reasons, including external pressures and internal fears of exposing one's own inadequacies.

At times like this supervision can be very important. It can give us a chance to stand back and reflect; a chance to avoid the easy ways out of blaming others – clients, peers, the organization, society, or even oneself; and it can give us a chance to engage in the search for new options, to discover the learning that often emerges from the most difficult situations, and to get support. We believe that, if the value and experience of good supervision are realized at the beginning of one's professional career, then the 'habit' of receiving good supervision will become an integral part of the work life and the continuing development of the worker.

In the last 30 years there has been an enormous increase in the use of counselling and therapeutic approaches in many of the helping professions. This has in part been fuelled by the move away from more traditional forms of institutional containment to 'community care' for those needing help and support. This move has led to an ever-increasing demand, not just on families and relatives, but also on the whole range of helping professionals who have had to learn new ways of relating to the distress, disturbance and fragmentation of their clients. At the same time there has been an increased acceptance by the general public that most people need some form of counselling or professional support at certain stages of their lives.

This enormous upsurge in both counselling and psychotherapy, and in counselling and therapeutic approaches within many of the helping and people professions, has brought in its wake the recognition that such work needs to be properly supervised. The need for skilled supervisors, good training in supervision, and for theory and research in this area has increased much faster than the provision. When we first wrote this book there were very few books on supervision in Britain, and those that did exist were mainly limited to one profession. There was also a dearth of theoretical papers and descriptive accounts by those practising supervision. Only in the late 1980s did the British Association of Counselling start to look at the training and accreditation of supervisors and psychotherapy training institutes started to provide training courses in this crucial area of work. Since the first edition appeared in 1989, there has been an enormous upsurge in both publications and training in this area. This has included important books by Carroll (1996), Page and Wosket (2001), Brown and Bourne (1996), Hughes and Pengelly (1997) Bond and Holland (1998), Carroll and Holloway (1999), Gilbert and Evans (2000), Holloway and Carroll (1999), Inskipp and Proctor (1993, 1995), Scaife (2001), Fleming and Steen (2004), Hawkins and Smith (2006) and Shohet (forthcoming) as well as many others.

In the United States they have been concerned with this core area of practice for much longer. There has been a great number of American papers and books on supervision. However, much of the work has been within the discipline of 'counselling psychology' and has mostly centred around one particular model – namely 'the developmental approach' (see particularly Stoltenberg and Delworth 1987). Although this offers a significant contribution (see Chapter 5), it attends to only one of the many important aspects of the supervisory process. Holloway has done important work synthesizing American approaches to supervision and creating an integrated approach (Holloway 1995; Holloway and Carroll 1999).

The supervisor has to integrate the developmental role of educator with that of provider of support to the worker and, in most cases, quality oversight of the supervisee's clients. These three functions do not always sit comfortably together (see Chapter 5), and many supervisors can retreat from attempting this integration to concentrate on just one of the roles. Some supervisors become quasi-counsellors or coaches to their supervisees; others turn supervision into a two-person case conference, which focuses on client dynamics; others may have a managerial checklist with which they 'check up' on the client management of the supervisees. It is our intention in this book to help the supervisor develop an integrated style of supervision. We are not only advocating integration of the developmental, resourcing and qualitative functions, but also a supervisory approach which is relationship based.

Sometimes, even in the best supervisory relationships, there will be times of being stuck, of wariness and even of avoidance. For one reason or another, fear and negativity can creep in and it is useful for both parties to be able to recognize this and have tools for dealing with it. This book is addressed to both supervisor and supervisees, for we think that both have some responsibility for the quality of supervision; both form part of the same system geared towards ensuring quality of work. As part of taking joint responsibility for the supervisory relationship which we are advocating, we have given guidelines to check out the process, especially around the initial forming of a contract for the working relationship. This working contract can be very important as it forms the boundaries and baseline to which both parties can refer. We also emphasize how contracting is not just something that happens at the beginning of a relationship or even at the beginning of each session, but is also a process that needs constant revisiting.

Before entering this relationship, however, we believe that supervision begins with self-supervision; and this begins with appraising one's motives and facing those parts of ourselves that we would normally keep hidden (even from our own awareness) as honestly as possible. By doing this we can lessen the split that sometimes occurs in the helpers, whereby they believe they are problem free and have no needs, and see their clients as only sick and needy. As Margaret Rioch (Rioch et al. 1976) says: 'If students do not know that they are potentially murderers, crooks and cowards, they cannot deal therapeutically with these potentialities in their clients.'

Our experience has been that supervision can be a very important part of taking care of oneself, staying open to new learning; and is an indispensable part of the helper's well-being, ongoing self-development, self-awareness and commitment to development. In some professions, however, supervision is virtually ignored after qualifying. We think that lack of supervision can contribute to feelings of staleness, rigidity and defensiveness, which can very easily occur in professions that require us to give so much of ourselves. In extremes, the staleness and defensiveness contribute to the syndrome that many writers have termed 'burn-out'. Supervision can help to stop this process by breaking the cycle of feeling drained, leading to a drop in work standards, which produces guilt and inadequacy and leads to a further drop in standards. Supervision is also not just about preventing stress and burn-out but also enabling supervisees to continually learn and flourish, so they spend more time working at their best than would otherwise be possible.

Supervision, like helping, is not a straightforward process and is even more complex than working with clients. There is no tangible product and very little evidence whereby we can rigorously assess its effectiveness, although in recent years more research on outcomes has been carried out (see Chapter 6). One person brings to another a client, usually never seen by the supervisor, and reports very selectively on aspects of the work. Moreover, there may be all sorts of pressures on either or both of them from the profession, organization or society in which they both work. So, as well as dealing with the client in question, they have to pay attention to their supervisory relationship and the wider systems in which they both operate. There is a danger that both the supervisees and the supervisor can be overwhelmed by the degree of complexity and become like the centipede who, when asked which foot it moved first, lost the ability to move.

In order to encompass the complex interconnecting levels of the supervision process and yet write a book that is comprehensible, we have divided the book into four parts. In Part One we have addressed the supervisees with the intention of encouraging them to be proactive in managing to get the support needed to do their work. Helping organizations and managers have an important responsibility to attend to the well-being of their staff, but it is only the workers themselves who can ensure that they get the particular type of support that is most appropriate for them and their work situation. There is a danger that workers may see support as coming only from higher up in their organization and to fail to see that it can arrive from many different directions. Even within the supervisory relationship it is important that supervisees can find a way of being active in ensuring that they make the most of the relationship. In this section we have also included a chapter on the motives for being a helper, which is relevant for supervisor and supervisees alike. Also, we have written a new Chapter 3 on continuing to learn and flourish at work.

In Part Two we look at making the transition from working with clients to becoming a supervisor, the different roles and functions that are involved, and the maps and models that we have found useful. Some of the same ground as Chapter 3 will be covered, but from the point of view of the supervisor. Chapter 7 is an in-depth exploration of the various aspects and levels of the supervisory relationship. This is addressed particularly to those supervisors who supervise counsellors, psychotherapists or other professionals who are working in intensive therapeutic relationships (such as psychiatrists, psychologists, nurse therapists, etc.) but has also been used to train supervisors of coaches, teachers, parent educators and those far from the therapeutic world.

Chapter 8 is on supervising difference which addresses issues of power both from one's own role as well as from the cultural differences that can exist between supervisor and supervisee and client. These cultural differences may be rooted in such areas as ethnicity, nationality, gender, class, sexual orientation or professional background.

The section ends with a chapter that explores the training needed for different types of supervisors – for beginning supervisors; those who supervise students or trainees; those who supervise teams and those who supervise departments or whole organizations. This chapter is both for those supervisors who want to think about what training they need for themselves and also for trainers, heads of training and others who are responsible for providing training in supervision.

In Part Three we look at forms of supervision other than the one-to-one, such as supervision in groups, peer groups and in work teams. This section explores the advantages and disadvantages of supervising individuals in a group setting and some of the ways of managing the group dynamics. It also explores how to supervise teams in a way that recognizes that the team is more than the sum of the individuals contained within it.

In the final part we focus on how to help an organization develop a learning culture where supervision is an intrinsic part of the work environment. We have found that the organizational context in which supervision occurs has a major influence on the supervisory relationship.

Focusing on this wider context helps in understanding the wider system in which supervision occurs. This understanding can be useful in not over-personalizing a problem, which is also a symptom of the organizational dynamics and in realizing that it is not just individual workers nor indeed just work teams that need supervision, but whole helping organizations. In Chapter 12 we also look at the need for supervising situations where a number of professional helpers and organizations are involved, and the specialized skills that this requires.

We end with a chapter that pulls together the various themes of the book, keeping our hearts and minds open, with the theme of Chapter 3 on learning and flourishing at work. We viewed the four parts as increasing in complexity, starting with one person, the helper, followed by the supervisory relationship, then groups, and finally, organizations. However, we recognize that looking at our internal processes can be as complex as looking at the organizational dynamics, it just involves fewer people. This choice of topic and order has been meaningful for us, but our hope is that the actual topics become less important in themselves and become triggers for your own experience and action.

A notion that we take from Winnicott is that learning is most creative when it emerges in play. In the supervision that we give we try to create a climate that avoids the sense of expert and student both studying the client 'out there', and instead creates a 'play space' in which the dynamics and pressures of the work can be felt, explored and understood; and where new ways of working can be co-created by both supervisor and supervisee working together. Likewise, in this book we have shared our experience of the feelings, issues and possibilities of supervision in order to create more choices and options for both supervisee and supervisors, rather than provide set prescriptions.

We also recommend that you choose your own order for reading the chapters, for as we have indicated above, each part (and indeed each chapter) is addressed to a slightly different audience. However, we suggest that all readers start with Chapters 2, 3 and 4 as, no matter how experienced you are as a supervisor, or even as a trainer of supervisors, we all commonly share the need to look constantly at why we are in the work, how we get appropriate support and how we continue to learn and develop.

2   Why be a helper?

Introduction
Facing the shadow
Exploring our own motivations
The lust for power
Meeting our own needs
The wish to heal
Conclusion

Introduction

> With great puzzlement and a furrowed brow he said, 'I don't understand why you are so angry with me. I wasn't trying to help you'.
>
> (attributed to Wilfred Bion and quoted by Symington 1986)

Helping and being helped is a difficult and often ambivalent process. In this chapter we look at some of the complex motives for wanting to work in the helping or caring professions. Ram Dass and Paul Gorman (1985) write very beautifully about the motivations and struggle to be a helper. 'How can I help,' they write, 'is a timeless enquiry of the heart.' They go on to say: 'Without minimizing the external demands of helping others, it seems fair to say that some of the factors that wear us down, we have brought with us at the outset.'

We believe that it is essential for all those in the helping professions to honestly reflect on the complex mixture of motives that have led them to choose their current profession and role. (Shohet 2005: 8) For as Guggenbuhl-Craig (1971) writes: 'No one can act out of exclusively pure motives. The greater the contamination by dark motives, the more the case worker clings to his alleged objectivity.

Exploring these mixed motives involves facing the shadow side of our helping impulse, including the lust for power and how we meet our needs through helping others.

Facing the shadow

The role of helper carries with it certain expectations. Sometimes clinging to our roles makes it difficult to see the strengths in our clients, the vulnerability in ourselves as helpers, and our interdependence. As Ram Dass says (Dass and Gorman 1985): 'The more you think of yourself as a "therapist", the more pressure there is for someone to be "patient".' In choosing to start here, we are again saying that a willingness to examine our motives, 'good' or 'bad', pure or otherwise, is a prerequisite for being an effective helper. Aware of what Jungians call our 'shadow' side, we will have less need to make others into the parts of ourselves that we cannot accept. The crazy psychiatric patient will not have to carry our own craziness, while we pretend to be completely sane; in the cancer patients who cannot face their impending death, we will see our own fear of dying. Focusing on our shadow, we will be less prone to omnipotent fantasies of changing others or the world, when we cannot change ourselves (see also Page 1999).

One aspect of his own shadow – the wish for praise/adulation – happened to Robin while we were writing this book.

> I was running a residential therapy group abroad on my own. After a group member had worked on her feelings involving the death of a child, the group began to share at a very deep level, with one person's work triggering off another's. As the group facilitator I found the work both rewarding and moving as people resolved some of their deep pain. Staying with the process was for me tiring, yet paradoxically effortless in the way people's openness allowed their work to unfold. I could not remember any group which had consistently managed to face such trauma, and work through it successfully. At times like this I remember how privileged I am to be a witness to such work. At times like this ego creeps in. 'Look what I have done as facilitator.' After the fourth session we sat around for dinner. I missed not having a co-leader and was wanting the group to give me some validation for (my) wonderful work. Just then a wasp came and joined us. I ran. There was much laughter. 'So you are human after all.' I laughed too, but not before I had caught a feeling of resentment at being lovingly mocked and not revered.

How often we find ourselves caught in the shadow side of helping, letting ourselves and others think we are special, creating that illusion, and then being disillusioned when people want to take us down a peg or two.

The idea that we are helpers as opposed to a channel for help is a dangerous one. We want the praise for the success, but not the blame for the failure. Both of us struggle with the idea of non-attachment, telling students and clients who thank us for good pieces of work that it is not us, but themselves they should thank, yet secretly saying '. . . and me'. It is hard really to accept the possibility of being only the vehicle of help. Yet this acceptance is the only way to get off the roundabout of being addicted to praise and fearful of blame, and to stop ourselves lurching wildly between impotence and omnipotence.

Non-attachment does not mean not caring. On the contrary, it may be the nearest we can get to real caring as we do not have to live through our clients, dependent on their successes for our self-esteem.

In different ways we were given the opportunity to learn this lesson early on in our helping careers working in a residential therapeutic community. The supervisor of the home came fortnightly to supervise the head of the establishment and then to do a group supervision for all the staff. In one of these sessions the staff were engaged in an intense exchange around how to treat one of the residents. The supervisor stopped the discussion in its tracks by saying: 'You are not here to treat the residents, nor are you here to heal them or make them better. The job of the staff is to maintain the structure and keep open the space in which the residents can learn and grow. You are merely the servants of the process.' We had to learn (and are still learning) to give up the struggle for omnipotence, to let go of the idea that we were the ones that cured people, and learn the humility of being the caretaker of the therapeutic space.

Yet humility too is not without danger. The word 'caretaker' reminds us of a Jewish joke.

> One day a rabbi has an ecstatic vision and rushes up before the ark in his synagogue and prostrates himself, saying: 'Lord, Lord, in Thine eyes I am nothing.' The cantor [singer] of the synagogue, not wishing to be outdone, also rushes up to the altar and prostrates himself saying: 'Lord, Lord, in Thine eyes I am nothing.' The shamash [caretaker] sees the other two and decides to do the same. He rushes up and prostrates himself with the same words: 'Lord, Lord, in Thine eyes I am nothing.' Whereupon the rabbi turns to the cantor and says: 'Look who thinks he's nothing.'

Exploring our own motivations

A book that deals very succinctly and challengingly with the shadow side of helping is *Power in the Helping Professions* by Guggenbuhl-Craig (1971). He writes (p. 79):

> To expand our understanding . . . perhaps it is necessary to go more deeply into what it is that drives the members of these ministering professions to do the kind of work they do. What prompts the psychotherapist to try to help people in emotional difficulty? What urges the psychiatrist to deal with the mentally ill? Why does the social worker concern himself with social misfits?

Here is Peter's story in response to that question.

> I originally believed that I would work in the creative arts and that I was destined for a career in the theatre or television, but I was drawn away from performance to working in community arts, drama therapy and from there into mental health work. I worked with people who were actively psychotic, who had murdered, burnt down churches, were violent, suicidal, alcoholic etc. – the whole gamut of human anguish, distress and pain. In this work I found relief, which many of my friends found strange, but which I now know was the relief that my own buried disturbance, hidden and denied within my family, school and culture within which I grew up, now had an outward reality. It was all being played out in the therapeutic community in which I worked.
>
> Looking back I can recognize that I both did some very good work which came from a genuine wanting (and needing) to meet these people in their pain, but also I had, eventually, to move on from this work as I had not got to the stage where I could re-own the full depths of my own shadow disturbance that these clients were living out for me. I had not truly faced my own inner

murderer, my paranoid fear, my fragmentation, my despair. So I was unable to meet them fully as equals and was only able to come alongside in an unequal relationship where they carried the dis-ease and I was reinforced in my role of the coping, caring and containing worker.

The journey from facing my own dark inner self through others, back home to facing the shadow deep within myself has been and is a long and painful process. It isn't one simple cycle, but many small waves of discovering depths within others that I then need to go back and find in myself. When I was working as a psychotherapist I had a simple rule that if I found myself saying something more than twice to different clients, trainees or supervisees, I assume that I am also saying this to myself and I go away, write it down and explore it.

The lust for power

For most of us the answer to the question of 'why' would include the wish to care, to cure, to heal – an attraction to the 'healer–patient archetype'. Alongside this, however, may be a hidden need for power, both in surrounding oneself with people worse off, and being able to direct parts of the lives of the people who need help. Guggenbuhl-Craig (1971: 8– 9) also addresses this issue:

> In my years of analytical work with social workers, I have noticed time and time again that whenever something must be imposed by force, the conscious and unconscious motives of those involved are many faceted. An uncanny lust for power lurks in the background … Quite frequently, the issue at stake appears to be not the welfare of the protected, but the power of the protector.

This is especially difficult to recognize, because at times of having to make decisions about clients, or their children, the worker very often feels incredibly powerless. This contrasts markedly with the power that he or she has and is seen to have. Here is an example which demonstrates the discrepancy in feelings of power, the value of super-vision, and the relevance of understanding motives even when it initially appears irre-levant to do so.

> A client with a record of considerable violence threatened to kill his experienced social worker for removing his child from home. The social worker was under-standably anxious at this, the anxiety escalated and could not be held within a loose framework of supervision. I was consulted and felt inadequate to contain this life-threatening anxiety. I decided that the only way I could help was to concentrate on a thorough understanding of the dynamics of the case, although this hardly seemed to be the crisis response that was being asked for. With this focus, we began to understand the covert rivalry between the worker and the parent to be the better parent, and the murderous, unmanageable rage the client experienced when his inferiority was confirmed and concretized by the making of a Care Order. An appreciation of the rivalry served to contain the anxiety in the worker, the agency and myself by providing pointers to planning the work.

This served to release the anxious paralysis. The client, I am thankful to say, responded sufficiently for the situation to become diffused. I quote this example to illustrate my point that agencies concerned with public safety, and indeed the safety of their workers ... let supervision go at their peril.

(Dearnley 1985)

We have come to believe that this case is not as exceptional as it may first look. In our experience, once workers have made a shift in acknowledging some aspect of their sha- dow side – in this case the competition – there is very often a shift in the client right from the start of the very next meeting.

The issue round the potential misuse of power was put very simply by one worker: 'We dabble in people's lives and make enormous assumptions about what we do. We don't sit back and think about what it really means. We can create dependency, under- mine the client's worth ...' (quoted in Fineman 1985). This can be done on a very subtle level. Here is an example from one of our supervisees. It comes from weekly psy- chotherapy where a male therapist had been seeing a female client in her mid-30s for about 18 months.

The client's presenting problem at the therapy session was her difficulties at work. There was a staff member there who was very offhand with her, treating her almost like some kind of servant, and she could not confront him with his obnoxious behaviour, although she very much wanted to. It transpired that this allowing him to treat her like an object even extended to his going to bed with her whenever he wanted. She did not know how to say no, and at some level they both knew this, which is why he could treat her with such contempt.

During the session the therapist suggested that she made an agreement with him, if she wanted, not to sleep with this man for three months, and see if it made any difference to her relationship with him. The following week she came back and said she had felt a lot stronger in the way she interacted with this man, and was very glad about the agreement. The therapist was pleased, but some- thing did not feel right. He took the case to his fortnightly supervision, and realized that he had become just another man telling her what to do – perhaps with more benign intentions, but nevertheless undermining her. The fact that she had agreed to the suggestion and was happy with the outcome almost completely missed the point – namely her underlying problem in all relation- ships with men, which obviously included the therapist, was that she could not say no. The therapist knew that his suggestion was not a permanent solution, but had not realized how much he and his helpful suggestion was also part of the client's process of giving power to men.

In supervision the therapist faced the fact that it was the 'victim' part of himself which he felt so uneasy about that had prompted his rush into this premature intervention. He came to realize that rushing into premature solu- tions was his way of attempting to deal with his own fear of powerlessness. In doing what he had done, he was creating an unnecessary dependence on himself for a behavioural solution instead of doing his job which was to help explore a fuller understanding of how she repeatedly got herself into such situations.

Meeting our own needs

Another aspect of shadow we would like to look at is the helper's attitude to needs – their own needs, both of the job and of their clients. As part of our training we are taught to pay attention to client needs, and it is often difficult to focus on our own needs. It is even considered selfish, or self-indulgent. Yet our needs are there nonetheless. They are there, we believe, *in our very motives for the work we do*. As James Hillman (1979: 16) writes:

> Analysts, counsellors, social workers are all troubleshooters. We are looking for trouble, even before the person comes in to take the waiting chair: 'What's wrong?' 'What's the matter?' The meeting begins not only with the projections of the person coming for help, but the trained and organized intention of the professional helper. In analysis we would say that the countertransference is there before the transference begins. My expectations are there with me as I wait for the knock on the door.
>
> In fact countertransference is there from the beginning, since some unconscious call in me impels me to do this work. I may bring to my work a need to redeem the wounded child, so that every person who comes to me for help is my own hurt wounded childhood needing its wounds bound up by good parental care. Or the reverse: I may still be the wonderful son who would lead his father or mother out of their mistaken ways. This same parent–child archetype may also affect us, for instance, in the need to correct and punish an entire generation, its ideals and values.
>
> My needs are never absent. I could not do this work did I not need to do this work ... just as the person who comes to me needs me for help, I need him to express my ability to give help. The helper and the needy, the social worker and the social case, the lost and the found, always go together. However we have been brought up to deny our needs. The ideal man of western Protestantism shows his 'strong ego' in independence ... Needs in themselves are not harmful, but when they are denied they join the shadows of counselling and work from behind as demands ... Demands ask for fulfilment, needs require only expression.

It is not the needs themselves, but their denial that we believe can be so costly. In Chapter 3 we look more at the denial of needs, particularly in relation to support. Another need we would like to mention here, however, is the need to be liked, to be valued, to be seen as doing one's best, to have good intentions even if we sometimes have to make difficult decisions for the 'client's own good': in short, to be seen as the good guy. It is not easy for us, even after many years of working with people and attempting to face our shadow side, to accept a picture of ourselves, painted by a client, which does not correspond with how we see ourselves. It seems so unfair to be told that one is cold, rigid or misusing power. The temptations are either to alter one's behaviour to be more 'pleasing', to counter-attack subtly or otherwise, or stop working with the person for 'plausible' reasons. The ingratitude is sometimes hard to accept. We may find ourselves thinking, '... after all I've done for you', words we heard from a parent or teacher, and which we promised never to repeat.

One of the best ways we have found of accepting some of these negative feelings from clients (which usually have at least a grain of truth in them) is for us to remember how *we* feel as clients. We can also remember how in our own supervision, when we feel inadequate, we want to criticize our supervisors in order to make them feel as we do.

The wish to heal

It would seem from the above that it is almost worth packing it in. This chapter has been full of lurking power drives, needy children, unclear motives, hostility to parents. To think this would be to miss the point alluded to above – namely it is only the *denial* of needs, shadow, image, power that makes them dangerous. Knowing ourselves, our motives and our needs, makes us more likely to be of real help. In that way we do not thoughtlessly use others for our own ends, or make them carry the bits of ourselves that we cannot face. For we believe that the desire to help, in spite of the unclarity surrounding it, is fundamental, and agree with Harold Searles (1975) when he says that:

> Innate among man's most powerful strivings towards his fellow men, beginning in the earliest years and even earliest months, is an essentially psychotherapeutic striving. The tiny percentage of human beings who devote their professional careers to the practice of psychoanalysis or psychotherapy are only giving explicit expression to a therapeutic devotion which all human beings share . . . I am hypothesizing that the patient is ill because, and to the degree that, his own psychotherapeutic strivings have been subjected to such vicissitudes that they have been rendered inordinately intense, frustrated of fulfilment or even acknowledgement, admixed therefore with unduly intense components of hate, envy and competitiveness: and subjected therefore to repression. In transference terms the patient's illness expresses his unconscious attempt to cure the doctor.

In other words, the wish to heal is basic to helpers and non-helpers alike.

Conclusion

We have found that when we have been able to accept our own vulnerability and not defend against it, it has been a valuable experience both for us and our clients. The realization that they could be healing us, as much as the other way round, has been very important both in their relationship with us and their growth. It is another reminder that we are servants of the process.

Finally, we believe that we are only in a position to give when our own needs go some way to being acknowledged and satisfied: to give when we feel that we have something to give, and not just when the client demands, or when we feel we 'ought' to. This puts a lot of responsibility on helpers to be active in trying to satisfy their own needs and continue to learn. It is this we turn to in the next chapter.

3 Continuing to learn and flourish at work

Introduction
Self-renewal: developing and resourcing ourselves
  Be in love with learning. Stay at your learning edge and have a learning project
  Be clear about your learning style and keep expanding it – models of learning styles
  Attend to your emotional well-being
  Increasing your capacity to relate and engage others
  Attend to your physical well-being – diet, exercise, sleep, breaks
  Have a personal or spiritual practice
  Find a group of good co-learners and fellow travellers
Mapping your resourcing system
Stress
Burn-out
Post-traumatic stress
Conclusion: learning to live: living to learn

> Most teachers enter the profession passionate about their work, keen to make a contribution and experiencing the work as personally developmental. By mid-career, many of these same teachers are finding work a chore, have lost the joy of teaching and have stopped learning and developing.
>
> (Hawkins and Chesterman 2005)

Introduction

The statement above could be made for many doctors, social workers, nurses, clergy, counsellors and psychotherapists – indeed nearly all of those in the helping and people professions. In the first two editions of this book, this chapter was more focused on stress, burn-out and how to avoid it. In our continuing work with many of the helping professions we have paid more attention to the positive and preventative aspects of flourishing at work. In this we have been influenced by such approaches as 'appreciative inquiry' (Cooperrider et al. 2000, www.aradford.co.uk), organizational learning (Senge 1990; Hawkins 1986, 1994b), well-being at work (www.worklifesupport.com), 'spirituality at work' (www.spiritualityatwork.org).

We have still maintained some of the useful models and understanding of stress and burn-out, from the second edition, at the end of this chapter. However, we have found that the best way to deal with stress and burn-out is to avoid it! The best way is to start taking responsibility for our own well-being from the beginning of our work life. Then we need to ensure that we are constantly attending to resourcing ourselves in a way that helps us to flourish and rekindle the joy in our work.

This chapter appears in the section to the supervisee, but we think is very relevant for both supervisor and supervisee. As we mention later, a good supervisory relationship is where both parties are committed to ongoing learning and development.

Self-renewal: developing and resourcing ourselves

In Chapter 6 we describe the three functions of supervision as 'Qualitative, developmental and resourcing' – to improve the quality of the work with the supervisee's clients; to develop the competence and capacity of the supervisee and to increase their ability to resource and sustain themselves. Previously, this function was called supportive or restorative. We decided that the earlier terms had elements of defining the supervisee as needy or dysfunctional and needing to be restored to a previously healthy state. We would like to think in terms of self-renewal to connote the process of connecting ourselves to our inner source, the place from which our energy, creativity and compassion for others flows; and to refer to the resources that maintain us from without; our family, relationships, colleagues, learning, physical exercise and beliefs.

To be effective at work we strongly believe that is vital to be constantly learning and attending to how we nourish and sustain all aspects of our being. This is not an easy task when often the job demands so much attention to the tasks that are urgent and immediate, which is why we think it requires a conscious decision to commit to taking care of all aspects of our being.

In talking to friends and colleagues who have managed to continue learning and flourishing at work for many years we inquired into what they considered the important activities that maintained their inner well-spring – the place from which they constantly renewed themselves. The answers we received were very similar and we clustered them into seven areas:

1   Be in love with learning. Stay at your learning edge and have a learning project.
2   Be clear about your learning style and keep expanding it.
3   Attend to your emotional well-being.
4   Increasing your capacity to relate and engage others.
5   Attend to your physical well-being – diet, exercise, sleep, breaks.
6   Have a personal or spiritual practice.
7   Find a group of good co-learners/fellow travellers.

Be in love with learning. Stay at your learning edge and have a learning project

Patrick Casement writes that for psychotherapy to be really effective not only does the client need to change, but the psychotherapist also has to change through the process. He tells the story of a difficult client, to whom, on her last session, he said that he thought the most important contribution he had made to her therapy was that he had survived. Her reply was that the most important contribution was not that he had survived, but that he had just survived! To have been of value not only had he needed to enable the learning of his patient, but constantly to have been at his own learning edge. This is just as important in supervision.

Many of the people who stay flourishing at work, see their work as a key area of their personal development. They view work as something that feeds the rest of their lives, rather than a chore or a drain on their energy. This mind-set makes a rewarding time at work far more likely.

In our work we have written extensively about how one's effectiveness does not just increase through training and experience, but is linked to the rate at which you are learning (Hawkins 1986, 2005): if you stop learning your effectiveness starts to atrophy. Helping another always happens in a relationship and the learning is relational with all parties learning.

> Good supervision, we believe, should allow for a two-way flow in which both supervisor and supervisee are responsive to each other's input. Supervision therefore becomes a dynamic learning and developmental process in which both parties learn and grow together.
>
> (Page and Wosket 1994: 40)

In our training work we utilize a very simple but useful model of three zones – comfort, learning and panic (see Figure 3.1). When we are in our comfort zone, we start to go on automatic, we treat the person in front of us as another example of type x, rather than a unique individual who requires a unique response. In our learning zone, we are always working at the edge, the boundary between what we already know and what is waiting to be learnt. In the learning zone we need to be able to always return to a 'beginner's mind'.

> The willingness to be a beginner is an essential ingredient to being a good learner – no matter what your level of expertise. It is the willingness to 'not know' and to be comfortable with not knowing that makes children and adults able to learn without fear.
>
> (Gallwey 1997)

This attitude of being willing not to know can carry over in our approach to making mistakes and believing that we have to be perfect. Not knowing is not an excuse to avoid finding out, or a way of justifying a doubtful course of action, but an approach which says that it is not possible for me to know everything, or never make a mistake, and I can still value myself. With this attitude it is possible to learn more and, paradoxically, make fewer mistakes, as a more relaxed attitude keeps us open and alert. Certainly we will stress ourselves less as we accept our imperfections and do not pretend to be something we are not.

In our panic zone we are too far out of our competence and capacity depth, so we panic and retreat to safe ground of being in control, or in known territory. Learning requires us to be able to tolerate not knowing, being vulnerable, risking looking foolish or making mistakes. These states potentially can trigger feelings of powerlessness, inadequacy, shame, inferiority and anxiety, all of which can take us into the panic zone. Guy Claxton described the four beliefs that get in the way of adults' learning as being:

- I must be *competent*
- I must be in *control*
- I must be *consistent*
- I must be *comfortable*.

(Claxton 1984)

For some people there is a very narrow band between comfort zone and panic zone so very little space for learning. With support and practice we can widen the learning band and increase our tolerance for being in the place of incompetence, out of control, inconsistent and uncomfortable and spend more of work life in the zone of learning.

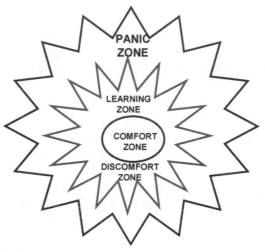

Figure 3.1 Increasing the learning zone

Be clear about your learning style and keep expanding it

Different people learn in very different ways. As you read this book, some of you will like the models and find they open up new ways of thinking about the field, for others the models might be baffling and they will find the stories and short case vignettes the most illuminating. For others, you will be taking the exercises mentioned and going off and doing them for yourselves. Some people will learn best not by reading this book, but by talking about it to others.

It is very useful to know about your own learning style, otherwise it is all too easy to feel inadequate when you find that others learn far faster than you in certain types of learning situations. Also, we all have a tendency to believe that others learn the way we do. Thus one of us (Peter) will provide more frameworks than most people can digest and the other (Robin) will tell stories, leaving some hungry to know how this connects with the wider theory! (See also Ryan 2004)

Your learning style is related to your sensory mode dominance (see Chapter 6). Some people learn to read through seeing whole words (visual), others through the phonetic sounds (auditory), while others learn by associating the word to a movement or feeling (kinaesthetic).

So it is important to answer the questions: 'How do you best learn?' and 'What have been your best learning experiences?'

A supervisee reported that one of his biggest learning breakthroughs was learning to swim at the age of 33, having previously been terrified of going out of his depth. He realized that the scene had been set in the first two minutes. The instructor looked at him and said, 'Get your head into the water and kick.' Very simple. But his tone of voice was such that the supervisee felt immediately that the instructor knew how scared he was and was gently but firmly going to contradict his fear. He sensed the instructor did not have anything to prove and was comfortable in his ability to teach and that his fear was going to be less powerful than the instructor's authority. And so it proved.

He said that this helped him to realize that what he needed from the supervisor was a person who: (a) knew what they were doing and enjoyed it; and (b) had nothing to prove and could lovingly bypass all the obstacles the supervisee was going to put in their way. The supervisee, in turn, needed to feel that they were seen and understood, and to know that any failures or resistances would not threaten the supervisor.

Models of learning styles

Kolb et al. (1971), Juch (1983), Revans (1982) and others have developed approaches that demonstrate that learning is richest when it follows a cycle that incorporates action, reflection on the action, new sense making and theorizing and then planning new action. This is sometimes referred to as the 'Cycle of Action Learning' (see Figure 3.2).

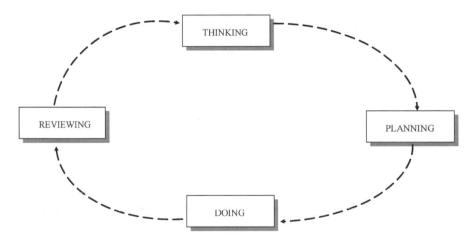

Figure 3.2 Action learning cycle

Different individuals have different learning styles, which affects where they are most comfortable starting on the learning cycle. Some prefer to start with practical action and then reflect on what does or does not work through reflection. Others like to have the theory and explanation before working out how to apply the model in action. Honey and Mumford (1992) have developed a number of methodologies for people to ascertain their learning styles and explore both how to utilize their dominant preference and to expand their repertoire of learning possibilities.

We have used this work to develop our own model of learning short circuits to help supervisees as well as those training in the helping professions to become more aware of their stuck learning patterns. There are five main limiting learning styles that we have identified.

1   *The fire-fighter: compulsive pragmatist.*   This is the plan – do – plan – do trap where the motto is: 'If what you plan does not work, plan and do something different.' The learning stays at the level of trial and error. This person does not reflect. As van Ooijen (2003) writes

> It is not sufficient to gain experience without also reflecting on what we experience in order to learn from it. Most of us can probably think of people who, despite having been in their professions for a long time, have not been in the habit of reflecting on their experience. As a result they do not appear to have learnt a great deal and may seem rigid in their approach to work. They seem to do things out of habit, and when challenged will say this is because 'We have always done it this way.'

2   *The post-mortemizer.*   This is the do – reflect – do – reflect trap, where the motto is: 'Reflect on what went wrong and correct it.' The learning here is restricted to error correction.

3   *The navel-gazing theorist.*   This is the reflect – theorize – reflect – theorize trap, where the motto is 'Philosophize on how things could be better, but never risk putting your theories to the test.'

4   *The paralysis by analysis.*   This is the analyse – plan – then – analyse some more trap, where the motto is 'Think before you jump, plan how to do it and think a bit more.' Learning is limited by the fear of getting it wrong or taking a risk.

5   *The totalitarian.*   This is the theorize – do trap, where the motto is: 'Work it out in private and then impose it on them.'

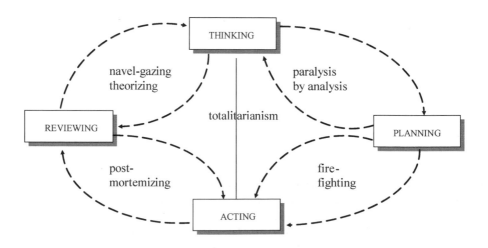

Figure 3.3   Learning cycle short circuits

Attend to your emotional well-being

To feel good about others, we also need to feel good about ourselves. Our own feelings of inadequacy, anger or distress get in the way of how we relate to others, or get projected on to colleagues or clients.

The BBC, in a recent large-scale experiment to increase the happiness and emotional well-being of a whole town, developed a happiness manifesto, much of which gives very simple and practical steps to increase your emotional well-being:

1 **Get physical**: Exercise for half an hour three times a week.
2 **Count your blessings**: At the end of each day, reflect on at least five things you're grateful for.
3 **Talk time**: Have an hour-long uninterrupted conversation with your partner or closest friend each week.
4 **Plant something**: Even if it's a window box or pot plant. Keep it alive!
5 **Cut your TV viewing by half**.
6 **Smile at and/or say hello to a stranger**: At least once each day.
7 **Phone a friend**: Make contact with at least one friend or relation you have not been in contact for a while and arrange to meet up.
8 **Have a good laugh at least once a day**.
9 **Every day make sure you give yourself a treat**: Take time to really enjoy this.
10 **Daily kindness**: Do an extra good turn for someone each day (www.bbc.co.uk/lifestyle).

Many of these we believe can make a real difference to your emotional well-being, but not all of them will work for everybody. You could build your own list using these as starter prompts.

Increasing your capacity to relate and engage others

At the core of all the helping professions is the capacity to relate to others. Often these will be people coming from very different backgrounds to ourselves and experiencing the world very differently. In Chapter 7 we write about how to work with difference in supervision, but this applies equally to our work with clients, patients, pupils or coaches. They become our teachers in finding new ways to expand our capacity to relate and engage. Our own family, children and friends can also be our teachers in new ways of relating, especially when we experience them as difficult!

In our work with teachers we wrote about four dimensions of relating (Hawkins and Chesterman 2005; Hawkins and Smith 2006). The first is our ability to broaden the range of people with whom we can achieve rapport. This involves moving beyond those who are like ourselves, to those from a wide breadth of different backgrounds, in gender, age, culture, personality type (see Chapter 8).

- Think of someone very different from you and with whom you would not naturally spend time. Make a conscious effort to find out about them and notice what happened to you.

The second dimension is the ability to stay very engaged with another without becoming reactive, when the relationship is full of difficult emotions. You may be being attacked, or restimulated by their distress or anxiety. It links closely with our first chapter where we talked about the good enough supervisor and the good enough worker, who can hear the communication of their client without becoming reactive to the client or feeling bad about themselves.

- Can you think of a time when your impulse was to defend or attack back and you did not. What were the reasons you decided to stay engaged? Did you use any special skills or strategies? How did it feel?

The third dimension is the level of the depth of engagement. Do you engage your clients (a) just about the problem out there, (b) their behaviours that are both part of the problem and also present in the conversation with you, (c) their mind-set or attitudes, (d) their feelings and reactions to the situation, or (e) their fundamental motivation or core beliefs?

- Can you think of a time when you did not just address the content of the problem, but went deeper and tried to connect with the other person's mind-sets or frames of reference, their feelings, their values and purpose. What questions did you ask? What was the result?

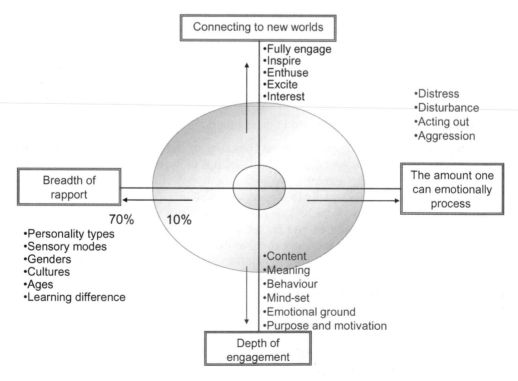

Figure 3.4 The four dimensions of relating

The final dimension is the ability to open new windows and doors for other people, to connect them with new worlds and possibilities. At its lowest level, this is the ability to interest another in an idea. This capacity proceeds through being able to excite another about a new possibility; enthuse them about a new direction; inspire them to take on new action or create a hearts and mind shift in how they engage with their work.

- Can you think of a time when you enthused or inspired another to enter a new world? What did you do? What made the difference? What was the result?

Attend to your physical well-being

Your body is the vehicle through which you think, feel, relate to others, carry out action, and yet many of us spend less time maintaining our bodies than maintaining our cars. To stay flourishing at work you need to be healthy. To be healthy requires a number of balanced flows in how we live:

- deep and balanced breathing,
- a healthy diet,
- quality sleep,
- refreshing breaks and periods of relaxation,
- different forms of exercise – swimming, jogging, anaerobic exercises, yoga and such like,
- connecting with nature.

Even simple things can make a difference. A number of our colleagues and supervisees have discovered the revitalizing effects of replacing their regular cups of tea or coffee with a glass of water or piece of fruit. Others described to us the difference created when they decided to cycle to work rather than queue for the bus, and others found that ensuring a walk in the fresh air at lunch time transformed the rest of the day.

It is also important to review how we use holidays and weekends as times of revitalization and renewal, and for each of us the answers will be different, which means that planning joint holidays with friends or family will often require careful negotiation.

Have a personal or spiritual practice

One important source of renewal can be having a personal or spiritual practice, which calms the mind, stills the body and provides inner space. Some workers get this from their religious affiliation, others through some form of meditation practice, or physical practice such as yoga or tai chi. We will illustrate the sustaining power of a simple spiritual practice with a personal story.

> One of us noticed that he was starting meetings in London irritated and impatient. He was treating everything, including the others present, as obstacles that had to be overcome. He reflected on this process and noticed that it started on his journey into London, where he was anxious about the train being late. He was rushing to the underground, getting impatient with the people in his way

on the escalators and stairs. He was fighting for space in the underground carriage.

He chose to interrupt this stressful process, with a simple spiritual practice of deliberately slowing down on the escalators, looking at each person coming in the other direction, and for each person, saying to himself: 'This is my brother, this is my sister, this is my child, this is my father, this is my mother', whichever was appropriate. He found himself arriving at meetings with a sense of delight and joy. His heart was open and he was ready to engage with the others who were present.

A personal or spiritual practice can also provide us with a sense of serving a higher purpose in our work, which can help us to be less reactive to the daily difficulties. If we see the whole of life as a learning journey, then difficult colleagues and clients each become our next teacher, the one who is most encouraging us to be at our learning edge, with all its discomfort and uncertainty.

A spiritual or religious belief can also underpin a strong set of values, which not only guide action but, in the midst of difficult times at work, give us a wider perspective. Some spiritual practices can also provide tools for interrupting our negative beliefs, helping us to move from blame to taking responsibility, from feeling hard done by to counting our blessings.

There has recently been a great deal of research on the place of spirituality at work, showing the positive benefits it can have both for the individuals and the wider organization: 'Research indicates that where organizations help people address their inner values and aspirations, morale is boosted and there are benefits to the bottom line' (Faith Regen 2005, referencing work by Weiler and Schoonover).

Find a group of good co-learners and fellow travellers

Most of those to whom we talked, who had sustained a flourishing work life in the helping professions for many years, referred to the important contribution of a few well-chosen colleagues. Some met informally, while others were part of established peer groups that met regularly, where they supported and challenged each other in their work and their development. Some of these were single gender groups, some mixed, some drawn from within one profession, others worked across a diversity of professional backgrounds.

Good colleagues can keep you honest and provide a way of interrupting your negativity or reactivity when you are unable to do it for yourself. One person mentioned having five minutes of 'BMW' with his peer group, which stood for: bitching, moaning and whingeing, as a way of discharging their built-up negativity. One of us has a long-term peer group that provides a form of co-mentoring, where each person has an hour to be fully listened to on their current state of transition and then receive encouragement and challenge. Such peer groups can also help you focus on what is important, as well as provide a safe place to discharge your emotions when times are tough. In Chapter 10 we provide some guidelines on setting up a peer group.

Mapping your resourcing system

As a way of exploring your own sources and resources that enable you to flourish at work we provide the following exercise.

We would like you to start by taking a large sheet of paper (A3 or bigger) and on it draw a map of your resourcing system at work. In the middle of the paper draw a symbol or picture of yourself. Within or attached to this symbol or picture represent symbolically the inner resources that sustain you in flourishing at work. Then around this picture or symbol draw pictures, symbols, diagrams or words to represent all the external resources (things and people) that support you in learning and being creative at work. These may be the walk to work, books you read, colleagues, meetings, friends, etc. We would like you to represent the nature of your connection to these supports. Are they near or far away? Is the link strong and regular, or tenuous or distant? Are they supporting you from below like foundations or are they balloons that lift you up? These are only suggestions: allow yourself to find your own way of mapping your resourcing system.

When you are satisfied with your initial map, we would like you to take a completely different colour and draw on the picture symbols that represent those things that block you from fully using these resources. It may be fear of being criticized or interruptions, or the relative unavailability of these resources. It may be blocks within you, within the support, or in the organizational setting. Draw whatever you feel stops you accessing the resources you need.

When you have done this, we suggest that you choose someone with whom to share your picture. This could be a colleague, partner, supervisor or friend, or even someone who has also done the exercise (you could get your whole staff team to do it!). When you have shared your picture with them, they should first respond to the overall picture. What impression does it create? Then they can ask you the following questions:

- Is this the kind of resourcing you want?
- Is it enough? What resources are missing? How could you go about developing them?
- What resources are essential for you to the extent that you must ensure that you nurture and maintain them?
- Which blocks could you do something about reducing?

Your partner could then encourage you to develop some specific action plans as to how you might improve your resourcing system. The action plan should include, what you are going to do; how you are going to do it; when and where you are going to do it; involving whom and the immediate first steps.

If there is no one that you want to share this process with, it is possible to do the exercise by yourself and ask yourself these questions, but it is much more difficult. But involving another is a good first step in proactively asking for support!

Stress

Even with a wide variety of ways of renewing yourself, we are aware that most people in the helping professions are stressed sometime during their careers. If we are taking good care of ourselves, this is less likely to happen, but we think it is useful to describe some of the symptoms and causes of stress.

We become stressed when we absorb more disturbance, distress and dis-ease from our clients and patients than we are able to process and let go of. We become overburdened by the work. Stress is not only absorbed from the clients but may also come from other aspects of the work and the organization in which we work. These stressors (factors causing stress) will in turn interact with our own personality and the stressors that are currently happening in our own life outside work. We can get caught into a negative cycle of stress making us less effective which gives us more stress.

Some stress is inevitable and can be positive in activating the body, mind and energies (Hawkins 2005). It can awaken our energies ready for action and for dealing with a threat or a crisis. However, so often in the helping professions the stressors of the work charge our mental and bodily systems ready for action, but there is no possibility for discharging this energy into action. We are left having to sit with the pain of the patient; or having to contain the frustration of not being able to secure the funding to meet client needs that we are in touch with; or having to cope with situations in which we feel undertrained or emotionally inadequate.

Stress that is not discharged stays within the body and can emerge as physical, mental or emotional symptoms. It is important to know your own tendencies for responding to stress, so you can be alert to the build-up of tension within you. In Table 3.1 we offer examples of some of the most common symptoms of stress, but suggest that you stop and make a note of the symptoms that inform you that you are overstressed. You might also take the opportunity to ask those who work with you, how they notice that you are under pressure.

Symptoms of stress can take many forms. Some like insomnia are loud warning bells. Others like turning to drink, overeating or over-smoking can be masked as they are part of the dominant culture at work: 'Everyone here gets pissed regularly – it's the only way we cope,' said one worker. Others such as pretending to care, or avoiding some clients, colleagues or situations can be hidden for some time. We would like to make clear that we may all occasionally go through phases where we over-indulge, avoid, or dislike our client group. We all go through phases when we put on an act. To feel that we have to be totally congruent all the time is unrealistic, and almost guaranteed to make us behave in an incongruent way, the very thing we were trying to avoid. What we are talking about is a chronic cynicism, despair or resentment about work or human nature which saps our energy, creativity and ability to be open to new learning. We go into this in more detail in the next section.

As an example of sharing stress, one of us (Robin) was working with a group of middle managers in a college of further education. There was considerable stress and anxiety, because many of them were likely to lose their jobs through cost-cutting, but it was not yet clear which ones. Robin started by saying that he guessed that there might be quite a lot of stress around because of the uncertainty, and he was interested to see if they

Table 3.1   Symptoms of stress

Physical
- Migraines or headaches
- Diarrhoea, indigestion, constipation
- Insomnia
- Over-tiredness
- Loss of appetite

Mental
- Inability to concentrate
- Compulsive worry
- Paranoid thoughts, seeing yourself as victim

Behavioural
- Pretending to care, and playing the role of carer, but the actions and feelings are incongruous
- Avoiding clients, colleagues or situations
- Turning to drink, overeating or over-smoking

Emotional
- Sudden swings in feelings
- Not wanting to get up in the mornings
- 'Floating anxiety'
- Hating clients

were willing to share some of their habitual ways of attempting to deal with stress, for example attack, withdrawal, alcohol, workaholism, over-responsibility, blame. Gradually they opened up and were able to not only name their own patterns, but recognize each others' patterns of coping. The level of trust in the group began to increase as they realized how everyone had different ways of coping. After the break the group was able to share specific anxieties and come up with a more collaborative strategy in what was potentially a competitive and anxiety-producing situation.

It is very important that, as helpers, we take responsibility for noticing the signs that our systems are overloaded: and that we ensure that we get the support, not only to deal with the symptoms of stress that are emerging within us, but also to tackle the cause of the stress. The earlier this is done the better. If we ignore the stress symptoms for too long then we are in danger of being overwhelmed and being left in a situation where the only things we can attend to are the resultant symptoms within us. When this happens we have entered the state that is often referred to as 'burn-out'.

Burn-out

The term 'burn-out' has become much overused in recent years. It has become the helping professions' equivalent to what the British army called 'shell shock' or the Americans 'battle fatigue'; what our parents' generation called 'nerves' and the present generation 'depression'. They become catch-all phrases that signify not coping. Burn-out is not an illness that you catch, neither is it a recognizable event or state, for it is a process that often begins very early in one's career as a helper. Indeed, its seeds may be inherent in the belief systems of many of the helping professions and in the personalities of those that are attracted to them (see Chapter 2).

Pines et al. (1981) define burn-out as:

> The result of constant or repeated emotional pressure associated with an intense involvement with people over long periods of time. Such intense involvement is particularly prevalent in health, education and social service occupations, where professionals have a 'calling' to take care of other people's psychological, social and physical problems. Burnout is the painful realization that they no longer can help people in need, that they have nothing left in them to give.

Fineman (1985) follows Maslach (1982) in saying that burn-out represents: '(a) a state of emotional and physical exhaustion with a lack of concern for the job, and a low trust of others, (b) a depersonalization of clients; a loss of caring and cynicism towards them, and (c) self-deprecation and low morale and a deep sense of failure.'

An earlier work (Hawkins 1986) explored another aspect of burn-out that is ignored in most of the literature, which is the apathy and loss of interest which develop in helpers who stop learning and developing in mid-career. They begin to rely on set patterns of relating to clients and patients and treat new clients as just repeat representatives of clients and patients they met earlier in their career. A preventative approach to burn-out needs to include creating a learning environment that continues right through one's career as a helper.

Edelwich and Brodsky (1980) explore how unrealistically high expectations of what can be achieved can create the background for the later development of disillusionment and apathy. Many professions also encourage their trainees to develop the image of themselves as heroic helpers who can continually provide for others, solving their problems, feeling their pain, meeting their needs, whilst remaining themselves strong and happy. This can be coupled with the personality of those attracted to such work who may have been the one who contained the pain and was always helpful in their own families.

The idea that we can help everyone was illustrated when Robin interviewed the editor of a medical journal in connection with a book he was editing. He was interested in the high rate of burn-out among doctors and the editor said that some of it could be put down to the doctors' training. They colluded with the idea that they were responsible for curing, so any failure was their fault. Combined with an idea that science can cure anything, the doctors allowed themselves to buy into an omnipotent role which was bound to fail.

Glouberman (2002) writes about the joy of burn-out and thus deliberately juxtaposes two words that would not normally go together. The message in her book is that burn-out is a state of mind, body and spirit reached by those who have come to the end of a particular road and not acknowledged it. Rather than being cured, it needs to be honoured and listened to. She thinks ultimately burn-out is positive if we are open to its message. She says that the major differences between depression and burn-out is that depression is to do with failure and loss, while burn-out has more to do with a profound disappointment in love, meaning and our ability to be of service.

James Hillman (1975) has written a classic paper on betrayal in which he shows that if we enter a relationship or a new organization with unrealistic expectations, we can see others or the system as letting us down – in Hillman's words betraying us. 'There's too much paperwork', 'I can't do what I came to do', 'You have to lose your integrity to get on.' Hillman contends that if we come in with a naivety or idealism, then when the world does not meet our expectations, we feel betrayed. He contends that this is part of life – what determines whether we grow or not is our response to this betrayal. Among his five dysfunctional responses to betrayal is 'self-betrayal'. He writes:

> It is a strange experience to find oneself betraying oneself, turning against one's own experiences by giving them negative values and by acting against one's own intentions and value system ... So we begin to cheat ourselves with excuses and escapes.
>
> (Hillman 1975)

Cynicism is another defence against betrayal and disappointment and we have learnt to listen carefully to the cynic for their idealism, rather than to buy into their often witty but disparaging comments about others and the system.

One supervisee we worked with started a new job, idealizing the organization she was going to join and heroically describing her vision of what she was going to achieve. Three months later she was furious with the organization. She felt betrayed, let down, disillusioned and stressed. She complained bitterly about how the organization had not delivered on what they had promised, and how it was impossible for her to do what she had set out to achieve. It was only after much reflection in supervision that she realized how her own idealization and heroism had created the reality she felt betrayed by and had blamed on others.

Since that episode she tells how she has a greater capacity to accept responsibility rather than blame others and sometimes laughs at herself or the situation.

We would contend that the best time to attend to burn-out is before it happens. This involves, as discussed above, being willing to see how your mind-sets can contribute; looking at your shadow motivation for being in the helping professions (see Chapter 2); monitoring your own stress symptoms and creating a healthy way of renewing yourself (see above); and ensuring that you have a meaningful, enjoyable and physically active life outside the role of being a helper.

Post-traumatic stress

More recently a cluster of symptoms known to be part of post-traumatic stress disorder (PTSD) has been recognized. It is now accepted that in dealing with traumatic incidents like shootings, fires, crashes, rapes, the workers can experience trauma that is parallel to that suffered by the people they work with. Whilst some of the symptoms are similar to those of stress and burn-out, one of the essential differences is that trauma happens suddenly and unexpectedly. This requires very different responses from managers and supervisors and some of these are formulated by Brown and Bourne (1996, ch. 7). They draw a very useful distinction between internal and external stressors. The latter originate from re-experiencing some of the effects of the traumatic incident and unlike external stress, could not be reduced, say, by simply lightening the workload.

It is also beginning to be recognized that it is not only front-line workers who are traumatized but such people as telephonists and clerical staff who receive distressed calls from relatives, friends and the media, legal secretaries, caretakers, cleaners, leisure centre staff, cooks, registrars of deaths who operate rest centres, body identification centres, drop-in centres, and help lines. Managers are in particular need of supervision as they are making key decisions, often without prior training, which affect the whole response and staff care process (Capewell 1997). The burden of responsibility they carry exacerbates the impact on them, yet they rarely feel they need support (doing so is seen as weakness) and believe those on the front line need or deserve it more.

Supervisors, if they are working with supervisees in this area, need to familiarize themselves with the symptoms, and how they differ from symptoms of stress which build up over time. Often those working on the front line can resort to denial to get the work done, and the symptoms can emerge much later.

We have included this short description in the chapter on learning and flourishing at work because it is impossible to learn in a PTSD state. Whereas stress and burn-out are potential learning situations, PTSD is a shut-down of all the ways we can renew ourselves.

Conclusion

A lecturer, when explaining stress management to an audience, raised a glass of water and asked: 'How heavy is this glass of water?'

Answers called out ranged from 20g to 500g. The lecturer replied: 'The absolute weight doesn't matter. It depends on how long you try to hold it. If I hold it for a minute, that's not a problem. If I hold it for an hour, I'll have an ache in my right arm. If I hold it for a day, you'll have to call an ambulance. In each case, it's the same weight, but the longer I hold it, the heavier it becomes.'

He continued, 'And that's the way it is with stress management. If we carry our burdens all the time, sooner or later, as the burden becomes increasingly heavy, we won't be able to carry on. As with the glass of water, you have to put it down for a while and rest before holding it again. When we're refreshed, we can carry on with the burden.

So, before you return home tonight, put the burden of work down. Don't carry it home. You can pick it up tomorrow. Whatever burdens you're carrying now, let them down for a moment if you can. Relax; pick them up later after you've rested. Life is short. Enjoy it!' Chesterman (Personal communication, 2006).

In this chapter we have suggested ways of increasing your capacity to resource yourself. We maintain that a commitment to ongoing learning is essential so that you can continue to grow and enjoy your work. Taking care of yourself enables you to be more effective. We look at seven aspects of resourcing yourself and offer suggestions on how to develop them. However, we recognize that even with these there can be stress in one's job. We refer to burn-out and pay particular attention to how our beliefs can substantially contribute to burn-out. However, even in the midst of stress and burn-out there can be much learning and we cite examples where people have benefited from finally listening to themselves. We briefly refer to post-traumatic stress as this is in a different category to stress and burn-out. Ongoing learning is not a possibility until this episode of trauma-induced stress has been addressed.

The important part supervision can play in resourcing ourselves is the subject of the next chapter.

4 Being an effective supervisee

Introduction
Resourcing yourself through supervision
Arranging the supervision you need and taking appropriate responsibility
    Contracting
    Evaluating your supervisor
Blocks to receiving supervision
    Previous experiences of supervision
    Personal inhibition and defensive routines
    Difficulties in handling authority
    Conflict of roles
    Assessment
    Practical blocks
    Difficulty in receiving support
    Organizational blocks
Overcoming blocks
Self-supervision
Conclusion

Introduction

In the previous chapter we talked about how you can resource yourself in all aspects of your life. In this chapter we look specifically at how to use supervision as a resource.

Supervision forms part of our continual learning and development as workers, including eventually helping us to learn how to be supervisors. A good supervisor can also help us to use our own resources better, manage our workload and challenge our inappropriately patterned ways of coping. We think that, if we are helping clients take more charge of their own lives, it is essential that we are doing the same. There is research to show that good supervision correlates with job satisfaction (Cherniss and Egnatios 1978).

We can give countless examples where supervision has enabled workers to go back to their work confident in their own abilities, with a new perspective. However, we can also give examples where supervisees have not been able to avail themselves of this kind of resourcing. We outline a few reasons and then go on to see how the blocks can be overcome. We want to encourage the supervisee to be proactive, not only in learning about their own learning style, but to know how to make best use of supervision.

Resourcing yourself through supervision

At regular intervals it is beneficial to stand back and reflect on the supervision you need and want in relation to what you are currently receiving, and then to ask yourself what are the blocks that prevent the supervision being more effective and what you can do to initiate the unblocking process. Here are some questions to help you consider ways of being more proactive about both your support and supervision, and your learning and resourcing. We would recommend you go through this with a colleague or friend as that will add another dimension. Others, even those we know well, can sometimes have a very different perception of us and our ways of coping:

- What are the strengths and weaknesses of your present resourcing system? What do you need to do about improving it?
- How do you recognize that you are under stress? What ways do you use to alleviate this stress? Do these coping mechanisms provide just short-term relief, or do they change the cause of the stress?
- What are your specific needs from supervision and how far do your present supervisory arrangements meet them?
- Do you need to renegotiate the contract with your supervisor, supervision group or work team? Make as many of the transactions and assumptions as explicit as possible. Are all/both parties clear about the purpose of supervision?
- Are there additional forms of supervision (peer-supervision, etc.) that you need to arrange for yourself?
- How open do you feel to supervision and feedback? If not, are there personal changes you could make to open up the communication?
- Are you frightened of being judged and assessed? Have you tried checking out whether your fears are justified or fantasy?
- Can you confront your supervisor and give him or her feedback? If not, are the constraints internal or external?
- What defensive routines do you fall into using? What do you need in order to move beyond these?
- Are you stuck in blaming others for what you yourself can change? We find that supervisees de-power themselves, by having an investment in believing that they cannot change what their supervisor or organization does to support them. Many supervisees discover that more changes are possible than they previously believed.
- Do you carry some of your supervisor's anxieties, so that you have to look after them?
- Is it feasible to have a more equal relationship? How far is it appropriate and is it what you want, given that more equality means more responsibility?

Arranging the supervision you need and taking appropriate responsibility

The need to be proactive does not stop at the point where you have set up a good support system and have found a good supervisor or supervisory situation. It is all too easy at this point to slide back into dependency and just accept the style and level of supervision that the supervisor provides. To ensure you get the supervision you want, you need to take full responsibility for your part in contracting and negotiating how the supervision will operate, what it will focus on and how the process will be monitored and reviewed.

Inskipp and Proctor (1993) have drawn up a list of responsibilities for the supervisee. By terming them responsibilities, they point out that being more active in getting the right sort of supervision also involves taking responsibility in an ongoing way. The responsibilities of the supervisees include the need to

- identify practice issues with which you need help and ask for help;
- become increasingly able to share freely;
- identify what responses you want;
- become more aware of the organizational contracts that affect supervisor, clients and supervisees;
- be open to feedback;
- monitor tendencies to justify, explain or defend;
- develop the ability to discriminate what feedback is useful.

In stressing the essential equality of the relationship we do not want to overlook the fact that in most supervisory relationships there is a managerial or quality responsibility carried by the supervisor. The supervisee needs to be aware of this, and both parties need to work at integrating the managerial and qualitative aspects of supervision so that they do not invalidate the opportunity for equality.

Contracting

Pat Hunt (1986) emphasizes the value of having a clear supervision contract: 'Supervision can become a more effective and satisfying activity for both supervisor and supervisees in any setting if there is a more *explicit* contract on what it is about.' She talks about the need for a supervisory alliance and this includes:

> more openness and clarity on the methods to use in supervision, and why they are used, the style of supervision, the goals of supervision, the kind of relationship it is hoped to achieve and the responsibilities of each partner in the supervisory relationship.

When contracting with your supervisor, both parties need to have the opportunity to say how they see the purpose of the sessions, explore how much their expectations match, and look at their hopes and fears concerning the working relationship. Where there is a mismatch in expectations, it is important that these differences are further explored and some form of negotiation takes place. As much as possible any conflict of purpose should be talked over, as should any issues of style, assumptions and values. Ground rules need to be established about frequency, duration and place and about how cases are to be brought; also how the supervision contract and the work will be reviewed and evaluated; finally, if relevant, what procedures there are for emergencies.

The need for such explicit contracting has been clearly expressed by Brigid Proctor (1988a).

> If supervision is to become and remain a co-operative experience which allows for real, rather than token accountability, a clear – even tough – working agreement needs to be negotiated. The agreement needs to provide sufficient safety and clarity for the student or worker to know where she stands: and it needs sufficient teeth for the supervisor to feel free and responsible for making the challenges of assessments which belong with whatever role – managerial, consultative, or training – the context requires.

She develops this further (Inskipp and Proctor 1993: 49) with guidelines for the exploratory contracting interview and also a checklist as to what the new supervisee might be looking for (p. 39). We explore contracting in greater detail in Chapter 6.

Evaluating your supervisor

When exploring blocks to receiving supervision (see below) we mentioned that one of the most common fears of supervisees is how they will be judged and evaluated by their supervisor. What most supervisees forget, or do not even consider, is that supervisors may also be anxious about how they are being judged or evaluated by their supervisees. Evaluation and review should be a two-way process and needs to be regularly scheduled into the supervision arrangements. This ensures that fears on both sides about 'how I am doing' can be brought into the open, and there is a chance to give clear feedback and, where necessary, to renegotiate the supervision contract.

Borders and Leddick (1987) provide a very useful checklist of 41 points for evaluating your supervisor. This list includes:

- helps me feel at ease with the supervision process;
- can facilitate and accept feedback from their supervisees;
- helps me clarify my objectives in working with clients;
- explains the criteria for any evaluation of my work, clearly and in behavioural terms;
- encourages me to conceptualize in new ways regarding my clients;
- enables me to become actively involved in the supervision process.

We would invite you to write your own evaluation criteria – some will be what you might ask of any supervisor and some might be of this particular supervisor at this particular time, related to the current work situation.

Blocks to receiving supervision

Part of arranging for good supervision is recognizing blocks and finding effective ways of overcoming them. In this next section we will briefly look at the following blocks: 1 Previous experiences of supervision; 2 Personal inhibition; 3 Difficulties in handling authority; 4 Role conflict; 5 Assessment; 6 Practical blocks, such as finance or geography; 7 Difficulties in receiving support; and 8 Organizational blocks.

Previous experience of supervision

Previous experiences of supervision, both good and bad can influence the current supervision. A bad experience can lead a supervisee to be wary, but a good one can lead to comparisons, that no one will be as good as my last supervisor. Taking a more positive stance, you might like to make a resume of past experiences of supervision and what you learnt from them both in terms of managing the relationship, yourself and skills. How do your needs differ now from then?

Personal inhibition and defensive routines

Sometimes just being in a one-to-one relationship can restimulate painful feelings. Here is an account of one supervision relationship from a supervisee:

> When I started supervision I found that I was not going to be directed in any way and that all the ideas had to come from me. This felt very uncomfortable and I felt very much 'on the spot' – in fact it gave an insight as to how a client would feel. Painful emotions were just below the surface brought there by the insecurity of the position I seemed to be in. I felt very vulnerable as if the supervisor's attention was scrutiny. My defensive reaction to this was anger and one week I was on the point of walking out. I actually started to gather my things together. The supervisor stopped me and I realized that I was checking to see if he could cope with my anger. I had a shock of recognition at this scene as it reminded me of how I test out other relationships.
>
> Although these sessions were painful I realized how important supervision was and how necessary for our particular work especially the 'coping collusion' which permeates our work, our denial of how much we are affected by the client group. Finally, the blocks in supervision were self-imposed and therefore having another supervisor would not have solved these blocks but brought out others.

The idea of being on the spot, even when objectively there is no assessment, can relate to internal judging. As the above supervisee said:

> In all the supervision sessions there was a third person present, a part of myself – very critical – who looked at all my thoughts, actions and feelings and commented on them. Somehow it seemed as if my own analysis of my behaviour

served to paralyse me. I always had a counter argument for anything I came up with. It seems as if this is the way I keep control.

We can certainly identify with this, and have often found ourselves being needlessly defensive in supervision, protecting ourselves from being judged, when, in fact, we are usually the worst judges of ourselves. It can certainly feel very exposing to bring cases to supervision to find out that one has missed something which, in retrospect, seems very obvious.

You might like to ask yourself here how much you hold back in supervision and for what reasons. Can you share any of these reasons with your supervisor even if it feels a bit risky? Kadushin (1968) has written about the various strategies adopted by supervisees for dealing with such anxieties. There is also a later paper by Hawthorne (1975) on supervisor strategies for dealing with their anxieties (see below). Ekstein and Wallerstein (1972) and Argyris and Schon (1978) both describe 'professional defensive routines', that we all can adopt to avoid being vulnerable, and open to new learning. These are developed by Gilbert and Evans (2000) in the following types of defensive routines:

- The pre-packaging approach: 'I've got it all sewn up in advance and here is my supervision contract for today.'
- The information flooding approach: 'You don't understand unless I give you every detail about my client.'
- Energetic denial of any need in the face of input from supervision: 'This is not really new to me ... I'm familiar with that already ... Yes, I've already tried that approach...'
- The self-flagellation approach (magnifying one's own shortcomings): 'I know I have made a mess of this session ... I'll just never get it right ... whatever you tell me, I seem to forget as soon as I sit in front of the client.'
- The approach to supervision as a personal assault: 'I know that you will criticize what I have done here ... I think the problem is really the difference in our orientations to clients ... I feel terrified in coming to supervision because it always ends in an argument...'
- The fault finding or 'nitpicking' approach to supervision: 'You make a good point there but I'm not sure it would apply to this particular client.'
- The displacing of the problem in supervision on to the supervisor: 'I certainly do not have any angry feelings towards this client: are you sure you are not angry here?'

Difficulties with authority

As one worker said in Fineman's study (1985): 'I fear authority and always feel I need to prove to my supervisor that I can do my work.' So supervisors are often not seen for who they are; sometimes they are given too much power, at other times they may be defensively seen as useless. Difficulties with the power and authority of the supervisor can relate to taking our own power and authority (see Chapter 8). Sibling rivalry can also occur in terms of who can manage the client better, and this can come just as much from the supervisor as the supervisees.

Conflict of roles

There can also be problems around the different roles contained within the supervision.

> I have regular meetings with my supervisor, but always steer clear of my problems in coping with my report work. Can I trust her? I need her backing for my career progress, but will she use this sort of thing as evidence against me? There are some painful areas that are never discussed but need discussing so much. It's an awful dilemma for me.
>
> (Fineman 1985: 52)

In Fineman's research there was also an appreciation of the dilemma of the supervisor. 'Currently I get supervised by the team leader – but he's in a conflict situation between being a manager and being my supervisor' (Fineman 1985).

The conflicting roles of support person and assessor can also create conflict when the supervisor is providing an evaluation (see Chapter 9 and below).

Although supervisors might try to protect their supervisees from their own stress, the stress was inevitably picked up. Sometimes the supervisees had the attitude, 'They've got enough on their plates without my problems', but often there was resentment at not having the support they felt they had a right to.

A mismatch of expectations that never get tackled can play a part in reducing the worth of supervision. 'My supervisor doesn't really provide what I want. He tends to pick on things which are important to him, not me' (Fineman 1985: 52).

Later in this chapter we explore the importance of ensuring that you have a clear supervision contract with your supervisor, and that roles and expectations within the supervision are explored and regularly reviewed.

Assessment

One of the biggest causes of anxiety (for both parties but especially supervisees) is around being assessed. When assessment is a feature of supervision, some supervisees say they are reluctant to bring cases where they might not be working well and don't feel safe. Any assessment procedure can often evoke feelings, and being able to talk to the supervisor about these can show a maturity that will benefit both parties. As well as talking about feelings, it is important to understand the assessment process, the criteria being used and how possible pitfalls can be overcome.

Practical blocks

Besides the many personal and organizational blocks to supervision, some people also face practical difficulties in getting the supervision that they need. These could be financial (I can't afford supervision), or geographical (living in a very isolated place) or availability (being head of an establishment and one's manager not having the specialized skills).

All these blocks require the supervisees to have an even higher degree of proactivity and also to think laterally. Isolated practitioners may have to look outside their own training to find a skilled professional of another orientation, but who is sympathetic enough to support them in developing within his or her own style and school of work. Some geographically isolated practitioners have arranged infrequent supervision with supervisors to whom they have to travel great distances, but have supplemented these visits with correspondence, telephone calls or teleconferencing.

In Chapter 10 we look at ways of setting up and conducting peer supervision and support groups. This can be either with a group of other similar practitioners in your area, or a reciprocal arrangement with one other practitioner who is also in the position of not being able to get appropriate supervision within their organizational structure. We also give examples of how one can use professional organizations or training courses to provide a network within which to establish such peer supervision contracts.

Difficulty in receiving support

Another difficulty or block in receiving support or supervision has been referred to in Chapter 2 – namely the difficulty in receiving. To receive makes one potentially more vulnerable and exposes need. It is often felt to be safer to work with clients who have to express their needs and leave us safe in our roles of providing.

Although this might be a personal difficulty, it is certainly culturally reinforced. As we quoted in Chapter 3, 'We have been brought up to deny our needs . . . To need is to be dependent, weak; needing implies submission to another' (Hillman 1979: 17). This attitude is certainly there in individuals and is strongly reinforced by work cultures. In Fineman's study (1985: 100–1) of social workers, when talking about the double standards of giving and not receiving, he quotes one worker as saying:

> This is a particular caring group of people, but they play a charade with each other's problems and stresses. There's a sort of collusive arrangement not to talk to people about their stresses. If it's linked to a home situation there's a shame that they, as social workers, feel stressed . . . No one stops to ask why this should be the case.

and continues:

> It was an odd feeling for those who found themselves facing, and contributing, to a wall of interpersonal evasiveness or even indifference inside the office, while professing just the opposite to clients outside the office . . . They felt helpless victims of a climate which provided little of the emotional support they desired.

Organizational blocks

From the above quotes it can been seen that there is an interplay between an individual's process and the way a work culture might reinforce an individual's own inner feelings about asking for help. The culture of some organizations will discourage individuals to expect and ask for supervision. In such cultures, in spite of grumbling about lack of good supervision, there can be an unwillingness to really do something about it. Other organizations will encourage individuals to overcome their inner resistances. This is explored at length in Chapter 13 on organizational cultures.

There is also a very useful exploration of the interface between the personal and organizational blocks in the nursing profession in Chapter 2 of Bond and Holland (1998): 'The hidden picture – resistance to clinical supervision and implications for the clinical supervision relationship'.

Overcoming blocks: Geraldine's story

Here is part of an article from one of our supervisees who is a speech therapist. She shows how her chosen profession's blocks around supervision reinforced her own, and she demonstrates the changes she made to break her personal patterns. She also ends by asking some very relevant questions which do not only apply to speech therapists but all helping professionals. You might try to answer these questions for yourself about your own work setting.

> As a disillusioned speech therapist who has considered leaving the profession several times I was interested to read that the majority of speech therapists in full-time posts were mainly newly-qualified, and those who have left the profession were mainly experienced full-timers. It struck me that these therapists had left without speaking out and saying why. Here is my story:
>
> I started training at the age of 21. I knew that speech therapy was a small profession and that therapists were poorly paid. In fact I was already earning more than a senior speech therapist in my previous job in catering. However I liked working with people and had a genuine interest in communication problems. I wanted job satisfaction and felt that this would be more satisfying than a large salary.
>
> I attacked my first job with a vigour and enthusiasm that I now recognize in many newly-qualified therapists. I was keen to put into practice all that I had learnt. I was highly motivated. However, I should have begun listening to the messages behind the questions and comments I was receiving from other professionals, friends and relatives:
>
> 'Speech therapy must be a very lonely job.' 'Who do you go to for support?' 'Do you receive supervision?'
>
> I can remember my replies were of the following nature: 'I like being my own boss.'
>
> 'I don't need support.'
>
> 'I am qualified and no longer need supervision.'
>
> My first senior post, two years after qualifying, was very challenging. My job was divided between setting up an advisory speech therapy service to a social services department and introducing speech therapy into a language unit which had been open for one year without a speech therapist. I felt I was appointed because I presented as a self-starter who could work without supervision and enjoyed challenges.

Even as I write this, a voice inside me is saying, 'What is wrong with that?' and, 'Maybe you just don't have what it takes to be successful.' I have enough faith in myself to know these voices are wrong. If we do not question the assumptions or challenge the rationale behind such management decisions, we become guilty of perpetuating these fantasies. Being a self-starter often means taking up a post which has been poorly set up, then not being given the power to make necessary changes. I feel the personality of those attracted to the caring professions lends itself to exploitation and denial of their own needs. How many times have you heard? 'We are here to help our patients.' This is, of course, what may have attracted us to our work, but at what price? The reverse side of the coin often appears to be 'My needs don't matter.'

Despite starting a counselling course, I still believed that I did not need support or require supervision. During the first year I refused to join a support group as it sounded too much like something found in a Californian suburb!

I found my new job very difficult and the team leader for the social work team started questioning me on how much support I received. She was shocked when she realized I saw my line manager very infrequently. She suggested that she and I met fortnightly to discuss the job. These meetings became supervision, even though the team leader was not my line manager, and were very supportive.

Through discussing my work during these supervision sessions and through greater self-awareness gained as a result of my counselling course, I began to realize that I was going through 'professional burn-out'. By this I mean that I had reached a point when I no longer had the enthusiasm to keep injecting into the job because I felt that my efforts were not effective or appreciated. The side effects of burn-out for me were tiredness, lethargy, poor time-keeping and boredom. I had believed that I would always remain as highly motivated as I had been in my first job only four years ago.

The two things that kept me going through this period were supervision and praise (something we tend to give to the patients much more than to other staff). I feel I achieved a lot during this period, by learning how to use the support systems both on the course and at work.

After two years in this post I felt the need for a change. Where did I go from here? I decided to move into an area of work that had always interested me, 'speech therapy within psychiatry'. I found myself with another challenging post. After the initial excitement of the new job etc., I realized I was back at the beginning of the long uphill struggle of getting a new service going.

There was no formal supervision or support system set up. The voice inside me said: 'Of course, you should be able to do this without support.' When I spoke about the difficulties of the post I heard the responses from others as criticism. I even found myself saying the job was going well. It was difficult to admit, the therapist in me did not want to admit, that I could not cope. Eventually I called out for support. Then my overworked and, probably, unsupported GP also wanted to find a solution to my problem and put me on anti-depressants.

The speech therapy profession is concerned about why so many experienced staff are leaving four or five years after being trained. I think my story illustrates one of the main reasons. Therapists who are working in the field need support and supervision. If they are not rewarded and valued by members of their own profession, what hope is there of receiving this from other professions and the government in the future?

I have thought about some questions that each speech therapist should ask before accepting a post:

- Does the district therapist see all new employees shortly after they commence and at regular intervals thereafter?
- Are there regular staff appraisals?
- Is there supervision for all staff members at all levels?
- Are support groups facilitated by an independent person encouraged?
- Are therapists encouraged to meet their colleagues regularly and is there provision made in the timetable for this?

Perhaps by identifying our needs and finding ways of getting them met, we will not have to take such drastic steps as leaving the profession.

(Geraldine Rose, unpublished work, 1987)

In view of what has been written above about the various personal, interpersonal, practical and organizational blocks to getting supervision, you might like to return to the map of your own resourcing system and review the blocks you experience. Awareness of the blocks is the first step in overcoming them.

Self-supervision

This is a form of supervision that is always relevant, even if you are receiving good supervision elsewhere. One aim of all supervision is to help practitioners develop a healthy internal supervisor, which they can have access to while they are working.

Later in the book when we look at the seven-eyed model (Chapter 7), we ask supervisees to monitor their responses to clients. This is a form of self-supervision. Some of the questions to ourselves we have found useful in monitoring our own responses to clients are:

- What would I least like my supervisor to know about my work with this client?
- How do I want to change this client (to access my implicit or explicit agenda)?
- Why did I make this intervention?
- What might I have held back in any way during the session?
- On a scale of 0 to 10, how well did the session go?
- What might have made it a higher score?
- What score might the client give?
- What residues from the session do I experience in my body/thoughts?
- What is an image for the session?

This reflection process can be deepened if the supervisee develops their own system of writing up their sessions. This should not only record the facts necessary for professional practice but, as described above, can reflect on the process of the work and monitor own body sensations, breathing, feelings, thoughts and actions, whilst with the client. If we can learn to self-monitor whilst engaging with another this is a very valuable skill, but it takes a long time and much practice to develop. However, we have made part of our work to check in with ourselves, and if necessary ask for a pause to reflect in the session.

Written processes of reflection can be further deepened by using audio and visual tape-recording of work with clients and patients and developing ways of using these tapes to further our own self-supervision. Kagan (1980) has done much to develop ways of learning through seeing tapes of ourselves at work and we will be writing further about our own systems for self-supervision (See the section on use of video in Chapter 9).

What is essential for all forms of self-supervision is giving oneself enough time and also being willing to confront one's own ways of working. Many of our trainees have found their first attempts to learn from listening to themselves on tape to be both challenging and instructive.

Conclusion

In this chapter we have stressed the importance of supervisees taking responsibility for receiving regular, good quality supervision. We explored how you might proactively overcome blockages to receiving supervision, both those inside yourself and those in the work environment. Your own efforts to improve your own supervision can become an important part of the organization developing its collective supervision practice and can contribute to a learning culture within the organization. In Chapter 14, we show how an organization can either introduce supervision or radically improve the policies and practice of supervision that it provides. Such change processes are often initiated by enough staff in an organization or agency responsibly speaking out about the need for better supervision. However, we do not have to wait for changes in policy, for there is much we can do personally to improve the supervision we receive.

PART TWO

Becoming a supervisor and the process of supervision

5 Becoming a supervisor

Introduction
Why be a supervisor?
Getting started
Qualities needed to be a good supervisor
Supervisor roles
Taking appropriate authority and power
Ethics
Conclusion

Introduction

Suddenly becoming, or being asked to be a supervisor can be both exhilarating and daunting. Without training or support the task can be overwhelming.

> Supervising is new to me. It's OK, I suppose, but I'm anxious – I'm never quite sure whether I'm giving the people I'm supervising exactly what they are wanting ... I'm really afraid about what they will say about me so I don't ask. To be judged by a colleague is just too much.
>
> (Fineman 1985: 52)

This chapter and the other four in this section will provide you with some core frameworks not only for carrying out supervision, but also for reviewing and evaluating your supervisory work and for receiving quality feedback on your sessions.

If you are reading this book, having just become a supervisor, we would encourage you not to start with this chapter, because as we mentioned in Chapter 4, you cannot expect to give good supervision unless you have first learnt how to receive supervision and be a proactive supervisee.

Why be a supervisor?

There are many reasons for becoming a supervisor. For some it is the natural progression that comes with promotion. They become nursing tutors, senior social workers or area youth officers, and discover that, instead of spending time seeing clients, for which they had been trained, they are now spending all their time seeing junior staff. Some counsellors or therapists become, over time, the most senior practitioners in their area, and supervisees start coming to them. Some staff find that they greatly miss the direct contact with clients and are nostalgic for their earlier days in the work. Such staff can be prone to turning their supervisees into substitute clients, to keep their hand in with therapeutic work.

Others turn to supervision to get away from the pressures of client work, in the false hope that seeing supervisees provides a quiet life! After several years as a helping professional they opt, not for a specialist post, but to go into student supervision or to become a tutor in their chosen profession. For some the role of supervisor fits more easily than for others. They find themselves at home in a role that requires both personal development and educational skills.

Others get promoted into management because they are better administrators than they are at working with people, but unfortunately for such people and their organizations management positions in the helping professions nearly always include some supervision responsibilities. These staff then become the reluctant supervisors, who are always too busy with 'important meetings' and finishing 'essential reports' to see their supervisees.

Some supervisors are so able to arrange their work that they can mix some direct work with clients, with being a supervisor of others. We would recommend that wherever possible staff who supervise or teach should still be practising whatever they teach or supervise. It is all too easy to get out of touch with the realities of being at the 'coal-face' and to wonder why your supervisees are making such heavy weather of what seems perfectly straightforward from your perspective as supervisor. The mix of work can have advantages in both directions. Many new supervisors in several professions have remarked to us how having to supervise other staff helped them revitalize their own work with clients and start to think afresh about what they did themselves.

Many people become and stay supervisors through being attracted to the challenge and scope of the role. Here is an account from a colleague:

> I feel most challenged and excited in supervision by the tension between the loving relationship and holding my own authority. Supervision is the place in my work where I can be at my most free ranging – playful, free to think aloud, able to comment on the process, challenge, take a journey into the unknown. Then there is the opposite side when I really have to hold the boundaries, own my own authority and risk the good relationship for the sake of the truth. Each time this has happened, I have found it risky, self-challenging, lonely for a while, but also very mind-clearing and transformational and ultimately very strengthening to both the supervisees, myself and our relationship.

Being a supervisor provides an opportunity to increase your development skills in helping others to learn and develop within their work. As a new supervisor you are impelled to stop, reflect upon and articulate the ways you have worked as a practitioner, many of which you may have begun to take for granted. The challenge is then to use your own experience to help supervisees develop their own style of working and their own solutions to difficult work situations.

Another reason, which is often denied, for becoming a supervisor can be that of becoming 'one up' on the other staff. Many of us will remember the joy when we entered our second year at a school – we were no longer the youngest or most gullible, there were now others we could tell 'what is what' to. New supervisors can be eager to mask their own anxieties by using their supervisees to bolster up their own pseudo-role of expert – the one who has all the answers.

Finally, another hidden motive in giving supervision can be that staff who do not know how to get decent supervision for themselves can compensate by giving to other staff the sort of supervision they need and want for themselves, in the vain hope that this will magically lead to someone offering it to them. This is equivalent to those who find it difficult to ask for counselling help, going into training as a counsellor, a pattern that Relate termed 'training as the preferred mode of treatment'.

Getting started

The first prerequisite for being a good supervisor is being able to arrange good supervision for yourself (see Chapter 4). A useful question to ask yourself is: 'Am I currently receiving adequate supervision, both for the other work I am doing and for being a supervisor?'

Before you give your first supervision sessions, we think it is useful for you to sit down and reflect on the overt and covert motives that you bring to supervision. This is not in order to suppress the more shameful motives but to find some appropriate way to meet the needs the motives represent.

It would also be worthwhile to sit down and write out examples of positive and negative supervision experiences you yourself have received. What are your positive role models and what sort of supervisory experiences would you want to avoid repeating for your own supervisees?

Your expectations may well set the tone of what happens in the supervision sessions you give. If you go into supervision expecting the sessions to be full of conflict or to be problematic they may well end up that way. If you go in expecting them to be interesting, engaging and cooperative, you may well produce the necessary climate for that to happen.

Brigid Proctor (1988a) suggests that it is most useful to start with the assumption that workers in the human service professions can be relied on:

- to want to monitor their own practice;
- to learn to develop competence;
- and to respond to support and encouragement.

Starting with this basic assumption, even though at times it may not appear totally true, is helpful in setting a positive tone.

It is, however, possible that you are part of an organization where a negative culture about supervision has already developed, or where supervision is totally absent. You may find it supportive to recognize that some of the difficulties are not all yours and to read Chapters 13 and 14.

Qualities needed to be a good supervisor

Carifio and Hess (1987: 244) quote a variety of sources in looking at the qualities of the 'ideal supervisor' which they see as similar to the qualities of the ideal psychotherapist, but employed differently. These qualities include empathy, understanding, unconditional positive regard, congruence, genuineness (Rogers 1957); warmth and self-disclosure (Coche 1977); flexibility, concern, attention, investment, curiosity, and openness (Albott 1984; Aldridge 1982; Gittermann and Miller 1977; Hess 1980).

Gilbert and Evans (2000) provide a much fuller list of supervisor qualities based partly on the work of Leddick and Dye (1987) and we have developed this in the following list.

1 **flexibility:** in moving between theoretical concepts and use of a wide variety of interventions and methods;
2 **a multi-perspectival view:** being able to see the same situation from a variety of angles;
3 **a working map of the discipline in which they supervise;**
4 **the ability to work transculturally** (see Chapter 8);
5 **the capacity to manage and contain anxiety**, their own and that of the supervisee;
6 **openness to learning** from supervisees and from new situations that emerge;
7 **sensitivity to the wider contextual issues** that impact on both the therapeutic and supervisory process;
8 **can handle power appropriately** and in a non-oppressive way (see Chapter 8);
9 **humour, humility and patience.**

You will notice that most of these qualities, awareness and skills are ones you will already have or have developed in order to be a competent practitioner within the helping professions. Good counselling or coaching skills are a prerequisite for being a competent supervisor.

Brigid Proctor (1988b) makes this point well when she says:

> The task of the supervisor is to help him (the supervisee) feel received, valued, understood on the assumption that only then will he feel safe enough and open enough to review and challenge himself, as well as to value himself and his own abilities. Without this atmosphere, too, he is unlikely to be open to critical feedback or to pay good attention to managerial instructions.
>
> It will also be the case that a worker often comes to supervision stressed, anxious, angry, afraid. It is our assumption that only if he feels safe enough to talk about these uncomfortable feelings, and fully acknowledge them for himself will he be 'cleared' to re-evaluate his practice.

As a supervisor you may recognize how relevant to this new task are the wealth and experience you have had as a practitioner. Some new supervisors need to be helped to

adapt their useful counselling skills to this new context; others hold on to their counselling skills too tenaciously and, as mentioned earlier, turn their supervisees into quasi-
clients.

To start supervising you will first find it important to understand the boundaries of
supervision and be able to make clear and mutually negotiated contracts. In Chapter 4,
we discussed the importance of contracting clear supervision for the supervisees, and in
Chapter 6 we will explore how the supervisor can manage this process. Many new
supervisors are concerned about where supervision ends and therapy or counselling
begins. Some new supervisors are anxious that they will be flooded by their supervisees'
personal problems. Others are only too eager to play therapist with their supervisees.
Sometimes supervisees want to turn their supervisor into a 'quasi-therapist'.

When training therapists, one of us became aware that several of his own supervisees
were half secretly wishing to have therapy with him rather than supervision. In exploring
this further he became aware of another factor in this dynamic; that their wish for
replacing the supervision of their work with the client with quasi-therapy for themselves
was partly due to envy of their clients, to whom they were not only giving the attention
in their therapy that they wished for themselves, but were having to give them yet more
attention in the supervision. He began to realize that this envy needed to be made
conscious and that the supervisees should be helped to look at what other forms of
support they needed or wanted for themselves.

Kadushin (1968) describes a similar pattern in social work, when supervisees play the
game of, 'Treat me, don't beat me.' This game can be extremely alluring to the supervisor
in several ways:

1   because the game appeals to the ... worker in him ... who is still interested in
    those who have personal problems;
2   because it appeals to the voyeur in him (many supervisors are fascinated by the
    opportunity to share in the intimate life of others);
3   because it is flattering to be selected as therapist;
4   because the supervisor is not clearly certain as to whether such a redefinition of
    the situation is not permissible.

First, good supervision inevitably focuses some of its attention on the dynamics of the
supervisees, but this must always arise out of work-related issues and be done in the
service of understanding and being able to manage the work better.

Second, you need to develop your framework for supervising, which is appropriate to
the setting in which you work. This framework needs to be clear enough to be explain-
able to your supervisees, but also flexible enough to be adapted to meet the changing
needs of different supervisees, at different levels and with a variety of situations.

The most difficult new skill that supervision requires is what we call the 'helicopter
ability'. This is the ability to switch focus between the following areas:

* the client that the supervisees are describing;
* the supervisees and their process;
* your own process and the here and now relationship with the supervisees;
* the client within their wider context, and help the supervisees do likewise;
* the wider context of the organization and inter-organizational issues.

This skill cannot be learnt before you start and indeed takes many years to develop. What is important is to know of the existence of all the possible levels and perspectives and then gradually to expand your focus within the sessions (see Chapter 7). However, do not try and get all the possible perspectives into every session, or your supervisees will get indigestion.

Finally, before we go on to present the different maps and models of supervision, we would like to spend some time looking at the complex roles that a supervisor has to combine. Clarifying your role(s) as supervisor is half the battle in achieving a clear framework.

Supervisor roles

As supervisor you have to encompass many functions in your role:

- a counsellor giving support;
- an educator helping your supervisees learn and develop;
- a manager with responsibilities for the quality of the work the supervisee is doing with their clients;
- a manager or consultant with responsibilities to the organization which is paying for the supervision.

Several writers have looked at the complexity of roles that this provides for the supervisor (Bernard 1979; Hess 1980; Hawkins 1982; Holloway 1984, 1995; Ellis and Dell 1986; Carroll 1996).

Among the sub-roles most often noted are:

- teacher,
- monitor evaluator,
- counsellor,
- coach,
- colleague,
- boss,
- expert technician,
- manager of administrative relationships.

In our training course on core supervision skills we involve all the trainee supervisors in looking at the variety of helping relationships that they have experienced in their lives and the expectations and transactions that these roles involve. We ask them to brainstorm types of people they have gone to for help in their lives; what needs they take to these people and what they expect to receive. We end up with a list that typically looks like Table 5.1.

When the roles are not clearly contracted for and defined in supervision and to a lesser extent even when they are, supervisors and supervisees will fall back on other patterns of relating which may be one of the typical transactions mentioned above. It is possible to have *crossed, collusive or named* transactions.

Table 5.1 Helping roles

Helping role	What you take to them	What you expect to receive
doctor	symptoms	diagnosis, cure
priest	sins, confessions	penitence, forgiveness
teacher	ignorance, questions	knowledge, answers
solicitor	injustice	advocacy
coach	poor performance	improved performance
judge	crimes	retribution
friend	yourself	acceptance, listening ear
mother	hurts	comfort
car mechanic	mechanical failure	technical correction and servicing

A collusive transaction happens when you go to your supervisor expecting a reassuring mum and your supervisor obliging plays out that role by constantly telling you that everything is fine. Such a collusive transaction may feel good to both parties at the time, but would be unproductive as it would be feeding the neurotic needs of both parties rather than the needs of the supervision.

If on the other hand you went expecting a reassuring mum and your supervisor played judge, you would have a crossed transaction. In the latter case you would probably feel misunderstood and put down, and that your supervisor was very unsupportive.

A named transaction is when one or other of the parties names the patterns and the games that are being played, so they become a choice rather than a compulsive process.

The supervisor has to be able to combine the roles of educator, supporter and at times manager, in an appropriate blend. As Hawthorne (1975: 179) notes: 'It requires effort and experience to integrate these into a comfortable and effective identity.'

Taking appropriate authority and power

Much of the conflict around the role of the supervisor emerges from the difficulty that many supervisors have in finding an appropriate way of taking authority and handling the power inherent in the role. Hawthorne (1975: 179) has written about this difficult and yet crucial task:

> Many supervisors, especially new ones, have difficulty adjusting to their new authority. . . . 'The balance which they have worked out for their personal lives between dominance and submission is upset by the new responsibility.' The supervisory relationship is complex, intense and intimate . . . Sometimes the effort (to take on authority) is hampered by the supervisor's unfamiliarity with the requirements of his role, by difficulties stemming from personal experiences with authority, or by discomfort in the one-to-one relationship.

Hawthorne goes on to describe the sort of games supervisors play either to abdicate power or to manipulate power. These draw on the work of Eric Berne and other writers in transactional analysis approaches to counselling, coaching and psychotherapy. Abdication games include:

- *'They won't let me'*   I would like to agree to what you are asking, but senior management won't let me.
- *'Poor me'*   I'm sorry about having to cancel our weekly conferences, but you have no idea how busy I am with these monthly lists for the director.
- *'I'm really a nice guy'*   Look at how helpful and pleasant I am being to you.
- *'One good question deserves another'*   How would you answer that question?

Manipulation of power games include:

- *'Remember who is boss'*   artificially asserting the power of one's role;
- *'I'll tell on you'*   threatening to pass on information about the supervises to more senior management;
- *'Father or Mother knows best'*   acting in a parental or patronizing manner;
- *'I am only trying to help you'*   defending against criticism from the supervises by pleading altruism;
- *'If you knew Dostoyevsky like I know Dostoyevsky'*   or showing off your knowledge to make the supervisees feel inferior.

In Chapter 8 on transcultural supervision, we explore the interplay between personal power, cultural power and role power. With the role of supervisor comes the responsibility to be aware of your own power in each of these three areas and to learn ways of utilizing this power in ways that are: appropriate, well-intentioned, anti-oppressive and sensitive to the particular background of the supervisee.

In Hawkins and Smith (2006) there is a useful model of how a supervisor can develop their own 'authority, presence and impact' and how all three are necessary to create both a safe place to explore and enough edge to enable a transformational shift with the supervisee.

In Chapter 6 we look at positive ways of combining the roles of educator, supporter and manager, and at taking the appropriate authority, depending on the experience of the supervisees and the supervision contract you have with them.

Ethics

It is important before starting supervising to revisit the ethical standards that underpin your professional client work and to consider how each of these standards apply to working as a supervisor. Alternatively you can start afresh and list the principles you would wish your supervisor and yourself as supervisor to espouse and enact. Page and Wosket (2001) provide a whole chapter where they build their ethical principles for supervision from studying writings in moral philosophy. Following on from their work we would propose six basic principles:

1   balancing appropriate responsibility for the work of the supervisee with respect for their autonomy;

2   due concern for the well-being and protection of the client with respect for their autonomy;
3   acting within the limits of one's own competence and knowing when to seek further help;
4   fidelity – being faithful to explicit and implicit promises made;
5   anti-oppressive practice (see Chapter 8);
6   openness to challenge and feedback combined with an active commitment to ongoing learning.

We should also be guided by Hippocrates' injunction to first and foremost, 'Do no harm'!

Bramley (1996) also has two very readable and useful chapters on ethics, which make informative links with the ethical importance of respecting cultural difference (see Chapter 8). Bramley ends her list of injunctions with 'Do for heaven's sake laugh!'

Michael Carroll (1996) acknowledges that acting ethically is full of complexity and ambiguity. He provides a four-stage process for ethical decision making:

1   *creating ethical sensitivity* – becoming aware of the implications of behaviour for others and insight into the possibility of ethical demands within interpersonal situations;
2   *formulating a moral course of action* – an interplay between the facts of the situation, professional ethical rules and our ethical principles;
3   *implementing an ethical decision* – the need to follow through and implement the ethical decisions made whilst coping with the resistances both inside and outside, such as politics, self-interest, protection of a colleague, fear of making a mistake;
4   *living with the ambiguities of an ethical decision* – coping with doubt and uncertainty.

We discuss this issue further at the end of the chapter on training (Chapter 9). We also include a copy of the British Association of Counselling *Code of Ethics and Practice for Supervisors of Counsellors* as an example of one profession's ethical framework for supervision. We recommend that you familiarize yourself with your own profession's latest code of practice and ethics for supervision.

Conclusion

To be a supervisor is both a complex and enriching task. It is deceptively similar to, and uses the same sort of skills as one's work with clients, but the supervisor must be clear about how it differs in content, focus and boundaries and entails a more complex ethical sensitivity. It is also important to explore your feelings, motives and expectations of being in the role of supervisor, as they will have a large effect on the supervision climate that you set in the sessions.

Above all, supervision is a place where both parties are constantly learning, and to stay a good supervisor is to return regularly to question, not only the work of the supervisees, but also what you yourself do as supervisor and how you do it.

6 Maps and models of supervision

Introduction
What is supervision?
The functions of supervision
Types of supervision
  Tutorial supervision
  Training supervision
  Managerial supervision
  Consultancy supervision
Process models of supervision
CLEAR supervision model
Useful questions and responses for each stage of the model
Forming the contract
  Practicalities and meeting arrangements
  Boundaries
  Working alliance
  The session format
  The organizational and professional context
  Taking notes
Negotiating the contract
Supervision arrangements
Supervisory styles
A developmental approach to supervision
  Level I: self-centred
  Level II: client-centred
  Level III: process-centred
  Level IV: process-in-context-centred
Reviewing the developmental approach
Research
Action research
Conclusion: choosing your framework

Introduction

In this chapter we want to pause and provide a theoretical background and framework for supervision. It is written particularly for new supervisors to help them take a broad survey of what supervision is, and the various types, aspects and styles that are possible, so that they can identify their own style of supervision and then find the one that is most appropriate for the supervisee and the setting within which they work. The chapter also covers the issues that a new or experienced supervisor needs to consider and provide the basis for thinking about what training you might need in supervision.

What is supervision?

Hess defines supervision as: 'a quintessential interpersonal interaction with the general goal that one person, the supervisor, meets with another, the supervisee, in an effort to make the latter more effective in helping people' (1980: 25). This is similar to the other most commonly used definitions of supervision by Loganbill, Hardy and Delworth (1982): 'an intensive, interpersonally focused, one-to-one relationship in which one person is designated to facilitate the development of therapeutic competence in the other person.'

For the field of coaching supervision we developed a definition that reads: The process by which a coach with the help of a supervisor, can attend to understanding better both the client system and themselves as part of the client – coach system, and by so doing transform their work and develop their craft (Hawkins and Smith 2006).

The British Association of Counselling and Psychotherapy have created some ground rules for supervision. In their first document on supervision (1987: 2) they also include an awareness of supervision being not only for the supervisee, but also for the benefit of the client. They state that: 'The primary purpose of supervision is to protect the best interests of the client.'

But this is only the beginning of the story, because the task of supervision is not only to develop the skills, understanding and ability of the supervisee, but, depending on the setting, may have other functions. Combining the multiple functions is at the heart of good practice.

The functions of supervision

Kadushin (1976), writing about social work supervision, describes three main functions or roles, which he terms as *educative, supportive and managerial*.

Proctor (1988b), makes a similar distinction in describing the main processes in the supervision of counselling, for which she uses the terms *formative, restorative and normative*.

Having worked with these two models for many years we have found both to be related to their own field, Kadushin in social work and Proctor in counselling and so have developed our own model that defines the three main functions as *developmental, resourcing and qualitative* Also Kadushin focuses on the role of the supervisor, Proctor on the supervisee benefit and our new distinctions on the process that both supervisor and supervisee are engaged in. We show the three together in Figure 6.1.

The developmental function, which is the one stressed in the definitions quoted above, is about developing the skills, understanding and capacities of the supervisees. This is done through the reflection on, and exploration of, the supervisees' work with their clients. In this exploration they may be helped by the supervisor to:

Hawkins	Proctor	Kadushin
Developmental	*Formative*	*Educational*
Resourcing	*Restorative*	*Supportive*
Qualitative	*Normative*	*Managerial*

Figure 6.1 The three main functions

- understand the client better,
- become more aware of their own reactions and responses to the client,
- understand the dynamics of how they and their client were interacting,
- look at how they intervened and the consequences of their interventions,
- explore other ways of working with this and other similar client situations.

The resourcing function is a way of responding to how any workers engaged in personal work with clients are necessarily allowing themselves to be affected by the distress, pain and fragmentation of the client, and how they need time to become aware of how this has affected them and to deal with any reactions. This is essential if workers are not to become over full of emotions. These emotions may have been produced through empathy with the client or restimulated by the client, or be a reaction to the client. Not attending to these emotions soon leads to less than effective workers, who become either over-identified with their clients or defended against being further affected by them. This in time leads to stress and what is now commonly called 'burn-out' (see Chapter 3). The British miners in the 1920s fought for 'pit-head time' – the right to wash off the grime of the work in the boss's time, rather than take it home with them. Supervision is the equivalent for those that work at the coal-face of personal distress, disease and fragmentation (see also Chapter 3).

The qualitative aspect of supervision provides the quality control function in work with people. It is not only lack of training or experience that necessitates the need in us, as workers, to have someone look with us at our work, but our inevitable human failings, blind spots, areas of vulnerability from our own wounds and our own prejudices. In many settings the supervisor may carry some responsibility for the welfare of the clients and how the supervisee is working with them. Supervisors may carry the responsibility for upholding the standards of the agency in which the work is being done. Nearly all supervisors, even when they are not line managers, have some responsibility to ensure that the work of their supervisee is appropriate and falls within defined ethical standards.

Brigid Proctor (1988b) gives some interesting vignettes to illustrate the different functions of supervision and to show how one can move from one to another.

A teacher in a young person's treatment centre is leaving after five demanding years. She asks for time to review the skills she has developed. It soon becomes clear that, before she can do that, she needs to talk about her feelings of loss and disorientation as she leaves the close, battering, intimate, structured environment. (*An apparently formative task becomes restorative or resourcing.*)

A pregnancy adviser talks about her ethical and legal dilemmas in respect of a 15-year-old client. After giving her the 20 minutes she asked for, the group decides to spend all the following week's supervision on issues of confidentiality that arise in their work. (*A normative or qualitative task*)

A teacher in a disruptive unit starts to discuss a boy he is counselling. Through a socio-drama initiated by the supervisor the group helps him notice the complex system he and the boy are in and the different expectations placed on them both by parents, headmaster, social worker and others. At the end, he says he is clearer about his chosen task and role. (*Formative, normative and restorative*)

In our work training supervisors we have elaborated the supervisory functions, by listing what we see as the primary foci of supervision, and relating these to the three categories.

Table 6.1 Primary foci of supervision

Main categories of focus	Function category
To provide a regular space for the supervisees to reflect upon the *content and process* of their work.	Developmental
To develop understanding and skills within the work.	Developmental
To receive information and another perspective concerning one's work.	Developmental/resourcing
To receive both content and process feedback.	Developmental/resourcing
To be validated and supported both as a person and as a worker.	Resourcing
To ensure that as a person and as a worker one is not left to carry unnecessarily, difficulties, problems and projections alone.	Resourcing
To have space to explore and express personal distress, restimulation, transference or counter transference that may be brought up by the work.	Qualitative/ resourcing
To plan and utilize their *personal and professional* resources better.	Qualitative/ resourcing
To be proactive rather than reactive.	Qualitative/ resourcing
To ensure quality of work.	Qualitative

Thus supervision has developmental, resourcing and qualitative components, although in different settings some aspects will be more prominent than others; and also the differing aspects are not totally separate but are combined in much of the supervisory focus. We have described elsewhere (Hawkins 1982) our own model that illustrates how these three areas are both distinct but also greatly overlap. A good deal of supervision takes place in the areas where developmental, resourcing and qualitative considerations all intermingle.

Types of supervision

It is important to form a clear contract for every supervisory relationship, and to decide what developmental, resourcing and qualitative responsibilities the supervisor is carrying. The first step in contracting is to be clear which of the main categories of supervision is being requested by the supervisees and being offered by the supervisor and what sort of match or mismatch exists. The main categories are as follows.

Tutorial supervision

In some settings the supervisor may have more of a tutor role, concentrating almost entirely on the developmental function, helping a trainee on a course explore his or her work with clients, where someone in the trainee's workplace is providing the resourcing and qualitative supervisory functions.

Training supervision

Here the supervision also emphasizes the developmental function and the supervisees will be in some form of training or apprenticeship role. They may be student social workers on placements or trainee psychotherapists working with training clients. The difference from tutorial supervision is that here the supervisor will have some responsibility for the work being done with the clients and will, therefore, carry a clear qualitative role.

Managerial supervision

We use this term where the supervisor is also the line manager of the supervisees. As in training supervision the supervisor has some clear responsibility for the work being done with the clients, but supervisor and supervisee will be in a manager–subordinate relationship, rather than a trainer–trainee one.

Consultancy supervision

Here the supervisees keep the responsibility for the work they do with their clients, but consult with their supervisor, who is neither their trainer/nor manager, on those issues they wish to explore. This form of supervision is for experienced and qualified practitioners.

So far we have described only supervision which is *vertical*, by which we mean a more experienced supervisor working with a less experienced supervisee. It is also possible to have horizontal supervision contracts, between supervisees of the same level. This will be addressed further in Chapter 10 when we consider peer-group supervision. It is also possible to have a one-to-one peer-supervision contract. This would normally be a form of consultancy supervision, but it may also have a peer-learning element.

Process models of supervision

There are a number of models that illustrate the typical stages a supervision session goes through. Page and Wosket (2001) have a useful five-stage model that shows supervision proceeding from Contract to Focus, to Space, to Bridge to Review. This is very similar both in number and progression to the CLEAR supervision model which was the first model of supervision we taught in the 1980s and have since adapted as a model of coaching (see Hawkins and Smith 2006).

CLEAR supervision model

- **Contract**: Supervision sessions start with establishing the clients' desired outcomes, understanding what needs to be covered and how the supervisor and the supervisory process can be most valuable. Also agreeing any basic ground rules or roles.
- **Listen**: By using active listening and catalytic interventions (see the Heron Model, Chapter 9) the supervisor helps the supervisee develop understanding of the situation in which he or she wants to effect a difference. The supervisor needs to let the supervisee know they have 'got their reality' – can understand and feel what it is like to be in their shoes. In addition the supervisor can help the supervisee hear themselves more fully, through reframing and making new connections in what has been shared.
- **Explore**: Through questioning, reflection and generation of new insight and awareness supervisors work with the supervisee to create different options for handling the relationship or issue.
- **Action**: Having explored the various dynamics within the situation and developed various options for handling it, the supervisee chooses a way forward and agrees the first steps. At this point it is important to do a 'fast-forward rehearsal', to enact the future first step live in the room.
- **Review**: Reviewing the actions that have been agreed. The supervisor also encourages feedback from the supervisee on what was helpful about the supervision process, what was difficult and what they would like to be different in future supervision sessions (see section on feedback, Chapter 9). Agreeing how the planned action will be reviewed at future supervision sessions completes the work.

Useful questions and responses for each stage of the model

The following examples of questions and interventions have been found to be useful in helping others to explore a situation more deeply.

1   Contracting: Starting with the end in mind and agreeing how you are going to get there together.
   - How do you want to use your time?
   - What do you most need to achieve in this session?
   - How could I (or other group members) be most valuable to you?
   - What in particular do you want us to focus on?
   - What challenges are you facing?

2   Listening: Facilitating the supervisee in generating personal insight into the situation.
   - Can you say more about that?
   - Are there any people involved that you have not mentioned?
   - How do other people – your boss, your colleagues, your team – see the situation?
   - Let us see if I can summarize the issue.

3a   Exploring 1: Helping the supervisee to understand the personal impact the situation is having on themselves.
   - How are you feeling right now?
   - Are there any feelings that you have not expressed?
   - Does this person remind you of anyone? What is it you would like to say to that person?
   - What pattern might you be repeating in this situation?

3b   Exploring 2: Challenging the supervisee to create new possibilities for future action in resolving the situation.
   - What outcomes do you and others want?
   - What behaviours need to be different in you or your team members to achieve the outcome?
   - Who might be of help to you whom you have not yet consulted?
   - Can you think of four different ways of tackling this situation?

4   Action: Supporting the supervisee in committing to a way ahead and creating the next step.
   - What are the pros and cons of each possible strategy?
   - What is your long-term objective?
   - What is the first step you need to take?
   - When precisely are you going to do that?
   - Is your plan realistic? What is the percentage chance of your succeeding?
   - Can you show me the opening line you are going to use in your next session?

5   Review: Taking stock and reinforcing ground covered and commitments made. Reviewing the process and how it could be improved. Planning the future review after the action has been tried.

- What have you decided to do next?
- What have you learned from this session?
- In what ways have you increased your own ability to handle similar situations?
- What did you find helpful about this supervision process?
- What could be better next time in this supervision process?

Review 2: Debriefing action taken between sessions.

- How did what you planned work out?
- How do you think you did?
- What feedback did you receive?
- What did you do well, and what could have been even better?
- What can you learn from what happened?

Forming the contract

All forms of supervisory relationship need to begin with a clear contract, which is created and formed by both parties, and also reflects the expectations of the organizations and professions involved. Page and Wosket (2001) propose that a contract should attend to the following:

- ground rules,
- boundaries,
- accountability,
- expectations,
- relationship.

Carroll (1996) elaborates four principle areas that need to be explored:

- practicalities,
- working alliance,
- presenting in supervision,
- evaluation.

We propose that in contracting there are six key areas that should be covered:

1 practicalities and meeting arrangements,
2 boundaries,
3 working alliance,
4 the session format,
5 the organizational and professional context,
6 taking notes.

Practicalities and meeting arrangements

In forming the contract it is necessary to be clear about the practical arrangements such as the times, frequency, place, what might be allowed to interrupt or postpone the session, and clarification of any payment that is involved, etc. Where possible it is important that supervision takes place in a private space that is conducive to learning. If it is an office or meeting room, it is important to have comfortable chairs where the supervisor and supervisee can face each other, without a desk or table interrupting the space between them. This both enables deeper and more personal relationship and provides a wider range of non-verbal communication of what might be happening beyond the words. It is also important to have telephones switched off and clear indications to others not to interrupt.

It is possible to carry out effective supervision by telephone or video phone, but our experience is that this is far more effective when the relationship has already been established face to face. We would also recommend that with ongoing telephone supervision, review meetings 'in person' are continued, in order to maintain direct contact. One of us supervised an English director of an addiction treatment programme in a foreign country where there were no experienced supervisors in this field. The supervision lasted several years, but was based on face-to-face work that had previously been established prior to going abroad, and was supported by yearly visits back to the UK, when he would come for extended supervision.

Boundaries

A boundary that often worries both supervisees and new supervisors is the boundary between supervision and counselling or therapy. Clearly working in depth in any of the helping professions can restimulate personal feelings, distress, anger or unhappiness. These feelings need to be shared and explored if the worker is going to be able to function well and learn from the re-stimulative event. To give an example from a youth club:

> A youth-club leader had spent a lot of time with a 14-year-old boy whose father had just died. He came to the supervision very angry about how the boy was receiving very little help at school. It gradually emerged that his own father left home when he was quite young and he had to support his mother emotionally, with very little outside help.

The basic boundary in this area is that supervision sessions should always start from exploring issues from work and should end with looking at where the supervisee goes next with the work that has been explored. Personal material should only come into the session if it is directly affecting, or being affected by, the work discussed; or if it is affecting the supervision relationship. Thus, in the above case, it would be important to explore how the youth-club leader's own personal material was being restimulated by the death of the young boy's father and how this was colouring his perspective on the boy's needs. If such an exploration uncovered more material than could be appropriately dealt with in the supervision, the supervisor may suggest that the worker might want to get counselling or other forms of support in exploring these personal feelings. Page and

Wosket (2001: 19) provide a very useful summary of the differences between counselling and supervision.

A supervision contract should also include clear boundaries concerning confidentiality. Confidentiality is an old chestnut which brings concern to many new supervisors. So many supervisors fall into the trap of saying or implying to the supervisees that everything shared in the supervision is confidential, only to find that some unexpected situation arises where they find it is necessary to share material from the supervision beyond the boundaries of the session.

Clearly, this is more likely to be the case of training or managerial supervision, where the supervisor has an agency function and responsibility, of which the supervision is part. But even in consultancy supervision there are circumstances in which material from the session may be appropriately taken over the boundary. The consultant supervisor may feel a personal need for supervision on how he or she is supervising this worker. Another, although less likely, possibility is that, within the supervision, gross professional misconduct may be revealed which the supervisee refuses to take active responsibility to redress. The supervisor may feel ethically or legally incumbent to take action, informing appropriate authorities.

Thus, in contracting the appropriate confidentiality boundary for any form of supervision, it is inappropriate either to say that everything shared here is confidential or, as in the case of one supervisor we knew, to say nothing here is confidential. The supervisor should be clear what sort of information participants would need to take over the boundary of the relationship; in what circumstances; how they would do this; and to whom they would take the information. Clearly, every possible situation cannot be anticipated, but by such a general exploration the possibility of sudden betrayal is diminished.

We also give our supervisees the undertaking that we will treat everything they share with professional respect and not gossip about their situation.

Working alliance

Forming the working alliance starts from sharing of mutual expectations. What sort of style of supervising the supervisees most want and which of the possible foci do they wish the supervisor to concentrate on. The supervisors also need to state clearly what their preferred mode of supervising is, and any expectations they have of the supervisees. We find it useful at the contracting phase to not only share conscious expectations but also hopes and fears. It can be useful to complete sentences such as: 'My image of successful supervision is ...'; 'What I fear happening in supervision is....'

Good working alliance is not built on a list of agreements or rules, but on growing trust, respect and goodwill between both parties. The contract provides a holding frame in which the relationship can develop, and any lapses in fulfilling the contract need to be seen as opportunities for reflection, learning and relationship-building, not judgement and defence (see Shohet and Wilmot 1991: 95).

The session format

As well as sharing hopes, fears and expectations, it is useful to ground the discussions in an exploration of what a typical session format might be like. Will all the time be spent on one case? Do they expect the supervisees to bring written-up case notes or verbatim accounts of sessions? Is there an expectation that all clients will be discussed within a certain time frame? Do they require the supervisees to check with them or inform them whenever they take on a new client?

The organizational and professional context

Most supervisory situations involve other critical stakeholders besides the direct parties in the contract. There are the expectations of the organization, or organizations, in which the work is being carried out. The organization may have its own explicit supervision policy where expectations of supervision are clarified (see Chapter 14). Where a clear policy does not exist, it is still essential that the implicit expectations of the organizations are discussed. This could include what responsibility might be expected of the supervisor in ensuring quality work and what report they require on the supervision. Likewise it is important to clarify the professional and ethical codes of conduct that both parties may be party to. In many cases the supervisor and the supervisee may be part of the same profession, but on many occasions the supervision may be happening across professions or across orientations with different codes.

Most professional associations have codes of conduct and statements of ethics which stipulate the boundaries of appropriate behaviour between a worker and a client or patient and also provide the right of appeal for the client against any possible inappropriate behaviour by the worker. Many professions are not as clear about their code of practice for supervision. We do not want to prescribe what we think are appropriate ethical standards for supervisors, because this must invariably vary from one setting to another. However, we do consider it imperative that all new supervisors check whether there are ethics statements covering supervision within their profession and/or organization. If no such statement exists, we suggest that you review the ethical standards for work with clients and become clear within yourself which of them you feel apply to the supervision context. It is important that all supervisors are clear about the ethical boundaries of their supervisory practice and are able to articulate these to their supervisees (see sections on ethics in Chapters 5 and 9).

Taking notes

It is important to be clear with the supervisee what sort of notes you, the supervisor, will keep on the supervision. There is a wide range of practice in this area, which ranges from those who take notes live in the session, to those who write up notes afterwards, and to those who do not keep notes at all. This depends partly on the style of the supervisor, but it also depends on the type of supervision relationship (see pp. 60). In training supervision or management supervision, where the supervisor has responsibility for 'overseeing' all the work of their direct report or trainee, it is useful to keep records to track which clients are being brought to supervision and which are not, and what progress is being made over time. The supervisor may also need to report on their supervision as part either of appraisal and evaluation processes, or as part of wider case management. In these cases it is important that the supervisor contracts clearly about what notes they are keeping, how they will be used, and whether the supervisee can see what is written.

The supervisor may also require the supervisee to bring case notes on their work with clients and suggest a format that is suitable for such notes. In our early days of managerial supervision, we would ask supervisees to bring notes on sessions that covered four areas:

- **Facts** (what phenomena happened in their session with the client);
- **Feelings** (what they experience while being with the client);
- **Interpretations** (what their reflective sense making was about what happened – making use of the facts and feelings); and
- **Goals** (what are the client's goals from the session and what are the supervisee's goals for taking the work forward).

We have found that when you reach the stage of seeing a large number of supervisees, each of whom may have a large number of clients, then notes become a very useful aide-memoire. Before the session starts, rereading the notes on the supervisee and their clients can create a reconnection, and the work will get underway more quickly. However, it is important that immersion in content from the past does not interrupt the supervisor from being fully present to what is happening live in the present. It can also help the supervisor to keep track of patterns which develop over time, such as the way a client may tend to miss sessions which follow a break.

A number of authors including: Page and Wosket (2001), Brown and Bourne (1996), Carroll (1996), Hewson (in Holloway and Carroll 1999) have detailed sections on the process of contracting.

Negotiating the contract

Inskipp and Proctor (2000) have provided a very helpful checklist for areas to be covered by a counselling supervisor in an initial exploratory contracting meeting. We have amended this slightly to be appropriate for all the helping professions:

Table 6.2 The exploratory contracting interview

Negotiate	The working alliance	Information to supervisee about me:
Time, length, when, frequency, where?	Beginning to set up a trusting relationship to produce a working alliance by communicating:	Theoretical background and training experience as a professional, supervisor, etc.
Cost: how much?		
Method of payment: who pays, when, invoice/cheque/cash?	EMPATHY, RESPECT,	Present work
		Support for supervision
Missed sessions: payment holidays, notice	GENUINENESS	Professional associations – memberships

Table 6.2 *Continued*

Discuss and negotiate	*Basic relationship skills*	*Information wanted from the supervisee:*
Recording	For relationship building, exploring and negotiating	Experience, qualifications
• client		Theoretical model/s
• supervision	Paraphrasing, reflecting, summarizing, focusing, questioning, self-disclosure, immediacy and purpose stating and preference stating	Professional organization, code of ethics
• agreement		
Boundaries		Freelance/organization/agency
Reviews		Where working
Evaluation/Assessment		Number of clients, and other counselling work
Code of ethics		Any agency requirements
		Professional needs and development
		In counselling or therapy?
Final decision	Can and will we work together?	

Source: Inskipp and Proctor (1995)

Supervision arrangements

So far we have concentrated on contracts for formal one-to-one supervision. However, it is also possible to have supervision arrangements that are more informal or ad hoc. In some residential or day-care agencies much of the supervision will be outside formal individual sessions. Payne and Scott (1982) have produced a format for recognizing the choices between formal and informal; planned and ad hoc supervision. This is very useful in helping teams to recognize that a great deal of supervision happens in times and places other than those officially designated for supervision. Once this is recognized, the quality of the informal or ad hoc supervision can also be negotiated and improved.

There are, however, dangers in informal supervision arrangements. Although there is a lot of creative scope for more informal types of supervision, it is easy to use these less structured types of supervision to avoid the rigours and concentrated focus of regular, formal individual sessions. We have talked extensively in this book about the natural resistances and defences to both giving and receiving supervision, and without a formal structure these resistances can produce a lot of avoidance behaviour from both the supervisor and the supervisee. It is easy to create a climate where supervision is only requested when you have a recognizable problem and at other times you have to be seen to 'soldier on'. The dangers of this type of culture are explored more fully in Chapter 13.

Supervisory styles

Having looked at the various functions and modes of supervision, we now look at how the style of supervision can vary within each of these different types. In this chapter we provide you with a broad-brush distinction between different supervisory styles and then in Chapter 7 we present our own model for more finely delineating and developing your own supervisory style.

One's style as a supervisor is affected by the style of one's practitioner work. If you are a Rogerian counsellor it is most likely that your style of supervision will be non-directive and supervisee-centred (see Rice, chapter 12 of Hess 1980). If your training has been psychoanalytic, as a supervisor you may tend to concentrate on understanding the unconscious processes of the client or the supervisees (see Moldawsky, chapter 11 of Hess 1980). If you are trained as a behaviourist, then as a supervisor you will tend to concentrate on client behaviour and the methodology of the worker (see Linehan, chapter 13 of Hess 1980). It is also possible to integrate several different therapeutic approaches into one's own supervision style, and this is explored by Boyd (1978).

Sometimes we are asked whether you should always ensure that your supervisor has the same type of training as the supervisee. There is no easy answer to this question, but both supervisor and supervisee need to share enough of a common language and belief system to be able to learn and work together. Sometimes having a supervisor with a very different training means that he or she is more able to see what your own belief system is editing out.

Supervisory style is also greatly affected by your own gender, age and cultural background, as well as your personality. It is important to be aware how these all affect the way you will view both the supervisees and the clients they will present to you. This is especially relevant when there is a match between the age, gender and background of the worker and the supervisor, but the client has a different age, background or gender (for example, if the client is an old working-class, West Indian man, and the worker and supervisor are both young middle-class, white women). In such cases the supervisor has to work doubly hard to help the supervisee explore how her own background and attitudes are affecting how she sees and works with the client. (This whole area is explored at length in Chapter 8.)

Ekstein (1969) offers a simple way of thinking about such issues, through considering our *blind spots, deaf spots and dumb spots*. Dumb spots are those where supervisees or supervisors are ignorant about what it is like to be in the position of the client. They lack the experience to understand what it means to be a homosexual; frightened of parental disapproval; or a member of an oppressed ethnic group. Blind spots are where the supervisee's own personal patterns and processes get in the way of seeing the client clearly (see the discussion of counter-transference in Chapter 7, Mode 4). Deaf spots 'are those where the therapist not only cannot hear the client, but cannot hear the supervisor either. These are likely to involve particularly defensive reactions based on guilt, anxiety or otherwise unpleasant and disruptive feelings, or hostility to authority figures' (Rowan 1983).

Thomas Kuhn the writer and historian wrote: 'You do not see something until you have the right metaphor to let you perceive it.' The emotional life often emerges first into conversation through the metaphors we use. Languages are by nature metaphorically extremely rich and many ordinary words are intrinsically metaphorical such as: illuminate, alignment, flourishing.

In training programmes we will often give one of the observer's role of noticing the metaphors of both the supervisee and supervisor and how they tune in or not to each other's metaphorical story line.

From research in Neuro Linguistic Programming (Bandler and Grinder 1979) we know that different people have different dominant sensory modes. Some people are:

- Visual and use visual metaphors and language such as: 'Can you look at the problem I have getting my team lined up behind my vision?'
- Auditory and use metaphors and language drawn from sound such as: 'Can you hear how my team does not seem to be in tune with me?'
- Kinaesthetic and use feeling, moving and tactile metaphors and language such as: 'Can you feel what it is like for me when my team members are out of touch with my hunger for change and I cannot get them moving?'

In supervision to achieve rapport with the supervisee it is important to:

- see the world through the eyes of the visually dominant supervisee and to align one's views and perspectives;
- attune to the supervisee who is dominantly auditory, to get on their frequency and be in harmony with them;
- to be in touch with the feelings and sensations of the kinaesthetic dominant supervisee, to move alongside them and get under their skin.

In the dominant culture of Europe and North America, the majority of people are visually dominant, which is partly a reflection of our education system. In achieving deeper levels of connection and rapport with another, not only do we need to start by matching their dominant mode but also move to closer connection through the language we use. When in a visual mode we are more likely to stand apart and look at what is going on. In auditory mode we listen, tune in and try to resonate with their story and in kinaesthetic mode we are moved by them or with them.

To do this authentically, it is important to be aware of your own sensory dominance and your metaphorical home ground and how that interplays with different clients. From this foundation one can then expand one's own metaphorical range and this provides a richness that one can use to help the supervisee to increase their emotional range and expressiveness and also how they can then help their clients do the same.

A developmental approach to supervision

In the sudden upsurge of literature on supervision in the field of counselling psychology in the United States, the main model that has emerged is the developmental approach. This approach suggests that supervisors need to have a range of styles and approaches, which are modified as the counsellor gains in experience and enters different, definable, developmental stages.

One of the first seminal works in this field was by Hogan (1964) working in the field of training psychologists as psychotherapists. Many writers have followed since then; most notably Worthington (1987) and Stoltenberg and Delworth (1987). Rather than describing each of these models (they are well described in Stoltenberg and Delworth 1987: 18–30) we integrate them into a combined developmental model of four major stages of supervisee development.

Level I: self-centred

The first stage is characterized by trainee dependence on the supervisor. The supervisees can be anxious, insecure about their role and their own ability to fulfil it, lacking insight, but also highly motivated. A study by Hale and Stoltenberg suggests that the two main causes of anxiety of new trainees are firstly evaluation apprehension and secondly objective self-awareness. Objective self-awareness is a term borrowed from social psychology and is used to suggest that the process of being videotaped, audiotaped, or otherwise made to focus on oneself . . . can elicit negative evaluations of one's performance and concomitant feelings of anxiety.

(Stoltenberg and Delworth 1987: 61)

New trainees have not had the experience to develop grounded criteria on which to assess their performance and consequently can feel very dependent on how their supervisor is assessing their work. This apprehension may be linked to the supervisor having some formal assessment role in their training or in their work evaluation. It will also be present on a more day-to-day basis in a concern about how the supervisor is viewing their work, and how they compare to other supervisees that their supervisor sees.

We have found this concern to be particularly present when taping sessions is employed, or where trainees are asked to bring 'verbatims' or accounts of sessions. However, supervision generally must help the supervisees to reflect back on themselves, and for the new trainee this is inevitably anxiety provoking.

Level I workers tend: 'To focus on specific aspects of the client's history, current situation, or personality assessment data to the exclusion of other relevant information. Grand conclusions may be based on rather discreet pieces of information' (Stoltenberg and Delworth 1987: 56).

It is difficult for workers in this stage to have an overview of the whole therapeutic process as they have usually only worked with clients in the early stages of therapeutic work. This may make them impatient or fearful that the process will ever move on from a current sticking place.

In order to cope with the normal anxiety of Level I trainees, the supervisor needs to provide a clearly structured environment which includes positive feedback and encouragement to the supervisees to return from a premature judgement of both the client and themselves to attending to what actually took place. 'Balancing support and uncertainty is the major challenge facing supervisors of beginning therapists' (Stoltenberg and Delworth: 64).

Level II: client-centred

Here the supervisees have overcome their initial anxieties and begin to fluctuate between dependence and autonomy; and between over-confidence and being overwhelmed.

We have written elsewhere (Hawkins 1980) about how this stage manifests itself in residential workers in therapeutic communities. This paper, entitled 'Between Scylla and Charybdis', describes how the trainee has to be supported by tutors and supervisors to steer a course between submergence and over-identification representing the Charybdis on the one side and flight into over-professionalism being the Scylla on the other side. This is how a supervisee disappearing into the Charybdis whirlpool was described:

> He stops reading books or writing letters; he becomes unable to objectify his experience in case conferences or supervision; he finds it difficult to set limits, say no to residents (clients) or to protect his off-duty hours ... unable to separate other people's difficulties from one's own intra-psychic dynamics, or investing one's own success or failure and validation in the success or failure of the residents.
>
> (Hawkins 1980: 195)

The staff member who is dashed on the rocks of Scylla becomes:

> Defensively over-clinical to avoid any personal involvement ... staff trainees become unable to meet clients on a person-to-person basis, desperately hold on to a false persona of adequacy and retreat into administration.
>
> (Hawkins 1979: 222–3)

In their work with clients the Level II trainee begins to be less simplistic and single-focused both about the development process of the client and their own training: 'The trainee begins to realize, on an emotional level, that becoming a psychotherapist [*or other helping professional*] is a long and arduous process. The trainee discovers that skills and interventions effective in some situations are less than effective at other times' (Stoltenberg and Delworth 1987: 71; we have inserted the italics section).

Loss of the early confidence and simplicity of approach may lead some trainees to be angry with their supervisor whom they see as responsible for their disillusionment. The supervisor is then seen as 'an incompetent or inadequate figure who has failed to come through when he or she was so badly needed' (Loganbill, Hardy and Delworth 1982: 19). Some writers have likened this stage of development to that of adolescence in normal human development, with Level I being similar to childhood; Level III early adulthood; and Level IV being full maturity.

Certainly Level II can feel to the supervisor like parenting an adolescent: the testing out of one's authority, fluctuation in moods and a need to provide both space for the trainees to learn from mistakes and a degree of holding and containment. In this stage the trainees can also become more reactive to their clients who, like the supervisor, may also be seen as the cause of their own turbulence.

The supervisor of Level II trainees needs to be less structured and didactic than with Level I trainees, but a good deal of emotional holding is necessary as the trainees may oscillate between excitement and depressive feelings of not being able to cope, or perhaps even of being in the wrong job.

Level III: process-centred

> The Level III trainee shows increased professional self-confidence, with only conditional dependency on the supervisor. He or she has greater insight and shows more stable motivation. Supervision becomes more collegial, with sharing and exemplification augmented by professional and personal confrontation.
>
> (Stoltenberg and Delworth 1987: 20)

The Level III trainee is also more able to adjust their approach to meet the individual and particular needs of their client at that particular time. They are also more able to see the client in a wider context and have developed what we call 'helicopter skills'. These are the skills of being fully present with the client in the session, but being able simultaneously to have an overview that can see the present content and process in the context of:

- the total process of the therapeutic relationship;
- the client's personal history and life patterns; the client's external life circumstances;
- the client's life stage, social context and ethnic background.

It is less possible to recognize what orientation the trainee has been schooled in, as they have by this stage incorporated the training into their own personality, rather than using it as a piece of learnt technology.

Level IV: process-in-context-centred

This stage is referred to as 'Level III integrated' by Stoltenberg and Delworth. By this time the practitioner has reached 'master' level 'characterized by personal autonomy, insightful awareness, personal security, stable motivation and an awareness of the need to confront his or her own personal and professional problems' (Stoltenberg and Delworth 1987: 20). Often by this stage supervisees have also become supervisors themselves and this can greatly consolidate and deepen their own learning. Stoltenberg and Delworth (1987: 102) quote a colleague: 'When I'm supervising, I'm forced to be articulate and clear about connections across domains and that makes it easier for me to integrate'.

 We often find that we say things to our supervisees that we need to learn. It is as if our mouth is more closely linked to our subconscious knowing than was our mental apparatus! The wise fool Nasrudin, when he was asked how he had learnt so much, replied: 'I simply talk a lot and when I see people agreeing, I write down what I have said' (Hawkins 2005).

 Certainly the stage of Level IV is not about acquiring more knowledge, but allowing this to be deepened and integrated until it becomes wisdom; for as another Sufi teacher put it: 'Knowledge without wisdom is like an unlit candle.'

 It is possible to compare the developmental stages of supervisee development to other developmental approaches. We have already mentioned the analogy to the stages of human growth and development. We can also posit the analogy to the stages of development within the medieval craft guilds. Here the trainee started as a *novice*, then became a *journeyman*, then an *independent craftsman*, and finally a *master craftsman*.

The model also has parallels in the stages of group development. Schutz (1973) describes how groups begin with the predominant concerns being *inclusion/exclusion*: Can I fit in and belong here? Once this has been resolved the group will normally move on to issues of *authority*; challenging the leader, dealing with competitiveness, etc. Only then will the group move on to look at issues of *affection* and intimacy; how to get close to the others and what is the appropriate closeness. This progression of themes seems to be paralleled in the supervision–developmental approach, particularly where supervision is part of a training, which is being carried out with other trainees (see also Chapter 9).

Finally the four stages can be seen as characterized by where the centre of their focus and concern is located (Table 6.3).

Table 6.3 Supervisee developmental stages

Level I	self-centred	'Can I make it in this work?'
Level II	client-centred	'Can I help this client make it?'
Level III	process-centred	'How are we relating together?'
Level IV	process-in-context-centred	'How do processes interpenetrate?'

We return to this map in the following chapter when we explore the developmental aspects of our own model of supervision.

Reviewing the developmental approach

The developmental model is a useful tool in helping supervisors more accurately to assess the needs of their supervisees and to realize that part of the task of supervision is to help in the development of the supervisee, both within stages and between stages of development. The model also stresses that as the supervisee develops so must the nature of the supervision.

However, the limits to its usefulness must be borne in mind. First, there is a danger of using the model too rigidly as a blueprint for prescribing how every supervisee at each stage should be treated, without enough reference to the particular needs of the individual, the style of the supervisor and the uniqueness of the supervisor–supervisee relationship.

Second, Hess (1987) points out that supervisors are also passing through stages in their own development and we must, therefore, look at the interaction of both parties' developmental stages. This challenge is taken up in part by Stoltenberg and Delworth (1987: 152–67). They suggest a parallel model for supervisor's development as follows:

- **Level 1**: The tendency of supervisors to be anxious to do the 'right' thing and to be effective in the role. This can lead to being overly mechanistic or attempting to play an expert role.
- **Level 2**: 'The supervisor now sees that the process of supervision is more

complex and multi-dimensional than he or she had imagined. It is no longer the "great adventure" it once was.' There is sometimes a tendency to go on one's own as a supervisor, rather than get support for one's supervision practice.

- **Level 3**: Most supervisors reach this level if they avoid stagnating at Level 1 or dropping out at Level 2. At this level the supervisor displays a consistent motivation to the supervisory role and is interested in constantly improving his or her performance. They are able to make an honest self-appraisal (see Chapter 9).
- **Level 4** (Stoltenberg and Delworth call this Level 3 integrated): At this level the supervisor can modify their style to work appropriately with supervisees from any level of development, from different disciplines, different orientations and across cultural differences (see Chapter 8). Such supervisors are able to supervise supervision practice and may also teach or tutor supervision training.

An individual should not embark on giving supervision until they have reached a Level 3 or Level 4 of development in their own practice. They then have to cope with being an advanced practitioner and an early stage supervisor. Stoltenberg and Delworth suggest that it is very hard for a Level I or Level 2 supervisor to supervise practitioners other than those who are at Level 1 in their development. They also need good supervision on their supervision practice.

It is important not to apply this model too rigidly, but it can be a useful map for matching the right supervisee to the right supervisor, or for exploring difficulties in the supervision relationship.

Carroll (1987) warns those working outside America of another of the limitations of this model, which is that it has been developed entirely within an American context and writes: 'We need to be careful that we do not transport theories that work well in other climates to Britain without serious investigation that they will adapt well to the changing environment. Counselling supervision may not be a good traveller.' He quotes the research by O'Toole (1987) which shows significant differences between the counselling climates in America and Britain. In other professional fields there are also major differences between the cultures on each side of the Atlantic.

Finally, we would do well to remember that we can become egotistic, over-inflated, in thinking that we are responsible for another person's development. Here is a story that beautifully makes this point.

> A man once saw a butterfly struggling to emerge from its cocoon, too slowly for his taste, so he began to blow on it gently. The warmth of his breath speeded up the process all right. But what emerged was not a butterfly but a creature with mangled wings.

Despite these reservations, we would particularly recommend some acquaintance with this model to all supervisors who work in the context of a professional training course, in order that they may plan what supervision is most appropriate for trainees in different stages of the course.

Research

Although since we wrote the first edition of this book (1989), there has been an enormous number of both books, papers and articles on supervision, the amount of research in the area has grown much more slowly. The area that has produced the greatest amount of research studies are the fields of counselling psychology and psychotherapy, particularly in the United States.

As Fleming and Steen point out, 'Supervision research is largely descriptive. Most studies have focused on supervisees; reaction to supervision with little attention paid to outcome' (2004: 171).

Their own study does provide a very useful summary of the top ten most helpful supervisor behaviours as assessed by supervisees and trainees (Fleming and Steen 2004: 178–9). Nick Ladany (2004, and Ladany et al. (1999)) have also produced some very useful research on how supervisees experience supervision and what they see as effective. Hawkins and Schwenk (2006) have carried out research for the Chartered Institute of People Development (CIPD) on the whole field of coaching supervision in the UK, looking at the various perspectives of the organizational buyer (mostly through the Human Resources department), the coach manager, the internal coach and the external provider of coaching. The research focuses on the role supervision can play in constantly improving the quality of the coaching and also ensuring greater learning and benefit for both the individual and organizational clients.

What is so far missing from the research is outcome-based studies that show the effect of supervision on the practice of the supervisee and the work with their clients. This is a far from easy task as Fleming and Steen (2004) point out:

> The acid test of effective supervision would be demonstrable proof that a particular form of supervisory intervention could be traced through a positive outcome for the client receiving help from the supervisee ... However, the number of causal links and intervening variables that must be accounted for in testing this hypothesis is formidable ... Unsurprisingly therefore no published research yet appears to have established a secure outcome between supervisor conduct and patient outcome.
>
> (Holloway and Neufeldt 1995)

Action research

While encouraging more research on the growing field of supervision, it is also important to recognize that supervision in itself is a form of research on practice and to discover ways of making this more effective. Of all the different types of research, action research is arguably the most suited to our approach, both as a method of researching supervision and because it has many similarities to supervision in its practice and philosophy. It is based on a non-dualistic, participatory philosophy, and so does not seek to divide the world into objective and subjective research but to understand the complex relationships within a 'field' of inquiry through multiple perspectives. It is possible to view our approach to supervision as small pieces of action research carried out on an ongoing basis. Reason and Bradbury write that action research: 'seeks to bring together action and reflection, theory and practice, in participation with others, in the pursuit of practical solutions to issues of pressing concern to people' (Reason and Bradbury 2001: 1).

Both action research and our approach to supervision are based on this kind of inquiry – one in which all those involved are acknowledged to interact within an intersubjective 'field'. In other words they act within a system of 'reciprocal mutual influence' (Beebe, Jaffe et al. 1992; Stolorow et al. 2002). It is an approach which accepts that we cannot be objective as our presence always makes us part of the field of inquiry.

For action researchers, as well as for supervisors, finding a greater understanding of our work is not sufficient; it must lead to improved practice. We do not engage in it solely to know more or discover the 'truth'; it is undertaken in order to improve our practice. We can see, particularly through the use of modes 5 and 6 of our model (see Chapter 7), that all parties in the supervision process (client, supervisor and supervisee) set up a mutually influencing 'field' which can be explored in rich, creative and complex ways. The process allows a sense of what is 'true' to emerge in the spaces between those involved. This may uncover something truthful, while not denying its relational rather than 'objective' nature. Stolorow, Atwood and Orange say: 'We must attend to truth-as-possible-understanding and not truth-as correspondence-to-fact' (2002: 119).

There is not one 'truth' that can be reached by the supervisor but, by reflecting on the stories, metaphors, images and feeling experienced both in the session, with the client and in the supervision session itself, we deepen our understanding and our ability to respond with sensitivity and care.

Action research methodology takes these philosophical assumptions into account. One method is called Co-operative Inquiry (Heron 1996) which is collaborative in nature. Heron and Reason (2001: 179) describe these research groups as being 'research with' rather than 'research on' others and that participants are all researchers and all 'subjects' as the perspective of each contributor is as valuable and significant as any other. They all have a stake in any 'outcomes'. All those involved are, therefore, called co-researchers. Various methodologies have been developed to help these groups be rigorous rather than collusive in their practice, the most significant of which are known as cycles of action and reflection (Heron and Reason 2001: 179). Iterative cycles of action are followed by a period of reflection both inside and outside the group. Each period of reflection leads to fresh action, which has benefited from the thoughts and ideas generated during the period of reflection.

We find that the Learning Cycle described by Kolb (1984) is useful for understanding why the apparently simple notion of cycles of action and reflection is so powerful, particularly when put together with Argyris and Schon's (1978) notion of single and double loop learning (see below). Kolb's learning cycle leads from concrete experience to reflective observation, to abstract conceptualization, to active experimentation and that leads again to concrete experience. This cycle shows the process from practical experience through reflection to a change in action. In Chapter 3, Section 2 we develop the Kolb model and describe the four stages of Action, reviewing, thinking and planning as all necessary parts of a full learning process and the dangers when one or more of these stages is left out.

Argyris and Schon (1978) developed a similar theory of learning which involved both a 'single loop' and a 'double loop'. In 'single loop learning', action and reflection lead to further learning that is completed within a single, coherent frame of reference. In 'double loop learning', the second loop reflects on the first learning loop in a way that explores its attitudes, values and assumptions. This second loop ensures that the learning is deepened beyond the most obvious layer. It is the second loop that actually digs below our questions and finds new ones. Adherence to the single loop alone may lead to finding an efficient way of behaving but does not lead to new understandings. For instance, a supervisee might learn within a single loop that clients may be erratic in their attendance if a clear contract is not made, but when the learning has a double loop they may understand, for example, why they are drawn not to make a clear contract with a client who shares with them a difficulty in accepting authority. The second loop digs below the simple cause-and-effect assumptions of the first and the supervisee learns more than simply understanding that not having a contract can result in erratic attendance. The change in the supervisee's behaviour is founded on a greater understanding of the assumptions behind their actions. One of us (Hawkins 1991) developed the notion of a third learning loop which attends to higher purpose where the learning is taken into the realm of the spiritual.

We can see by this example that supervision practice can be understood as small pieces of action research constantly carried out within the practice of the supervisee and supervisor. At its most simple the 'action' of the session with the client is reflected upon in the supervision and new action is suggested as a result of the reflection. However, as the supervisee develops an 'internal supervisor' (Casement 1985), these cycles can be experienced within each client session and then further reflected upon in supervision. In fact, the supervision session can ensure that the learning has a double loop quality so that attitudes, values and assumptions are explored and not just accepted from within a single frame of reference. Supervision which just relies on single loop learning may result in more efficient practice but would not deepen the quality of the work.

Action research can also provide a number of mechanisms for ensuring that we are continuously researching the efficacy of our supervision practice, by providing spaces within the supervision sessions whereby both parties can reflect on the process they are part of. This can involve structured feedback from both parties, the use of some of the many models in this book to evaluate the supervision process, or the joint decision for both parties to experiment with different ways of operating. Appreciative inquiry, which we describe in some detail in Chapter 13, is a type of action research and has a similar methodology. It focuses on a collaborative discovery of appreciative questions and subsequent exploration. This type of inquiry is one of the ways that research can be brought right to the heart of the supervision process.

Supervision, then, can be understood as a type of action research built into the working life of the practitioner so that each is a researcher as well as a practitioner. This is true, of course, of the practice of supervision itself. Supervisors can thus be considered, not only as researchers, but as teachers of research as they encourage their supervisees to structure ongoing inquiry into their practice. It is a small step from here to more full-blown research in which supervisees and supervisors collaborate in an inquiry which gathers knowledge and experience together to improve the practice of supervision further. This can be further enhanced when supervisors, either from the same organization, or indeed across organizations, meet as a group to explore the nature of their supervision and experiment with new more effective ways of supervising. In Chapter 13, in the section on the learning organization and learning profession, we argue that such mechanisms are essential to ensure that learning flows back from the front line of practice into the organizations and professions of which it is part. We hope such research will be carried out more frequently in the future.

Conclusion: choosing your framework

Our hope is that this chapter will provide readers with the tools to choose and/or clarify:

- the supervision framework they wish to use;
- how to structure the supervision process of each session using the CLEAR model;
- how they will amend their basic framework depending on the work, needs and developmental stage of the supervisee;
- how they will balance the competing demands of the qualitative, developmental and resourcing functions of supervision;
- what sort of supervision contract they will negotiate, and what issues it will include;
- how they can build action research into their practice so that their supervision practice is constantly evolving and developing.

However, the map is not the territory. Before setting off on an expedition into new terrain, you need to ensure that the map is as good as you can get, but once you have embarked on the journey you do not want to spend the whole time buried in your map. You only need the map to send you in the right direction, or to redirect you when you get lost and also to make periodic checks that you are all going in the right direction.

Finally, it is important that the map you develop is accessible to and understandable by your supervisees. Supervision is a joint journey and works best where there is a shared model and framework.

7   Seven-eyed supervision: A process model

Introduction
The double-matrix or the seven-eyed supervisor model
  Focus on the client and what and how they present
  Exploration of the strategies and interventions used by the supervisee
  Exploration of the relationship between the client and the supervisee
  Focus on the supervisee
  Focus on the supervisory relationship
  The supervisor focusing on their own process
  Focus on the wider contexts in which the work happens
Mode 1: Focus on the client and what and how they present
Mode 2: Exploration of the strategies and interventions used by the supervisee
Mode 3: Focusing on the relationship between the client and the supervisee
  Attending to the client's transference
  Learning from the patient
Mode 4: Focusing on the supervisee
Mode 5: Focusing on the supervisory relationship
Mode 6: The supervisor focusing on their own process
  Mode 6A: Supervisor–client relationship
Mode 7: Focusing on the wider contexts in which the work happens
  7.1 Focusing on the context of the client
  7.2 Focusing on supervisee's interventions in the context of their profession and
       organization
  7.3 Focusing on the context of the supervisee–client relationship
  7.4 Focusing on the wider world of the supervisee
  7.5 Focusing on the context of the supervisory relationship
  7.6 Focusing on the context of the supervisor
Integrating the processes
Linking the model to a developmental perspective
Critiques of the model
  The model is hierarchic
  The model is claiming to be integrative but is biased to one specific orientation
  Mode 7 is of a different order and needs to be contained in the other six modes
Conclusion

Introduction

This chapter was originally written especially for those who supervise counsellors or psychotherapists, but over the last 20 years, we have found that it has been a useful model for those supervising right across the range of people professions from teachers to coaches; from general practitioners to management consultants. So we have now developed the model and changed some of the terminology to make it more available to the many different people professions.

Having presented, in Chapter 6, many of the maps and models of supervision that are currently available, we now turn to our own model of the supervision process. Our double matrix model, which we first presented in 1985 (Hawkins 1985), differs significantly from the other ways of looking at supervision. In this model we turn the focus away from the context and the wider organizational issues (discussed in the models in Chapter 6) to look more closely at the process of the supervisory relationship. This model has since been referred to as the 'Seven-eyed model of supervision' (Inskipp and Proctor 1995), a name we have since adopted.

The double-matrix or the seven-eyed supervisor model

Our interest in this dimension began when we were trying to understand the significant differences in the way each member of our own peer group supervised and the different styles of supervision that we had encountered elsewhere. These differences could not be explained by developmental stages, our primary tasks, or our intervention styles. From further exploration came the realization that the differences were connected to the constant choices we were making, as supervisors, as to that which we focused on.

At any time in supervision there are many levels operating. At a minimum all supervision situations involve at least four elements:

- a supervisor,
- a supervisee,
- a client,
- a work context.

Of these four, normally only the supervisor and the supervisee are directly present in the supervision session, except in live supervision. However, the client and the context of the work are carried into the session in both the conscious awareness and the unconscious sensing of the supervisee. They may also, at times, be brought indirectly into the session in the form of audio and videotapes or written verbatims of sessions or through role-play.

Thus the supervision process involves two interlocking systems or matrices:

- The client/supervisee matrix;
- The supervisee/supervisor matrix.

The task of the supervisory matrix is to pay attention to the supervisee/client matrix, and it is in how this attention is given that supervisory styles differ.

Our model divides supervision styles into two main categories:

- supervision that pays attention directly to the supervisee/client matrix, by reflecting on the reports, written notes or tape recordings of the client sessions;
- supervision that pays attention to the supervisee/client matrix through how that system is reflected in the here-and-now experiences of the supervision process.

Each of these two major styles of managing the supervision process can be further subdivided into three categories, depending on the emphasis of the focus of attention. This gives us six modes of supervision, plus a seventh mode that focuses on the wider context in which supervision and the client work happens.

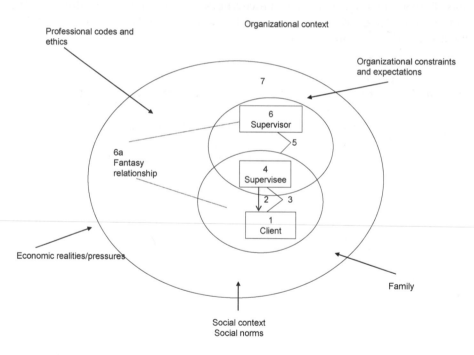

Figure 7.1 The seven-eyed model of supervision

Focus on the client and what and how they present

Attention is concentrated on the actual phenomena of the session, how the clients presented themselves, what they chose to share, which area of their life they wanted to explore, and how this session's content might relate to content from previous sessions. The aim and goal of this form of supervision are to help the supervisee pay attention to the client, the choices the client is making and the connections between the various aspects of the client's life.

Exploration of the strategies and interventions used by the supervisee

The focus here is on the choices of intervention made by the supervisee; not only what interventions were used but also when and why they were used. Alternative strategies and interventions might then be developed and their consequences anticipated. The main goal of this form of supervision would be to increase the supervisee's choices and skills in intervention.

Exploration of the relationship between the client and the supervisee

Here the supervisor will pay particular attention to what was happening consciously and unconsciously in the relationship between the supervisee and their client. This will include: how the session started and finished; what happened around the edges of the sessions; metaphors and images that emerged; and changes in voice and posture of both parties. The main goal of this form of supervision will be to help the supervisee to step out of their own perspective and develop a greater insight and understanding of the dynamics of the working relationship with a particular client.

Focus on the supervisee

Here the supervisor concentrates on how the supervisee is consciously and unconsciously affected by the work with their clients. It includes focusing on the supervisee's development and how they resource themselves (see Chapters 3 and 6). The main goal of this form of supervision is to increase the capacity of the supervisee to engage with their clients and more effectively to use their responses to the clients.

Focus on the supervisory relationship

Here the supervisor focuses on the relationship in the supervision session. This is essential in two ways; firstly to ensure that regular attention is given to the quality of the working alliance between the two parties; and secondly in order to explore how the relationship might be unconsciously playing out or paralleling the hidden dynamics of the work with clients (Mattinson 1975; Searles 1955). Thus, if the client was covertly acting in a passive-aggressive way to the supervisee, this might emerge in the supervision by the supervisee's becoming unconsciously passive-aggressive to the supervisor as they discuss that particular client. The goal is to enable the supervisee to surface unaware dynamics.

The supervisor focusing on their own process

Here the supervisor primarily pays attention to their own here-and-now experience in the supervision; what feelings, thoughts and images are emerging for them both in working with this supervisee and in response to the material that is shared about the work. The supervisor uses these responses to provide another source of information about what might be happening in the supervisory or client relationship. The unconscious material of the supervisee/client session which has been unheard at the conscious level by the supervisee may emerge in the thoughts, feelings and images of the supervisor.

Focus on the wider contexts in which the work happens

Although the six modes of focus are inclusive in so far as they include all the processes within both the client and supervisory matrices, the supervisory and client relationships also exist within a wider context which impinges upon and colours the processes within it. The supervisor cannot afford to act as if the client-supervisee-supervisor threesome exists on an island without a context. There are professional codes and ethics, organizational requirements and constrictions, relationships with other involved agencies as well as social, cultural, political and economic contexts. All of these need to be attended to and taken into consideration.

In Chapter 8 we explore how the organizational roles, power dynamics and issues of culture may affect the supervisory process and in the final section of the book (Chapters 13 and 14) we explore the wider organizational context in which supervision takes place and how to work with it.

It would be very unusual to find a supervisor who remained entirely in one of these seven modes of supervision and we would hold that good supervision must inevitably involve the movement between modes. However, distinguishing between the modes in their pure form has many advantages. It allows supervisors to be clearer about their own style, its strengths and weaknesses and which possible modes of supervision they might be avoiding out of habit or lack of familiarity and practice.

Not only does the model provide a way of increasing the options for the supervisor, it also can be used by the supervisee as a language within which to negotiate changes in supervision style and can be used as a tool in a regular two-way review and appraisal of the supervision.

The model is also useful in training supervisors to work with various elements of the supervision process, learning the refinements of each focus separately, so that they can then develop their own style and method of putting the different processes together (see Chapter 9). We liken this to musicians learning to play scales before performing concert pieces.

We now look at each of the processes in more detail.

Mode 1: Focus on the client and what and how they present

> It is the task of the supervisor to enable the supervisees to become more aware of what actually takes place in the session.
>
> (Shainberg 1983)

To a supervisor, focusing on what actually happened in the client session may sound deceptively easy. But as Shainberg points out in her excellent paper, 'Teaching therapists how to be with their clients' (Shainberg 1983), the difficulty for therapists in staying with their 'not knowing' causes them to fear their powerlessness and rush to try and make sense too quickly. This can lead on to premature theorizing and over early interpretation. Supervisors can both collude with and intensify this process through their own anxiety, their need to be potent, and their need to have answers for their supervisees.

Shainberg is not the first to point out this phenomenon. Freud relates how a store of ideas is created, born from a man's need to make his helplessness tolerable (Freud 1927: 18) and Bion in his writings on therapy constantly entreats us to stay empty and unknowing, uncluttered by premature judgement, theory and interpretation. 'In every consulting room there ought to be two rather frightened people' (Bion 1974). 'True knowing,' Shainberg writes, comes from 'being able to observe and describe what is going on in the present in accurate, concrete, and complete detail. This is different from wanting to change or get rid of or compare or assume a fixed meaning about what is happening' (Shainberg 1983: 164).

Often the first task in every supervisory exploration is to ask the supervisee to accurately describe their clients; how they came to be having sessions; their physical appearance; how they move and hold themselves; how they breathe, speak, look, gesture, etc; their language, metaphors and images and the story of their life as they told it. It is almost impossible to do quality supervision on a particular client until the client has metaphorically 'fully entered the room'.

The task requires the clear focus of a portrait painter or Zen archer and the supervisor's job is to help the supervisees to stay with this difficult task. This involves challenging the assumptions that the supervisees make and asking them to return to what they saw or what the client said, rather than their interpretations. It also entails watching for the supervisees' 'ideological editor' or belief system that edits what information the supervisees are relating to and forms the frame in which they present the clients.

Shainberg shows, in her paper, how often new therapists have a fixed notion of how the work with the client should go. They are anxious to apply the theory that they have learnt about personality types and pathology to the patients they see before them. This leads them to stop seeing the actuality of the unique human being that they are with and can lead to 'objectification': the seeing of the patient as a challenge to their therapeutic prowess. In the second of her two illustrations, Shainberg describes the 'objectification process' in one of her supervisees:

> She then said she did not experience the patient in the same way as she would 'a fellow human being'. She could not feel other than that the patient was 'so far a test of my being a therapist'. I said she had turned the patient into an object 'to be worked on' at this point. She said she felt the gist of it was that 'if it is a person you can feel free, but if it is a patient you have to do something to change things. Otherwise what are you doing there?' I did not comment on the use of her word it but heard it as how remote she experienced the patient at this point from herself, as though the patient were not her fellow being sharing the human condition of suffering, daily conflict, having a mother and a father, being in fear, facing the inevitability of death.
>
> (Shainberg 1983: 168)

Shainberg gradually helps supervisees become aware of the internal dialogue inside their own heads, the judgements, expectations, self-doubt, etc., so that they can return to the actuality of the experience of *being* with the patient prior to *doing*.

> Focus all your attention on seeing as clearly as you can the way this person behaves and what you think and feel being with her. Do not try to find

meanings, make connections, or understand. Observe what takes place and your responses.

(Shainberg 1983: 169)

There is a place for theorizing and using theory to understand what is happening in work with clients, but it must always come after direct encounter with the client in the fullness of their unique being. Between the stage of concentrating on the direct observation and the content of what the client said and turning to theoretical consideration, there are several further steps that need to be taken:

- an exploration of the connections between the content of one part of the session with material from elsewhere in the session;
- listening for the connecting pattern that is contained within each of the parts;
- the tentative linking of material from one session to material and sequences from previous sessions. Supervisees who are new to the work so often treat each session as if it was a closed system, rather than part of an ongoing process.
- an exploration of the links between the content of sessions and the life of the client, both outside and prior to these sessions. In this we can look at the content in the supervisee/client session as a microcosm of the macrocosm of the client's life and relationships as a whole.

We have found two techniques particularly useful when exploring Mode 1. One is to attend to the opening moments of the session, even before you think the session has started; to see how the clients first presented and revealed themselves before the conversation got fully underway.

The other useful approach is to use video or audio recordings of sessions. Here one can move between the phenomenon of the material and the feelings of the therapist (see Chapter 9, and Kagan 1980).

Mode 2: Exploration of the strategies and interventions used by the supervisee

In this mode the supervisor focuses on what interventions the supervisees made in their work with the clients, how and why they made them and interventions they would rather have made. One psychotherapy trainer that we interviewed uses this approach as the main focus of her supervision:

I ask them what interventions they have made; what reasons they had for making them; where their interventions were leading them; how they made their interventions and when and then I ask what they want to do with this client now?

(Davies 1987)

It is useful to bear in mind Abraham Maslow's aphorism: 'If the only tool you have is a hammer, you will tend to treat everything as if it is a nail' and it is important to make sure that your supervisees not only have a wide range of interventions in their tool box, but also that they use the tools appropriately and are not blunting their chisels by using them to turn screws!

We have often found that when supervisees bring to supervision their concerns about what intervention to use they can get stuck in dualistic thinking. They will make statements which we term 'either-or-isms' such as:

- I either have to confront his controlling behaviour or put up with it.
- I didn't know whether to wait a bit longer, or interpret his silence as his aggression towards me.
- I don't know whether to continue working with him.

As you can see they do not always contain the words 'either or', but they are always based on the supervisees seeing two opposing options. The job of the supervisor is to avoid the trap of helping the supervisees evaluate between these two choices, and point out that they have reduced numerous possibilities to only two. Once the supervisees have realized that they are operating under a restrictive assumption, the supervisor can help them generate new options for intervening.

Generating new options can be undertaken by using a simple brainstorming approach. The basic rules of brainstorming are:

- Say whatever comes into your head.
- Get the ideas out. Don't evaluate or judge them.
- Use the other person's ideas as springboards.
- Include the wildest options you can invent.

Brainstorming is helped by setting a high target for the number of options, as it is only when we have exhausted all the obvious rational choices that the creative mind starts to get going. Often it is the craziest idea that contains the kernel of a creative way forward. In a group supervision you could try brainstorming 20 ways of dealing with a supervisee's impasse: in individual supervision you could ask the supervisee to invent six or seven different ways of handling the situation with which they are supposedly stuck.

Group supervision offers a great number of creative possibilities. The group contains a greater variety of styles and can avoid the potential dualism between the supervisor's or the supervisee's approach.

Group supervision also offers a greater range of active role-playing possibilities. Different group members can choose one possible approach they would like to try out from the list of brainstormed possibilities. Then, with supervisees playing the client, several different possible strategies can be tried and evaluated (see Chapter 10). Even in individual supervision the supervisees can try out different options. It is possible to use an empty chair or the supervisor to represent the client. If necessary, after trying the intervention, they can role-reverse and respond from within the role of the client.

Many supervisors, when focusing in Mode 2, offer their own intervention. There are dangers in doing this. It is easy as supervisor to want to show off your intervention skill without fully acknowledging how much easier it is to be skilful in the relative ease of the supervisory setting than when face to face with the client. The other danger is that the approach of the supervisor will be introjected (swallowed whole) by the supervisees rather than helping them to develop their own improved interventions.

In Chapter 9 we describe John Heron's classification of six categories of interventions. We point out that one intervention is not better than another, but that all can be used, *appropriately, degenerately or perversely*. We explore these different types of interventions in order that supervisors may look at which forms they compulsively use and which they mostly avoid using. From this they can discover some aspects of the strength and weakness of their style, and how they might want to change the balance in the sort of interventions they are using. We find that monitoring our own interventions in such a way sharpens our awareness of the interventions of our supervisees.

Focusing on strategy should not be confused with 'strategic' approaches to therapy, for all those who work enabling others, use some form of strategy, be it interpretation, reflection, silence or the active facilitation of bodywork.

Mode 3: Focusing on the relationship between the client and the supervisee

In this mode the focus is neither on the client, the supervisee, nor their interventions, but on the system that the two parties create together. In this mode the supervisor focuses on the conscious and unconscious interaction between supervisee and client. To start with the supervisor might say one or more of the following:

- How did you meet?
- How and why did this client choose you?
- What did you first notice about the nature of your contact with this client?
- Tell me the story of the history of your relationship.

These interventions must clearly be requesting something different from a case history and must help the practitioner to stand outside the client relationship in which they might be enmeshed or submerged and see its pattern and dynamic.

Other techniques and questions that encourage this distancing and detachment are:

- Find an image or metaphor to represent the relationship.
- Imagine what sort of relationship you would have, if you and the client met in other circumstances, or if you were both cast away on a desert island.
- Become a fly on the wall in your last session; what do you notice about the relationship?

These are all techniques that help the supervisee to see the relationship as a whole rather than just their own perspective from within the relationship. The supervisor can be listening to the relationship even when the supervisee is talking about the client out of relationship. In this way, the supervisor acts like a couple counsellor, in so far as he or she must hold the interests of both parties in balance, and at the same time attend to the space and relationship between the two parties.

The supervisor listens to the relationship in a variety of different ways. All approaches involve listening with the 'third ear' to the images, metaphors and 'Freudian slips' that collect around the supervisee's description of this particular client. Through this form of listening the supervisor is trying to discover the picture that the unconscious of the supervisee is painting of the relationship.

Attending to the client's transference

The supervisor is also interested in the transference of the client. By this we mean feelings or attitudes that may have been transferred from an earlier relationship or situation. In Mode 4 we look at how the supervisee might be doing something similar, transferring attitudes and feelings from another relationship. This is called counter-transference and in many ways it is necessary to move between these two modes and consider the transference and counter-transference together. However, for the time being, we will separate the focus and look only at the client's transference.

Many of the questions used above, and paying attention to the images and metaphors, will give important clues to the transference that is happening. If, for instance, the supervisee said that the relationship was like that of two sparring partners in a boxing ring, the transference would be very different from that of a supervisee who answered that their relationship was like a frightened rabbit wanting to cuddle up to its mother.

Learning from the patient

When attending to the process between the client and supervisee it is important to recognize that somewhere both parties probably know what is going on at a deeper and less conscious level and what is getting in the way of their healthy open meeting. This knowing is most likely unconscious, otherwise the case would not have been brought to supervision. The job of the supervisor is to listen to how the unconscious of the client is informing the supervisee about the client's needs and how the supervisee is helping or getting in the way. Robert Langs (1978, 1985) has developed a complex and very detailed system for attending to and then decoding the latent and unconscious communication of the client and then relating this to the interactions of the supervisee and how they were unconsciously received by the client.

A simple way to use this approach is to listen to all the reported content of the client, (such as stories they told, feelings they have about other people, asides and throw-away comments), as all relating to how the client experiences the work and the practitioner, especially recent interventions.

Langs (1985: 17, 20) gives a good example of this process.

> The final session with a 45-year-old woman who was seen in once weekly psychotherapy for episodes of depression. She begins this last hour as follows:
>
> *Patient:* One of the boys in the class that I teach at religious school is leaving town. I don't know if I will ever see him again. I wanted to hug him goodbye. My son is leaving for an out-of-town college. I thought of the time my father left us when I was a child. Yesterday, at religious school, I thought of having an affair with the principal.

> The patient has largely made use of displacement and symbolization in her allusion to the external danger situation. Rather than alluding directly to the therapist's abandonment ... the patient mentions the loss of a boy in her class, of her son, and of her father in childhood. Each involves an aspect of loss and termination and each expresses in some disguised form a meaning of the ending of the patient's psychotherapy.

Patrick Casement has written about a very similar approach to Langs in a more easily readable book called *On Learning From the Patient* (1985). Here he writes about 'the patient's unconscious search for the therapeutic experience that is most needed'. He gives a number of examples of how the client or patient's unconscious is constantly informing the therapist about its need *for structure, responsiveness* and the appropriate *space*. However, he cautions us to distinguish between patients' growth needs and their wants: 'I am here making a distinction between needs that need to be met and wants ... The therapist should ... try and distinguish between libidinal demands, which need to be frustrated, and growth needs that need to be met' (Casement 1985: 171–2).

Here is an example illustrating the difference between these wants and growth needs, drawn from the work of a psychotherapist that one of us supervises:

> The therapist was a female worker who looked and acted in a motherly fashion. The client was also a female whose own mother had been very depressed, often not leaving the house for weeks at a time. The client went through periods of wanting the therapist to hug and cuddle her and of trying every way possible for the sessions to overrun the ending time. The libidinal demand was for unboundaried symbiotic mothering, whereas the unconscious growth need was for a therapist who would provide the clear boundaries that her own mother was unable to give her. Once this had been realised in the supervision, the therapist's anxiety with this client lessened considerably and she was able to set clear boundaries for the client, in a way that the client was able to accept.

Mode 4: Focusing on the supervisee

In this mode the focus of the supervision is on the internal processes of the supervisee and how these are affecting and being affected by the work and the relationship. This includes the emotional reactions and resonances of the supervisee, often called counter-transference. We would like to distinguish between five different types of counter-transference:

- Transference feelings of the supervisee stirred up by this particular client. These can be either the transferring of feelings about past relationships or situations on to the relationship with this client; or the projection of part of the supervisee on to the client.
- The feelings and thoughts of the supervisee that arise out of playing the role transferred on to him or her by the client (for example, if the client responds to

you as if you were her mother, you may find yourself feeling alternatively protective and angry, in the way her mother did).

- The supervisee's feelings, thoughts and actions used to *counter the* transference of
  the client. The client treats you as a mother figure and you find yourself
  becoming very masculine and businesslike to avoid the mother transference.
- Projected material of the clients that the supervisee has taken in somatically,
  psychically or mentally.
- Finally, we would like to mention a particular form of counter-transference that
  can very easily creep into the modern pressurized world. It is what Rowan calls
  aim attachment counter-transference where we want the client to change for our
  sake, not theirs. This could be because we want to see ourselves as successful,
  seeing the client's cure or otherwise as a reflection of our own well-being as a
  professional. This can also be fuelled by professional demands to produce results.

What all forms of counter-transference have in common is that they involve some form
of predominantly unaware reaction to the client by the supervisee. It is essential for the
supervisee to explore all forms of counter-transference in order to have greater space to
respond to, rather than *react*, to the client. Counter-transference used to be thought of as
something that had to be made conscious and removed as it formed a negative barrier.
Now many professionals realize that in the counter-transference can be found the clues
to understanding their work and their clients better.

It is clear from what we have said above that it would be hard to work with the counter-
transference without reference to the client's transference and so Modes 3 and 4 most often
work together. However, there is a difference in focusing predominantly on trying to
understand the client 'out there', or on concentrating on the supervisee's own process.

The simplest way to focus on the counter-transference is for the supervisor just to
pose the question 'What is your countertransference to this client?'; but, as we suggested
above, most counter-transference is outside awareness and predominantly unconscious,
so this question has only very limited effectiveness.

Another slightly more sophisticated technique is 'Checks for identity' which we have
adapted from 'Co-counselling' (see Heron 1974). In this technique the supervisor takes
the supervisee through five stages in order to elicit their counter-transference:

> *Stage 1:* The supervisee is encouraged to share their first spontaneous responses
> to the question: 'Who does this person remind you of?' The supervisor keeps
> repeating the question until the supervisee discovers an answer, which could be
> a person from their past, a well-known personality, a historical or mythic figure
> or part of themselves.

> *Stage 2:* The supervisee is asked to describe all the ways their client is like this
> person.

> *Stage 3:* The supervisee is then asked what they want to say to the person that
> they discovered in stage 1, particularly what is unfinished in their relationship
> with that person. This can be done in role-play by putting the person on an
> empty chair and expressing their feelings to them.

Stage 4: The supervisee is asked to describe all the ways their client is different from this person.

Stage 5: The supervisee is then asked what they want to say to their client. If the previous stages have been completed satisfactorily then the supervisee will be able to address the client differently.

This exercise can lead to surprising discoveries about the most unlikely connections and unfinished thoughts and feelings, which are getting in the way of seeing the client.

The more unconscious material is often found at the edges of the supervisee's communication. It can be in their images, metaphors or Freudian slips of the tongue; or it may be in their non-verbal communication. The supervisor can elicit this material by getting them to free-associate to images or 'slip' words; or by getting them to repeat and exaggerate a movement or gesture that carries a charge. From these interventions can emerge strong feelings that then need to be related back to the work with the client.

Also when looking at the supervisee's counter-transference it is important to include an exploration of what Frank Kevlin (1987) calls 'the ideological editor'. This is the way the supervisees view the client through their own belief-and-value system. This includes conscious prejudice, racism, sexism and other assumptions that colour the way we mis-see, mis-hear or mis-relate to the client. This is explored more fully in Chapter 8.

One way of eliciting this ideological editor is through awareness of the supervisee's use of comparatives or associations. If a supervisee says about a client: 'She is a very obliging client', the supervisor can ask, 'How is she obliging?', 'She is very obliging compared to whom?', 'Tell me how you think clients should oblige you?' Thus the supervisor is seeking to discover the assumptions about how clients should be that are hidden in this comparative term 'very obliging'. Construct theorists (Kelly 1955) might describe supervisees as having a bipolar construct obliging/non-obliging.

Here is another example which shows the eliciting of counter-transference through spontaneous association. It is taken from a supervision session where Robin is supervising a senior manager in a social services department, whom we will call John:

> *Robin:* Why are you allowing this staff member to drift and not confronting him?
> *John:* Well, I do not want to be a punitive boss.
> *Robin:* What would that be like?
> *John:* As you asked that, I got the image of a little boy outside a headmaster's office.
> *Robin:* So there is a link for you between confronting and being a punitive head teacher. If you were this staff member's head teacher, how would you want to punish him and what would you be punishing him for?

Having explored this together, Robin then encouraged John to try out other ways of confronting the staff member, which were less polluted by the punitive counter-transference. Thus having started with Mode 4 he then moved back into Mode 2.

Mode 4 also includes attending to the general well-being (resourcing aspect) and development (developmental aspect) of the supervisee's needs. Unless time is given to these aspects, there is a danger that supervision will become overly reactive, always responding to the impact of the latest difficult client, rather than proactively helping to build the capacity of the supervisee over time.

We have often noticed that supervisees can be less stressed by the difficulties with their client group, than by the response or lack of it from their organization (Morrison 1993; Scaife et al. 2001: 31). They may also have as their central concern their difficult relationships with colleagues. When collegial relationships are brought to individual supervision it is important to ask why they have not been addressed directly instead; and to view the issue from a systemic perspective. It is also essential to remember that the only part of the system that you can help to shift is the part that is present with you in the room. In later chapters we explore how collegial relationship and organizational politics with a small 'p' can also be explored in teams, networks and organizations. One reason it may have been brought to individual supervision is the lack of suitable team or organizational supervision processes.

Mode 5: Focusing on the supervisory relationship

In the previous modes the supervisor has been focusing outside him- or herself. In Mode 1 the focus has been on the client and then increasingly in Modes 2 to 4, on the supervisee. Increasingly the supervisor has been encouraging the supervisee to look less for the answers out in the client and to pay more attention to what is happening inside themselves. But the supervisor has so far not started to look inside him or herself for what is happening. In the final two modes the supervisor practises what he or she preaches, and attends to how the work with the clients enter and change the supervisory relationship, and then in Mode 6 how these dynamics affect the supervisor. Without the use of Modes 5 and 6 the supervisors would lack congruence between what they were asking the supervisee to do and what they were modelling, that is, to look inside themselves.

Harold Searles, an American neo-Freudian, has contributed a great deal to the understanding of this supervision mode in his discovery and exploration of the paralleling phenomenon (Searles 1955):

> My experience in hearing numerous therapists present cases before groups has caused me to become slow in forming an unfavourable opinion of any therapist on the basis of his presentation of a case. With convincing frequency, I have seen that a therapist who during occasional presentations appears to be lamentably anxious, compulsive, confused in his thinking, actually is a basically capable colleague who, as it were, is trying unconsciously by his demeanour during the presentation, to show us a major problem area in the therapy with his patient. The problem area is one which he cannot perceive objectively and describe to us effectively in words; rather, he is unconsciously identifying with it and is in effect trying to describe it by way of his behaviour during the presentation.

In the mode of paralleling, the processes at work currently in the relationship between client and supervisee are uncovered through the way they are reflected in the relationship between supervisee and supervisor. For example, if I have a client who is very withholding (who had a mother or father who was very withholding, etc.), when I present them to my supervisor, I may well do this in a very withholding way. In effect I become my client and attempt to turn my supervisor into me as therapist. This function, which is rarely done consciously, serves two purposes for the supervisee. One is that it is a form of discharge – I will do to you what has been done to me and see how you like it; and the second is that it is an attempt to solve the problem through re-enacting it within the here-and-now relationship. The job of the supervisor is to tentatively name the process and thereby make it available to conscious exploration and learning. If it remains unconscious the supervisor is likely to be submerged in the enactment of the process, by becoming angry with the withholding supervisee, in the same way that the supervisee was angry with the withholding client.

The important skill involved in working with paralleling is to be able to notice one's reactions and feed them back to the supervisee in a non-judgemental way (for example, 'I experience the way you are telling me about this client as quite withholding and I am beginning to feel angry. I wonder if that is how you felt with your client'). The process is quite difficult as we are working with the paradox of the supervisee both wanting to deskill the supervisor and at the same time work through and understand the difficult process in which they are ensnared.

Here is a clear example of paralleling written by our colleague Joan Wilmot:

> I was supervising a social work student on placement to our therapeutic community who was counselling a resident with whom she was having difficulty. He was a man in his forties who had been in the rehabilitation programme in the house for about seven months and was now to move on to the next stage which was finding himself some voluntary work. He was well able to do this but despite the student making many helpful and supportive suggestions, he 'yes but' everything she said. In her supervision with me, despite her being a very able student, her response to all my interventions was 'yes but'. I took this issue to my supervisor, in order as I thought, to obtain some useful suggestions with which to help the student. However, despite the fact that I was usually very receptive to supervision, I responded to every suggestion my supervisor made with a 'yes but'. He then commented on how resistant I was sounding and how like the resident in question I was being. This insight immediately rang so true that we were both able to enjoy the unconscious paralleling I had been engaged in and I no longer needed to engage in a resistance game with my supervisor. I shared this with my student who no longer needed to resist me but was able to go back to her client and explore his need to resist. His issues around needing to feel his power by resisting could then be worked on separately from his finding voluntary work and he was able to arrange some voluntary work within the week.
>
> (Wilmot and Shohet 1985)

Margery Doehrman (1976) has done one of the very few pieces of research on paralleling that exist, in which she studied both the therapy sessions and the supervision on the therapy of twelve different people. In the introduction to her study Mayman writes:

What is strongly suggested by Dr Doehrman's study, a result that she herself admits took her by surprise, was the fact that powerful parallel processes were present in every patient–therapist–supervisor relationship she studied.

(in Doehrman 1976: 4)

Doehrman discovered that paralleling also went in both directions; not only did the unconscious processes from the therapy relationship get mirrored in the supervision process, but also the unconscious processes in the supervisory relationship could get played out within the therapy process. Mayman concludes by saying:

I believe parallel processing ... is a universal phenomenon in treatment, and that the failure to observe its presence in supervision may signal only a natural resistance on the part of the supervisor and/or therapist against facing the full impact of those forces which they are asking the patient to face in himself.

(in Doehrman 1976)

Mode 6: The supervisor focusing on their own process

In Mode 5 we explored how the relationship between the supervisee and their client can invade and be mirrored in the supervisory relationship. In this mode we focus on how that relationship can enter into the internal experience of the supervisor and how to use that.

Often as supervisors we find that sudden changes 'come over us'. We might suddenly feel very tired, but become very alert again when the supervisee moves on to discuss another client. Images, rationally unrelated to the material, may spontaneously erupt in our consciousness. We may find ourselves sexually excited by our image of the client or shuddering incomprehensibly with fear.

Over the years, we have begun to trust these interruptions as being important messages from our unconscious receptors about what is happening both here and now in the room, and also out there in the work with the client. In order to trust these eruptions supervisors must know their own process well. I must know when I am normally tired, bored, fidgety, fearful, sexually aroused, tensing my stomach, etc., in order to ascertain that this eruption is not entirely my own inner process bubbling away, but is a received import.

In this process the unconscious material of the supervisee is being received by the unconscious receptor of the supervisor, and the supervisor is tentatively bringing this material into consciousness for the supervisee to explore.

Supervisors need to be clear about their feelings towards the supervisee: 'What are my basic feelings towards this supervisee?', 'Do I generally feel threatened, challenged, critical, bored etc?' All that has been said above about transference and counter-transference is relevant to supervisors when they relate to their supervisees. Unless supervisors are relatively clear about their basic feelings to the supervisees, they cannot notice how these feelings are changed by the import of unconscious material from the supervisee and their clients.

In order to use this mode supervisors must not only be aware of their own processes, but must also be able to attend to their own shifts in sensation, and peripheral half-thoughts and fantasies, while still attending to the content and process of the session. This may sound a difficult task, but it is also a key skill in being effective in any of the helping professions and it is, therefore, important that supervisors can model its use to those that they supervise.

Supervisors might use their awareness of their own changing sensations and feelings by making statements like:

- While you have been describing your work with X, I have been getting more and more impatient. Having examined this impatience it does not seem to be to do with you, or something I am bringing into the session from outside, so I wonder if I am picking up your impatience with your client?
- I notice that I keep getting images of wolves with their teeth bared, as you describe your relationship with this client. Does that image resonate with your feelings about the relationship?
- I am getting very sleepy as you 'go on' about this client. Often when that happens to me it seems to indicate that some feeling is being shut off either to do with the client or right here in the supervision. Perhaps you can check what you might be holding back from saying?

Mode 6A: Supervisor–client relationship

So far this model explores the interplay between two relationships: that of the client/supervisee and that of the supervisee/supervisor; but it ignores the third side of the triangle – namely the fantasy relationship between the client and the supervisor. Supervisors may have all sorts of fantasies about their supervisees' clients, even though they have never met them. The client may also have fantasies about the supervisor of the person who works with them, and we have known some clients to direct a lot of their attention at the unknown supervisor and their fantasies about what happens in their supervision! These fantasy relationships complete the triangle and like all triangular processes are laden with conflict and complexity. 'Any pairing ousts the third party, and may at an unconscious level, even revive the first rivalrous oedipal threesome' (Mattinson, quoted in Dearnley 1985).

The thoughts and feelings that the supervisor has about the client can clearly be useful, especially in Modes 1 and 6, as described above. Where the feelings of the supervisor are at odds with the experience of the supervisee, it can be that some aspect of the client/supervisee relationship is being denied and experienced by the supervisor.

Mode 7: Focusing on the wider contexts in which the work happens

Here the supervisor moves the focus from the specific client relationships that are figural in the session to the contextual field in which both the client work and the supervision work takes place.

The contexts surround all aspects of the supervisory process. We have gradually become aware that it is useful to sub-divide Mode 7 into various aspects.

7.1 Focusing on the context of the client

For many who are psychologically trained it is all too easy to fall into the trap of seeing how the client presents as deriving solely from their psychological patterns. This is only one aspect of the client. In Mode 7.1 it is important to also ask some of the following questions:

- Tell me about the client's background/their work/their culture, etc?
- What resources do they have that they are not utilizing or could utilize more?
- What is the client carrying for their family or team or organization?
- Why have they come for help now? Why you?
- When and where else have they had these difficulties?

7.2 Focusing on supervisee's interventions in the context of their profession and organization

The interventions and strategies that a supervisee utilizes will not just be the result of personal choices, but framed by the context of the tradition they work within and the policies, culture and practice of their organization. Even when the supervisee is an independent practitioner, they will still be part of a professional community with its standards, ethics and professional mores.

In this mode the supervisor may well ask, 'How does your handling of this situation fit with the expectations of your professional body?' Although the supervisor has some responsibility for ensuring ethical and professional work, the focus should not be just on compliance, but also helping the supervisee question how they may be over-constraining their practice because of their assumptions about 'expected practice standards' or fear of judgement.

If the supervisor gets trapped into seeing themselves as the channel of the current wisdom of the profession to the supervisee, then the danger is that the profession stops learning. Where supervision is an active inquiry process between supervisor and supervisee, it can become an important seedbed for the profession, where new learning and practice are germinated (see Chapter 12).

7.3 Focusing on the context of the supervisee–client relationship

Not only do the client and the supervisee bring aspects of their separate contexts into their working relationship, the relationship itself has a context and a pre-history. In this sub-mode it is important to ask questions such as:

- How did the client come to see the supervisee?
- Did they choose to come themselves, or were they sent or recommended to come by somebody else?
- If so what is the power relationship with that person or organization?
- How do they see this helping relationship and how does this relate to their experience of other helping relationships?
- How are such relationships viewed in their culture?

7.4 Focusing on the wider world of the supervisee

In Mode 4 we focus not only on the aspects of the supervisee that are triggered by the work with the particular client, but also their overall development and their general patterns of working. This has its own context, for it will be affected by, among other things;

- their stage of professional development (see Chapter 6),
- their personality and personal history,
- their role and history in the organization in which they work.

7.5 Focusing on the context of the supervisory relationship

The supervisory relationship, like that of the client and the supervisee, has its own context and pre-history. A key element of this context will be the nature of the supervisory contract. Is this supervision: training, managerial, tutorial or consultancy? (Chapter 5). If the supervisee is still in training it may be necessary to focus on the nature of that training and any role the supervisor has in an assessment process.

Other elements of this sub-mode include:

- the previous experience of both parties in both giving and receiving supervision;
- the race, gender and cultural differences between both parties (see Chapter 8);
- different theoretical orientations;
- how both parties hold power and authority and respond to the power and authority of other.

7.6 Focusing on the context of the supervisor

In order to reflect skilfully on sub-mode 7.5, the supervisor needs to be able to reflect on their own context and how it enters the supervisory relationship. This requires an advanced form of self-reflexive practice (Schon 1983). It necessitates a high awareness of one's own racial, cultural and gender biases and prejudices (see Chapter 8) as well as the strengths and weaknesses of one's own personality style, learning style and patterns of reactivity. This awareness is not to exclude these from the relationship, but to be aware of the lenses through which one is experiencing the supervisee and the system they are presenting.

In the final section of the book (Chapters 12, 13 and 14) we explore the wider organizational context in which supervision takes place and how to work with it.

Integrating the processes

It is our view that good supervision of in-depth work with clients must involve all seven processes, although not necessarily in every session. Therefore, part of the training with this model is to help supervisors discover the processes they more commonly use and those with which they are less familiar. We have found that some supervisors become habituated to using just one mode.

Gilbert and Evans (2000: 7) also stress the importance of a balance of attention:

> A systems approach to supervision involves the supervisor's capacity to retain a sensitivity to her own counter transference reactions in relation to their origins. In addition the supervisor must, at the same time, enter into the supervisee's world of experience in relation to interpersonal or intrapsychic events and achieve a view that takes into account the intersubjective nature of the supervisory process. At any point in supervision, any one of these elements may be the focus of the supervision intervention: 1) the psychotherapist's reflection on and understanding of client dynamics or of his own counter transference, 2) the psychotherapist's empathic engagement with the client and 3) sharpening his awareness of the delicate dance between them.

A parallel model to ours is suggested by Pat Hunt (1986) in her article on supervising couple counsellors. She suggests that supervision styles can be divided into three types:

- *Case-centred approach:* where the therapist and the supervisor have a discussion on the case 'out there'. This is similar to our Mode 1.
- *Therapist-centred approach:* which focuses on the behaviour, feelings and processes of the therapist. This is similar to our Modes 2 and 4.
- *Interactive approach:* this focuses both on the interaction in the therapy relationship and the interaction in the supervision. This is similar to our Modes 3 and 5.

Hunt illustrates the dangers of using one of these approaches exclusively. If all the attention is on the client 'out there', there is a tendency to get into an intellectual discussion 'about' the client. There is also a danger of a large 'fudge-factor' – the supervisees hiding material from the supervisor for fear of judgement. If the approach is exclusively supervisee-centred it can be experienced by the supervisee as intrusive and bordering on therapy. Hunt writes: 'I am not sure how supportive this kind of supervision would feel. I guess quite a lot of learning would occur, but I suspect assessments might be made in terms of the trainee therapist's willingness to open up and talk about himself' (Hunt 1986: 7).

If the approach is exclusively interactive-centred, there are fewer dangers than in the other two approaches, but a great deal of important information could be ignored in the immersion of the attention in the complexities of the two interlocking relationships.

Thus the trainee supervisor, having learnt skilfully to use each of the main processes, needs help in moving effectively and appropriately from one process to another. To do this, it is important to develop the supervisory skills of appropriateness and timing. The supervisor needs to be aware of how different modes are more appropriate for different supervisees, and for the same supervisees at different times. The most common pattern of the use of different modes in a supervision session is to begin with Mode 1, discovering what happened in the session; for this to naturally lead on to Modes 3 and 4, what happened in the relationship and how this affected the therapist; and if and when this triggers unconscious communication to switch the focus to Modes 5 and 6. At any of these stages one might move from the specific mode to the appropriate sub-mode of 7, so as to reflect on that which is colouring the situation in the wider field. At the end of the exploration of a particular client the supervisor might then focus back on Mode 2 to explore what new interventions the supervisee might utilize at their next session with this client.

Linking the model to a developmental perspective

It is also helpful for the supervisor to be aware of the developmental stage and readiness of the individual supervisees to receive different levels of supervision (see Chapter 6).

As a general rule supervisees who are new to the work need to start with most of the supervision focusing on the content of the work with the client and the detail of what happened in the session. At first supervisees are often over anxious about their own performance (Stoltenberg and Delworth 1987) and they need to be supported in attending to what actually took place. They also need help in seeing the detail of individual sessions within a larger context (Modes 1 and 7); how material from one session links to the development over time; how it relates to the clients' outside life and to their personal history. In helping supervisees develop this overview, it is very important not to lose the uniqueness of the supervisee's relationship with their client, and for the supervisor not to give the impression that what is new, personal and often exciting for the supervisee can easily be put into a recognizable category.

As supervisees develop their ability to attend to what *is*, rather than to premature theorizing and over-concern with their own performance, then it is possible to spend more time profitably on Mode 2, looking at their interventions. As stated above, here the danger is that the supervisor habitually tells the supervisees how they could have intervened better. We have found ourselves saying to supervisees statements such as 'What I would have said to this client would have been ...' or 'I would have just kept quiet at that point in the session.' Having said such a line we could kick ourselves for not having practised what we preach and wish we had kept quiet in the supervision session!

As the supervisees become more sophisticated, then Modes 3, 4, 5 and 6 become more central to the supervision. With a competent and experienced practitioner, it is possible to rely on their having attended to the conscious material and having carried out their own balanced and critical evaluation of their sessions. In such a case the supervisor needs to listen more to the unconscious levels of both the supervisee and of the reported clients. This necessitates focusing on the paralleling, transference and counter-transference processes being played out within the supervision relationship.

We find that this model holds good for those of all theoretical approaches and orientations and that all supervisors are helped to be more effective by increasing their range over all seven modes. This is not to say that for some supervisors it may be more appropriate to focus more often on specific modes. So for example, supervisors who are behavioural clinical psychologists may favour Modes 1 and 2, whereas psychodynamic supervisors may favour Modes 3 and 4.

The developmental stage of the therapist is only one factor which will cause the experienced supervisor to shift the dominant mode of focus. Other factors that should influence the choice of focus are:

- the nature of the work of the supervisee;
- the style of the supervisee's work; their personality and learning style;
- the degree of openness and trust that has been established in the supervision relationship;
- the amount of personal development and exploration the supervisee has undertaken for themselves;
- the cultural background of the therapist (see Chapter 8).

Critiques of the model

Since the model was first published in 1985, and then in the two earlier editions of this book (1989 and 2000), we have received many interesting and valuable critiques which have expanded and developed the model. Other critiques have shown us where we have not been clear enough, and have led to a misunderstanding of our model or intention.

Some of the most common critiques include (a) the model is hierarchic, (b) the model is claiming to be integrative but is biased or limited to a specific orientation; (c) Mode 7 is of a different order and needs to be contained in all the other six modes.

The model is hierarchic

A number of trainees have objected on egalitarian grounds to the supervisor being at the top of the diagram and the client at the bottom with the supervisee in the middle. Tudor and Worrall put this position clearly when they write: 'In Hawkins and Shohet's model, the fact that, of the three related circles signifying people, the supervisor is at the top, signifies a certain hierarchy and authority given to the person of the supervisor' (2004: 75).

We believe that this position is based on a misunderstanding that comes from confusing systemic hierarchy and political domination, and greater responsibility and authority with being authoritarian. In a systemic hierarchy a tree is 'higher' to the bough. The forest is 'higher' to the tree. This in no way implies the forest is superior to the tree, in fact the forest is dependent on the trees for its existence and being. In the same way a supervisor can only exist if there are supervisees, and the supervisees can only exist if there are clients. The hierarchy in the process model does not imply that higher is more important, more powerful or wiser. It does imply that in supervision the supervisor has responsibility for attending to themselves and both the supervisee(s) and the client(s), and that supervisees have responsibility for attending to themselves and their clients. However, the responsibility does not flow in the same way in the opposite direction. Those who want to learn more about this way of thinking should refer to Bateson (1973) and Whitehead and Russell (1910–13).

The model is claiming to be integrative but is biased to one specific orientation

For us the model is essentially integrative on two accounts. Firstly, it fundamentally draws on understanding from systemic, psychodynamic, inter-subjective, cognitive, behavioural and humanistic approaches to understanding relationships. The systemic understanding of how change in the supervisory matrix, impacts the client–supervisee relational matrix, which in turn impacts the client system is fundamental to the model. The model clearly draws on the psychoanalytic understanding of transference and counter-transference, particularly as developed by those working in the field of object relations or adopting the inter-subjective approach. Much of the creativity in ways of intervening draws heavily on the work of many humanistic innovators from psychodrama, Gestalt, psychosynthesis, transactional analysis, to name just a few.

Our second integrative claim is pragmatic. When we first developed the model we did not know the range of its usefulness, but were committed to taking it into different professional groupings to test out the limits of its ability to work with people from different orientations. We have been surprised and pleased to find that practitioners from most psychotherapeutic orientations have been able to use the model to develop their own practice, if they were able to think outside the frameworks of their original training.

Mode 7 is of a different order and needs to be contained in the other six modes

We found this challenge from Mathews and Treacher (2004: 200) very useful, and we fundamentally agree that Mode 7 is of a different order. The move from any of the other six modes to Mode 7 is a move from focusing on what is figural to focusing on the contextual field in which the phenomena is happening. We also have become aware that there are almost as many levels of context as there are modes of focus on the figural phenomena, and thus have developed the variety of sub-distinctions in Mode 7.

We still believe that it is important not to subsume Mode 7 into the other six modes, for this would lose the constant challenge that nearly all of us need: regularly to move our attention from what is naturally in the field of our vision, to the wider domain in which we are operating. This is a theme we pick up in Chapter 8 when we explore the cultural, race and gender issues that may be happening both within the relationships but also in the social context that surrounds them.

Conclusion

We have explored in detail the 'seven-eyed supervisor model' that we first developed in 1985. We have continued to teach and develop this model ever since and have found that it continues to provide a framework for new levels of depth and ways of creatively intervening in a supervision session. For us, the power of the model is that we continue to learn and gain new insights even after 20 years. It has proved useful beyond our original horizons, and has been used in a great variety of cultures and in different 'people' professions, from youth work to palliative care; from psychiatry to management development; and from education to couple therapy. We have become increasingly convinced that to carry out effective supervision of any client work it is necessary for the supervisor to be able to use all seven modes of supervision.

The model also provides a framework for the supervisee and the supervisor to review the supervision sessions and to negotiate a change in the balance of the focus. Different supervisees will require different styles of supervision and in Chapter 8 we explore how the supervisor can increase their ability to work with a greater range of difference. We also revisit each of the seven modes and provide case examples of working with each mode transculturally.

8 Supervising across difference

Introduction
Understanding culture
Cultural orientations
Acknowledging cultural difference
Awareness of culture and other differences in supervision
Working across faith communities
Power and difference
Difference in relation to the seven modes
  Mode 1
  Mode 2
  Mode 3
  Mode 4
  Mode 5
  Mode 6
  Mode 7
Developing transcultural supervision
Supervision of asylum seekers and refugees
Conclusion

Introduction

In this chapter we focus on the sensitivity and awareness needed to work with those whose backgrounds and ways of looking at the world are different from ours. We show how this sensitivity and awareness applies as much, if not more, to our own culture and cultural assumptions as it does to that of others. White, western people tend to see themselves as culturally neutral (Ryde 2006) so that non-western cultures are defined in reaction to western 'normality'. Those who are 'white' need to be particularly careful not to assume that cultural norms which deviate from theirs need to be 'corrected'. We concentrate in particular on the area of culture as it has implications not only for 'race' and ethnicity, but also for class and other groupings which develop their own 'sub' culture. Even different organizations and families develop their own cultures so that differences between them need to be acknowledged and understood.

Although it is important to take steps to understand cultures that are different from our own, we have found that our usual stance of openness to inquiry is also useful. This is partly because we believe that an open attitude to learning keeps our work alive and creative rather than formulaic; but also because, if we are to really honour rather than deny cultural diversity, we need to find a way of dialoguing across difference. If we see our task as merely to understand the other's perspective then no real meeting has happened. We are ourselves absent. In a supervisory relationship this means not only a willingness to encourage and explore difference in the supervisee/client relationship, but also an openness to our selves and our own cultural assumptions and our relationship with our supervisees. Those who are 'white' need also to be aware of the power and privilege that this affords them (Ryde 2006).

Tyler, Brome and Williams (1991, quoted in Holloway and Carroll 1999) distinguish between three ways of responding to culture:

- **The universalist** denies the importance of culture and puts difference down to individual characteristics. In counselling a universalist will understand all difference in terms of individual pathology.
- **The particularist** takes the polar opposite view, putting all difference down to culture.
- **The transcendentalist** takes a view more similar to our own. Coleman (in Holloway and Carroll 1999) discusses this perspective as follows:
  both the client and the counsellor have vast cultural experiences that deeply influence their worldviews and behaviour.
He says that:
  it is the individual who has to make sense of and interpret those experiences. The transcendent or multicultural perspective suggests that there are normative assumptions that can be made about individuals based on cultural factors such as race, gender and class, but that it is just as important to understand how these normative assumptions become reality through the idiosyncratic choices made by individual members of a group.

Eleftheriadou (1994) makes a helpful distinction between cross-cultural work and work that is transcultural. In the former we 'use our own reference system to understand another person rather than going beyond our own world views'. Transcultural work 'denotes that counsellors need to work beyond their cultural differences' and be able to operate within the frame of references of other individuals and groupings.

An open attitude to inquiry enhances the ability to work transculturally from a transcendentalist perspective. This inquiry optimally takes place within a dialogue in which both parties participate in the learning.

One particularly complex area is the way issues of power and authority are present for all those concerned. The supervisory relationship is already complicated in this way because of the authority vested in the role of supervisor and in the role of the profession of the supervisee. In working with difference, power dynamics are compounded because of the inequality of power between majority and minority groups. We look at how power invested in different roles, cultures and individual personalities come together to make a complex situation which is, nevertheless, better explored than ignored or denied.

In this chapter we see how supervision can play its part in ensuring that differences are understood and responded to appropriately. We explore the importance of taking culture and other areas of difference into account when supervising; cultural factors that need to be worked with; power dynamics and difference and an exploration of how difference affects the seven modes of supervision (see Chapter 7). Finally, there is a discussion of best practice in supervision which is sensitive to difference. But first we explore what we mean by 'culture'.

Understanding culture

> My new client will never be able to use counselling. She kept saying, 'I'll do whatever you suggest, doctor.' Actually, I wanted to laugh. Of course, I told her I wasn't a doctor and I wouldn't tell her what to do. She looked really confused when I said that.

This supervisee was a recently qualified English counsellor. Her client was from Southeast Asia and had recently come to England with her husband. She was working as a nurse and was lonely and frightened much of the time. Her husband's work took him away from home a good deal so she did not even have him as a familiar reference point. A nursing officer had suggested counselling as she was struggling to cope at work. However, the counselling never got beyond the second session as she was told that counselling was not appropriate for her.

This event happened several years ago. We wonder whether the counsellor and the supervisor would now be more aware of the cultural implications in how the client understood the counselling relationship. Would they now be more likely to consider that, by trying to understand the cultural context including her own cultural assumptions, some useful work could have been done, even if it were just a place where the client could have articulated the loneliness and confusion she felt in this very alien culture? We recognize here that the difference in culture had led to an inappropriate response. But what precisely do we mean by 'culture'.

We understand 'cultural differences' as referring to the different explicit and implicit assumptions and values that influence the behaviour and social artefacts of different groups (Herskovitz 1948). An understanding of culture in relation to our clients must also include an understanding of our own cultural assumptions and beliefs.

Culture is not just something within us, which we *have*, but rather resides in the milieu in which we live. Culture affects primarily not *what* but *how* we think, although what we think may alter as a result of our cultural assumptions. It exists in the spaces between us, just as an organism is grown in a 'culture' in a laboratory. Hawkins (1995, 1997) has developed a model of five levels of culture, each level being fundamentally influenced by the levels beneath it:

- artefacts: the rituals, symbols, art, buildings policies etc.;
- behaviour: the patterns of relating and behaving; the cultural norms;
- mind-sets: the ways of seeing the world and framing experience;
- emotional ground: the patterns of feeling that shape making of meaning;
- motivational roots: the fundamental aspirations that drive choices.

This model is further explored in Chapter 14.

Cultural orientations

Both national and ethnic groups, and different sub-groups, based on gender, class, sexual orientation, profession, religious affiliation etc., have different cultural norms, behaviour, mind-sets, emotional ground and motivational roots, that distinguish them from other groups. To try and learn the cultural orientations of the myriad different cultures would be an impossible task, but we can become sensitized to the different dimensions of cultural orientations. Rosinski (2003: 51–2) provides a useful 'Cultural orientation framework' that has seven dimensions:

- sense of power and responsibility;
- time management approaches;
- identity and purpose;
- organizational arrangements;
- territory – both physical and psychological;
- communication patterns;
- modes of thinking.

Other variables that have been identified by a variety of writers (Hofstede and Stodtbeck 1961; Sue and Sue 1990; Trompenaars 1994) include:

- equality versus hierarchy;
- self-disclosure;
- outer-directed versus inner-directed;
- cause and effect orientation;
- achievement orientation;
- universalist to particularist;
- adaptive versus protectionist;
- time as sequence versus time as synchronization.

Ryde (1997) has written about two dimensions very pertinent to coaching across cultures. These are:

- a continuum between the valuing of the experience of individuals and the valuing of the group;
- a continuum between emotional expressiveness and emotional restraint.

The ways these dimensions interact may be arranged in a diagram (Figure 8.1).

We may then place a particular culture on the diagram at a position which demonstrates the culture's position in regard to these polarities. For example the dominant British and most north European cultures can be plotted in the individual/ emotional restraint box. While the diagram does not cover all possible cultural differences, it does help us to orientate ourselves more easily to two important variables and, therefore, to think in a more culturally sensitive way.

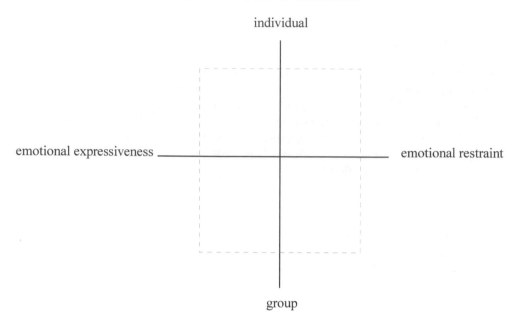

Figure 8.1 Supervision across cultures

Acknowledging cultural difference

The more we can understand how different the world looks through different cultural lenses, the more able we are to work well across cultures. Weerdenburg and Brinkmann (Weerdenburg 1996; Brinkmann and Weerdenburg 1999) have created and researched a developmental model of Intercultural Sensitivity based on the work of Dr Milton Bennett (1993) which maps the stages that individuals go through as they become more transculturally effective. These are:

- *Denial:* where one sees one's own culture as the only real one;
- *Defence:* against cultural difference, where one sees one's own culture as the only good one;
- *Minimization:* in which elements of one's own cultural world view are experienced as universal;
- *Acceptance:* in which there is a recognition that one's own culture is just one of a number of equally complex world views;
- *Cognitive adaptation:* where one can look at the world 'through different eyes';
- *Behavioural adaptation:* where the individual can adapt their behaviour to different cultural situations and relationships.

The first three stages of this development are termed 'ethnocentric' and the later three stages 'ethnorelative'. We would contend that the first two stages represent culturally insensitive work, the second two the beginnings of cross-cultural practice; but only the last two stages equate with transcultural supervision.

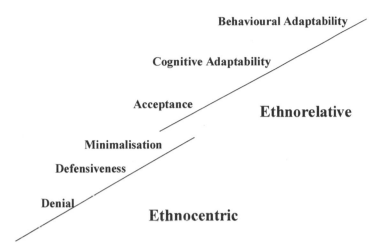

Figure 8.2 From ethnocentric to ethnorelative

Source: Oscar van Weerdenburg (1996)

These stages provide a parallel developmental path to the general stages of supervisor development outlined in Chapter 6.

Awareness of culture and other differences in supervision

Several other writers on supervision (Brown and Bourne 1996; Carroll and Holloway 1999; Inskipp and Proctor 1995, Gilbert and Evans 2000) have pointed out that the supervision situation creates a more complicated set of relationships than relating one-to-one. In supervision there are at least three relationships: client–supervisee, supervisee–supervisor, client–supervisor. (There are more than three in group supervision, and also if there is a supervisor of a supervisor.) This is complicated further in a situation of cultural difference. Any one of the three may be culturally different and, indeed, all three may be culturally different from each other. In the situation where the client comes from a different cultural background from the supervisor and supervisee it is particularly important that they do not collude to misunderstand factors which are based in culture rather than personal psychology, as we see below.

Where there are smaller ethnic groups within a dominant, usually 'white', western culture, it is not uncommon for the second generation of these groups to experience problems in trying to exist in two cultures at once.

> An Asian came from a culture which emphasised the group and emotional restraint. The father of this client lived for some time in America and, whilst there, trained as a Rogerian therapist. Here he learnt to value the individual and emotional expression. Then, when he returned to his own country, he married and had a family. This family became an island of Rogerian values within the predominant culture. The effect on the son was to create a situation which was very similar to that confronting a second generation immigrant with an alien

culture. One set of values pertained at home and another in the world beyond it. In going to a psychotherapist in this country he chose someone with a similar but not identical theoretical basis to his father. This possibly showed some 'unconscious hope' (Casement 1985) that the differences in the two cultures could be reconciled. He needed someone who would be somewhat similar to his father but not identical. The impulse of his psychotherapist was to stress the importance of finding his own direction, meeting his own needs and getting in touch with feelings he needed to express. Whilst this may indeed have had value, his supervisor pointed out that this approach did not recognise or help to resolve the cultural differences and tensions that had become almost unbearable for this client.

We can see here how necessary it is for both supervisor and supervisee to be aware of, and sensitive to, cultural difference. It is also important to notice and honour differences even when they are being denied.

Perceived cultural differences are often focused on physical characteristics, the colour of the skin, the shape of the nose, eyes, etc. The dominant group can often be ruthless in denigrating and marginalizing those with real or perceived differences. Rather than face this vicious prejudice people will go to much trouble to disguise the difference or deny their affects.

One client of mixed race denied that the colour of her skin led to any difficulties for her. She was a good-looking and popular woman and the question of her being black did not seem to arise in her circle of friends or in the counselling. The supervisor remarked on this but found it difficult to engage the supervisee with the issue or keep a focus on it himself. The issue drew itself to the attention of all three rather forcefully when the client related an incident in which a motorist had called her a 'black bastard'. Upon hearing this she had chased him and pulled him out of his car! Subsequently memories and feelings arose about being black which had been previously unexplored.

Other marginalizing differences may not be immediately obvious to the eye but can cause as much alienation through the cultural rejection of people with these differences. Differences in sexual orientation is one of the less visible. While moves are being made to ban discrimination on this and other grounds, prejudice remains and is likely to be found, consciously or unconsciously in the supervisor and supervisee.

Working across faith communities

Another often neglected element of working transculturally is the ability to work with people from different faith communities. We can assume that we live in a dominantly secular society and yet that is a great deal of evidence to show that religion and spiritual belief plays a large part in influencing the culture and value base of many workers. In the UK national census of 2001 over 75 per cent of people reported belonging to a religion.

Seventy-two per cent said their religion was Christianity, 3 per cent Muslim and there was also a sizeable population of Hindus, Sikhs, Jews and Buddhists.

Three other factors make a sensitivity to religious belief critical for supervisors:

- Research shows that one of the 'defining characteristics for some ethnic minorities is their religion' and that religion 'is perhaps the key area where the minority groups manifest a cultural dynamic which is at least partly at odds with native British trends' (Modood and Berthhoud et al. 1997).
- There is a higher preponderance of those with strong religious beliefs in the helping professions than in other sectors, and particularly in the voluntary sector many helping organizations have a strong faith basis in their foundation.
- 'Research indicates that where organizations help people address their inner values and aspirations, morale is boosted and there are benefits to the bottom line' (Faith Regen UK 2005, referencing work by Weiler and Schoonover 2001).

Faith Regen (2005) in their very useful *Faith Communities Toolkit* written for the UK further education sector, provide guidance on how to work sensitively with people from different fundamental beliefs. They also provide a very concise guide to the major faith communities and the impact this has on their work life, including holidays, diet, regular practices, ethical codes and what constitutes acceptable and unacceptable behaviour.

Power and difference

Society may be greatly enriched by the multitude of differences brought by populations of different cultures living side by side. However, the culture with economic and political power – usually those who are 'white' and western – is more powerful in the community and imbalances of power are inevitably played out in professional relationships, including the relationship between supervisee and supervisor and between supervisee and client. As we saw above, Brown and Bourne (1996) have pointed to the different combinations of relationships present in supervision, and they also explore in some depth the different power relationships. They show (1996: 39) all the different possible combinations that can arise when someone from a minority group is in each of the possible roles and the complex power dynamics that result. They particularly emphasis race and gender, although other factors such as sexual orientation, disability and class also have inbuilt power imbalance.

Inskipp and Proctor (1995) have also illustrated the dynamics in relationships between black and white in a series of eight triangles showing all the possible combinations of supervisor, client and counsellor with each being black or white. Each triangle has its own dynamic, which is influenced by the different power dynamics inherent in the roles and the ethnic grouping.

To draw this out further, we consider another triangle: one which demonstrates the complex power dynamics inevitably present in cross-cultural supervision. At each corner we can have three different types of power: role power, cultural power and individual power (Figure 8.3).

Role power

Cultural power   Personal power

Figure 8.3   Complex power dynamics in cross-cultural supervision

- *Role power* points to the power inherent in the role of supervisor, which will vary depending on the organizational setting in which supervision is taking place. This includes what has been termed *legitimate* power, invested in the role; *coercive and reward* power (the power to require the supervisee to do something and the power to offer or withhold rewards), and *resources* power, the power a supervisor may have to offer or withhold resources (French and Raven 1967, discussed by Kadushin 1992, chapter 3).
- *Cultural power* derives from the dominant social and ethnic group. Often this would be someone who was born within the 'white', western majority group. This power is emphasized if that person is male, middle class, heterosexual and able-bodied. Certain professions tend to hold more cultural power too. Doctors, for instance, tend to hold more power within the culture of health professionals.
- *Personal power* points to the particular power of the individual which may be over and above that given to the person through role or culture. It derives both from the authority of their expertise, as well as from the presence and impact of their personality. It also comprises what French and Raven term *referent* power, that derives from the supervisee wishing to identify with or be like their supervisor.

When all three sources of power are brought together in the same person the effect may be quite overwhelming. The dominant cultural and/or personal power do not necessarily lie with the supervisor. When they are, the power dynamics may be simpler but could well be insensitively misused or even overlooked as they are taken for granted. When cultural and/or personal power is not with the supervisor there may be conflict in establishing authority or a need to compensate by over-emphasizing it. Whatever the case, power relationships in the supervision are better explored than ignored as we have shown in the paper 'Anti-Discrimination and Oppression in Supervision' (Centre for Supervision and Team Development (CSTD) 1999).

While it is spurious for power and, therefore, authority to be automatically invested in those from a cultural majority, it may be appropriate for a supervisor to carry greater authority through their role.

One well-intentioned white supervisor felt nervous but excited about having her first black supervisee. The supervisee was a counselling student who had been taken on to a counselling course in spite of the fact that she did not have the initial experience of counselling normally expected of students starting the course. This 'positive discrimination' had been one clear factor that had led the supervisee to struggle to be able to understand and use basic counselling techniques and theories.

The supervisor, not wanting to appear racist, was very tentative in confronting the supervisee on her tendency to advise clients rather than listen to them. In fact the supervisor's worst fears were realized when the supervisee complained to her tutor that her supervisor was racist. This led to a further backing off from confrontation.

In order to understand this complex situation it is helpful to bear in mind Karpman's drama triangle (Karpman 1968), which illustrates the interconnecting dynamics of the persecutor, victim and rescuer. This dynamic is characterized by the way in which these roles, having been established, tend to revolve between the players (see also Chapter 12). Here the supervisor appears to be the persecutor, the supervisee the victim and possibly the tutor the rescuer. In this example, the roles changed with the accusation of racism so that the supervisor apparently became the victim.

In fact, the role power dynamic was with the supervisor. Had she been more experienced and confident she may have been able to work with the supervisee more effectively in the first place to explore the situation in all its complexity: the way the power dynamics of the supervisee/supervisor relationship is compounded by the cultural context of a difference in 'race'; the cultural context in which a student is taken on to a course without the usual preparatory experience; an exploration of the difference experienced by clients in being listened to rather than given advice; and any cultural meanings given to 'being listened to' and 'being given advice' in the different cultures of supervisee and supervisor.

By appropriately keeping her authority and not being afraid to open up the complexity of the issues knotted up in this situation, the supervisee (and supervisor) would have received a rich learning experience which any student might rightly expect where appropriate authority is taken.

If the supervisor had hounded this supervisee out of the course it would have been a clear abuse of power. As it was, the misuse of power was much more subtle: appropriate authority was not taken and the supervisee's difficulties with her course were compounded. One might go so far as to say that the supervisor exhibited, if not racism, then clear cultural prejudice in her assumption that these issues could not be tackled openly and honestly.

Learning to take appropriate authority, while being sensitive to the various aspects of power operating in the therapy and supervision relationships is an important and challenging task. As Kadushin (1992) writes: 'The supervisor must accept, without defensiveness or apology the authority and related power inherent in his (sic) position. Use of authority may sometimes be unavoidable. The supervisor can increase its effectiveness if he feels, and can communicate, a conviction in his behaviour.'

Difference in relation to the seven modes

The seven modes of supervision (presented in Chapter 7) can be used to increase the ability of the supervisor to attend to the cultural differences between client, therapist and supervisor, as well as the cultural and power dynamics at play in both sets of relationships.

- *Mode 1:* a focus on the culture of the client and their context. This includes attending to possible culture-specific behaviours (for example, the avoidance of eye contact).
- *Mode 2:* finding ways of responding to the cultural differences and the hidden cultural assumptions implicit in the supervisee's interventions.
- *Mode 3:* the culture inherent in the relationship between the client and the supervisee. How the cultural material manifests in the process of the work including any 'unconscious supervision' (Casement 1985) which might correct the approach to the work.
- *Mode 4:* a focus on the cultural assumptions of the supervisee. Also the counter-transference of the supervisee which seems to be responding to the cultural material (for example, racist fantasies).
- *Mode 5:* cultural difficulties experienced in the here-and-now cultural dynamics between client and supervisee and how they are mirrored in the supervision relationship. Also attending to cultural differences in the supervisee–supervisor relationship.
- *Mode 6:* the supervisor attending to their own cultural assumptions and their own counter-transference which seem to arise as a result of the cultural material.
- *Mode 7:* the cultural norms and biases in the wider context in which the work is done, particularly organizational, social and political. This will include institutional racism and oppressive practice.

Mode 1

In Mode 1 the client's world is explored through the content of the actual material brought to the sessions both in terms of their behaviour and through the narrative of the client's life. Here cultural material may be brought explicitly or implicitly. Explicit problems within the client's world may be experienced through clashes or difficulties with people from the majority culture. Implicitly, difficulties may turn out to relate to cultural differences, even though the client is unaware that this is the case when the matter is first approached. In Mode 1 the supervisee and supervisor will engage with trying to understand the client's world from the material brought, both verbally and non-verbally. The therapist may try, for instance, to understand to what extent the client's experience is rooted in their culture and how much is owing to their individual character.

> A Japanese client was married to a successful Japanese businessman living in England. Since coming to England she had been very depressed. She felt displaced and missed her home and family. This led to her feeling unable to act as

the sparkling hostess that both she and her husband expected of her. This inability intensified her depression and feelings of inadequacy. In supervision the counsellor brought her feelings of outrage at what she understood to be the client's acquiescence to her husband. The supervisor, however, quickly returned to the phenomenal world of the client to better understand her cultural position.

Mode 1 will often involve paying close attention to the non-verbal behaviour of the client in order to become aware of their phenomenal world. It is important in supervision not to jump to conclusions about the meaning of non-verbal behaviour so that the 'interpretation' of what is seen becomes mistaken for the real thing. This is particularly true when working cross-culturally. Within our society we tend to have culturally determined ways of interpreting non-verbal signs. For instance, a client who likes to shake hands with the therapist may be considered inappropriately formal or trying to please. This view would be mistaken if the client came from a culture in which it would be considered unthinkably rude not to shake hands. The avoidance of eye contact also has different meanings in different cultures. In western cultures it is often thought of as shifty and defensive but in some cultures it is considered to be very impolite to look directly at someone with whom you are not on familiar terms, or has a higher status to yourself.

Mode 2

In Mode 2 the supervisee and supervisor explore the interventions made in the session.

> In the example of the Japanese client mentioned above, the supervisor was able to challenge the cultural assumption of the supervisee that it was dependency in the client that led to this attitude to wifely duties rather than it being a normal response within her culture. The therapist's intervention had been to say, 'Are you angry with your husband for putting you into such an inferior role?' The supervisor was able to challenge the counsellor's cultural assumption that the client may be 'angry' and that the 'role' was 'inferior'. The two then explored different interventions that could have been made and decided that it might be useful to ask what it was like for the client to be a hostess in England and in Japan. This would have opened up the area of differences between the two cultures and how it felt for the client to be in both. With a better understanding of the cultural differences it led the counsellor be able to intervene in a more genuinely empathetic way and to a useful and non-defensive exploration within the context of cultural difference.

Mode 3

Here the supervisory exploration involves the way unconscious material is shown in the process of the work and in particular in the process between the supervisee and the client. It may, for example, be shown in dreams or the kinds of anecdotes that the client tells. In the example of the mixed-race client who related the story of how she chased a motorist and pulled him from his car, the telling of the anecdote could be understood as being brought as an unconscious prompt to explore the issues. Maybe at some level she wanted to metaphorically pull the supervisee, and, indeed, herself, from her chair and shake them both into realizing the importance of this issue.

> A West African client told of being sent to an aunt in England at the age of six. She was given an apple to eat on her arrival, a fruit she had never tasted before. It was so delicious that the client thought life in England would be as wonderful as the apple tasted! She soon discovered that this would be far from the case and in fact never returned to her parents in Africa. This was, of course, a very formative experience in the client's life, but it became clear that she had also told the story unconsciously because of a fear that the apparently benign nature of the first few sessions of the psychotherapy may be illusory in the same way.

Following an exploration in supervision her fear was picked up by the supervisee and the work was able to deepen.

Mode 4

In Mode 4 the supervisee explores how their own issues may affect the process of the work. In order to work with these modes it is necessary for the supervisee to be aware of their own prejudiced attitudes and feelings. Again, with the example of the Japanese client, we saw how the counsellor's own concerns about being disparaged by men led to an inappropriate intervention. Understanding our own issues more clearly and how they relate to our own culture can bring a vital and very fruitful way of working with cultural difference. It brings the whole question right into the room rather than being seen as something that only happens out in the big bad world.

> One supervisee had a paraplegic client who was in a wheelchair. When first discussing this client in supervision she stressed on several occasions how 'intelligent' the client seemed. The supervisor remarked on this and it led to an exploration of the supervisee's expectations of people in wheelchairs. The supervisee discovered in himself an expectation that they were not very bright.

It is often useful in uncovering unconscious prejudice to discover what 'scale' is being used when a description is given. In this example the client was described as 'intelligent' so the supervisor asked what measure was being used in making this observation. In this way the unconscious prejudice was uncovered and not allowed to affect the progress of the work.

Mode 5

In this mode the supervisor and supervisee explore ways in which the relationship with the client is mirrored within the supervisory relationship. This is particularly interesting where there is a cultural difference as it may provide a taste of the way in which a client from a non-dominant culture feels.

One supervisee started to feel stupid and ridiculed during supervision sessions and the supervisor noticed that he was beginning to feel unusually critical. Things became so difficult that the supervisee had started to look elsewhere for supervision. He announced his intention to leave the supervision rather abruptly while he was presenting a client. This client had felt ashamed in adult life of having failed the eleven plus and being sent to a secondary modern school. Now, in the session being presented, the therapist related that the client had started to act as if he were being examined. The supervisor also noticed that he was in danger of being seen as critical and so had become patronizingly protective to the supervisee. The parallels between what was happening in the supervision and the therapy struck the supervisor. This led to an exploration in which the supervisee discovered his identification with his working-class client and the hostility he felt to his middle-class supervisor. This enabled the whole area of feeling ridiculed to be opened up between them and led to the supervisee staying with his present supervisor. It subsequently led to a greater ability to work with his client's lack of self-esteem and his emerging judgmentalness in the relationship with the client.

Mode 6

Mode 6 involves the reactions and responses that the supervisor notices in themselves during a session.

One supervisor often found herself feeling uneasy when a certain client was being presented. When she focused on this feeling she thought it was fear. As this feeling grew she mentioned it to her supervisee saying she wondered how her feeling might be related to what was being shared. The supervisee was at first very surprised. He felt rather in awe of this very bright client who was a foreign student newly in this country but who was having difficulties concentrating on his work. The supervisor's feelings of fear became the first clue to the terror that the student felt at being away from home. In his own culture it was rare to leave the village, let alone the country. The supervisor was experienced enough to value rather than fear her own responses and had faith that they may provide valuable counter-transference clues. She also knew that this was often true when the supervisee and supervisor had different responses. In this case it provided much needed insight for helping the work to move on.

We have also described a slightly different form of Mode 6 called Mode 6(a). Here the emphasis is on the supervisor's specific responses to the client which may be quite different to those of the supervisee.

In the example above the feeling was pervasive rather than attached to the particular client. The following is an example of Mode 6(a):

A supervisee tended to find a client interesting while the supervisor found that she dreaded having to listen to accounts of the client's life. In this case both the supervisor and the client came from the same African country. The supervisor's unease eventually became a clue to unexpressed feelings that were disguised by the client often telling an apparently interesting story. The supervisor and supervisee had different responses to these stories: the supervisor was irritated and the therapist was beguiled by hearing unfamiliar stories about life in Africa. By paying attention to her counter-transference, the supervisor was able to draw attention to important material.

Mode 7

In applying the modes to working across cultural differences we are, in some ways, applying Mode 7 to each of these as this mode concerns the context in which the supervision takes place. Difference in culture is, of course, an important aspect of this context. We will, nevertheless, show how the different aspects of this mode apply to cultural difference.

In Chapter 7 we show how Mode 7 has six subsections. All of these have relevance for working across difference. *Mode 7.1* reminds us of the importance of taking into account the client's phenomenal world which may be interpreted differently to their supervisee and supervisor as we saw in Mode 1.

Mode 7.2 focuses on the supervisee's professional development and shows the importance of their education and training in helping her to understand her own cultural assumptions and position of privilege and be sensitive to cultural differences. Encouraging the work to be undertaken within an organizational culture that supports a developing understanding of the supervisee's own cultural standpoint is also important in Mode 7.2.

Mode 7.3 underlines the importance of taking into account the context of supervisee–client relationship including the way in which the relationship is culturally determined. This might be revealed in the way in which the client was referred and how counselling might be viewed within this intercultural situation.

Mode 7.4 focuses on the wider world of the supervisee and what her social and cultural context means to her, including bringing to awareness that which has been taken for granted.

Mode 7.5 focuses on the supervisee–supervisor relationship and how cultural differences may be played out in that context. Where the social and political context for working with culture in supervision is hostile then it is harder for supervisors to focus clearly on these issues. The necessity to work towards a more conducive environment in the social and political world may become pressing. It may become part of the supervisor's task within Mode 7 to ensure that the context for doing the work is supportive. Some of this work may be by raising awareness within the session but may also entail work outside it on the political stage (such as within national and local professional bodies) or by having more personal contact with key people within organizations such as those with training programmes.

Developing transcultural supervision

Transcultural supervision as well as transcultural practice with clients are both still in very early stages of development. Leong and Wagner (1994) in their review of the literature, conclude that little has been written about cultural issues in supervision, and most of what has been is very recent. As we increasingly operate in a transcultural society, it is essential that both individuals and organizations put a strong emphasis on developing their ability to work transculturally.

Coleman (in Holloway and Carroll 1999) stresses the need for trainings to ensure that students are well-versed in cultural awareness and that supervisors bear this in mind in the same way as they would ethical practice. Evans and Gilbert (2000) provide a very useful case example of one training institution's attempt to address its own oppressive practice and develop its ability to work more transculturally. They provide a very useful simple audit for training organizations to examine their own 'make-up in terms of ethnicity, gender, sexual orientation, religion, political affiliation, class, status, age and disability'. This includes examining:

- recruitment from different groupings;
- the make-up of the staff;
- patterns of interaction between the staff;
- the make-up of the client groups;
- the training curriculum.

As well as looking at how much time is given to addressing the issues of culture and difference and developing the skills of transcultural work, it is also important to reflect on cultural biases inherent in all aspects of the theories taught, the learning processes adopted and how trainees are evaluated. Supervision training needs to include specific focus on both transcultural supervision, and awareness of power imbalances in supervision practice.

At the personal level, all of us as supervisors need to continually develop our ability to work with a greater range of difference and with more awareness of our own culturally defined behaviour, mind-sets, emotional ground and motivational roots. Working in a culturally sensitive way is never easy. We cannot be culturally neutral and so we will inevitably view the world from our own cultural perspective.

In order to increase our transcultural ability it is useful to hold in mind the following:

1 It is important to become conscious of our own culture.
2 Habitual ways of thinking may arise out of cultural assumptions and not out of personal pathology.
3 We as professionals also exist in a culture which is no more or less valid than the client's, but may lead to us holding different values and assumptions.
4 The dialogue between us will throw up cultural clashes and may be a fruitful way of understanding and negotiating cultural differences.
5 We will work more sensitively if we familiarize ourselves with the types and

range of differences that may exist in order that we can recognize them when they arise.

6   It is good to be sensitive to the differences that might emerge both in the supervisory and the therapy relationship. To facilitate this sensitivity we need not only to take an active interest in other cultures and areas of difference but never to assume that we understand the client's cultural world. We can then start with an interest in finding out from the other whilst also accepting our own not knowing.

If we are to be non-dogmatic we cannot hold on to our own theories tenaciously. We may need instead to be more interested in phenomena as we experience them. This may be a more useful guide to our practice than rigid theories. This phenomenological approach to the work means that the focus of interest, both for the supervisor and the supervisee, is their own experience and their interest in that of the client. The work thus becomes like a research project (Reason and Bradbury 2004) in which the experienced world of all three is made known more richly.

It is important to understand in working transculturally that we ourselves are not culturally neutral. Every individual is embedded in their culture and, if we are to work effectively with people from cultures different from our own, we need to have an understanding of our own culture and the assumptions we take as read because of this cultural context. If the supervisor espouses this attitude it will help the supervisee to be less defensive in presenting work in the supervision. Certain attitudes and feelings cease to be either wrong or right but *interesting*. This approach helps to open up a space in which real experience can 'come in' and be valued.

It is not enough just to rely on an openness to another's experience. The professionals also need to have, or acquire some knowledge of, the sorts of differences that may be found cross-culturally or they are likely to miss vital pieces of information. Pat Grant cogently points out the arrogance of assuming that it is not necessary to know the cultural background of a client (Grant, in Carroll and Holloway 1999). The factors mentioned at the beginning of the chapter begin to alert us to the kinds of differences we may find. Nevertheless, we need to guard against assuming that we know everything about a person's culture by having read about it. We are unlikely to know the subtleties and we could be in danger of reducing all to culture (Coleman, in Holloway and Carroll 1999).

Supervision of asylum seekers and refugees

Although supervision is a vital part of work in any of the helping professions, it is extremely important where asylum seekers and refugees are concerned, as the severity of the issues brought can render it difficult to keep a reflective space open for the work (Papadopoulos 2002; Trivasse 2003: 9). Refugees and asylum seekers are a very diverse group with many different cultures and nationalities and are no more or less likely to be vulnerable to difficulties with mental health problems than any other group (Loizos 2002). However, they have all suffered persecution, often of an extreme nature. The unusually horrific and sustained level of trauma experienced by these clients can make it hard to listen in an open, reflective and empathic way, particularly over long periods and the professionals involved often find it difficult not to be become reactive or 'shut down'. This is in addition to the usual difficulties and issues thrown up by cultural difference, as we showed earlier in this chapter.

Woodcock (Woodcock 2005), who researched the affect of work with asylum seekers and refugees on counselling and psychotherapy staff, advocates a type of supervision that is 'a cross between supervision and supportive psychotherapy' as the material is likely to be very disturbing. He suggests that supervisors 'engage more actively in the themes that cross the boundary between personal history and resonant themes in work with patients and clients'. He stresses the need to keep a reflective space open in spite of the extreme nature of the work and that supervision is essential in ensuring this.

Judy Ryde, who works with The Bath Centre for Psychotherapy and Counselling's Project (BCPC) for work with asylum seekers and refugees, described the following in which supervision helped her both 'stay with' difficult feelings and discover a way to reach a client's potential strength. It is interesting that in this example it is not so much the suggestion that the supervisor made that was useful, but permission to think more creatively to meet a need. Although the supervisor's suggestion was not taken up in the form offered, it helped the thinking to change in a productive way:

> I work with a man who had sunk into a depression following his flight to England, having been very severely tortured in his country of origin. His experiences seem to have all but broken his spirit. He has no energy, he has a constant severe headache as well as other pains inflicted by the torture, and images and memories that are constantly with him that he finds degrading, disturbing and shameful. I find in myself a desire to escape the room. I feel sleepy and look at the clock. Still half an hour to go. Then I am overcome by a feeling of sadness and despair into which I momentarily sink. I then come back to myself and feel helpless. How can I help such a wounded man? I think he is wounded in his body and in his soul. I want to reach out to him. I try to put into words what I have felt and how I imagine he must feel.
>
> He explains to me that he was a rich and important person in his community at home. He often helped members of his family with money and jobs as well as young people in the wider community whose education he ensured. I try to imagine what it is like for him in this country where his status is very low and where he has lost his ability to concentrate and cannot act from a position of strength. His wife, who would normally defer to him, makes all the decisions. My own thoughts about gender roles seem unimportant in the face of his shame at losing his power in this way.
>
> My supervisor acknowledges my struggle to stay with and to understand his difficult feelings on the one hand but the need for the client to find a sense of hope for the future on the other. As we reflect we think it may be time to help him to move on more actively but in a way that does not deny his reality. My supervisor suggests a meditation exercise which would help him to ground himself in his body, thus providing a stronger container for his feelings. At the following session I try to introduce this idea. He looks puzzled and confused. The strangeness of my suggestion even produces a small smile. The idea doesn't sit

well between us but I know that something is needed. I ask myself what I really want to achieve. At that instant I have an idea. I explain that I am trying to find within him a small feeling of hope. It seems to me that this feeling is like a seed – a seed of hope. I grab some paper and roughly draw a garden with flowers and sky. I draw a seed in the ground. I say it is a seed of hope and suggest we think about what potential might lie within the seed. I mention his children's future, his family's love for him, his loving heart, the great ability and generosity he showed in his country of origin, his love for his community, the respect shown to him by them and his ability to survive terrible events. I ask him if he can add anything to these pieces of potential within the seed. He says he can't but seems pleased with what I have done and reads them over, asking me about them. I draw some stones round the seed to indicate feelings of which he cannot let go such as anger and fear and distrust. These, I say, make it hard, but maybe not impossible, for the seed of hope to grow. I draw the sun and the rain which will be needed to encourage growth. I ask what the sun and the rain might represent. He cannot answer this and I suggest that we both think about it.

This talk of seeds leads to him talking about the farming he did in his early adulthood when he owned a farm. He remembered how much he enjoyed sowing seeds and watching them grow and come to fulfilment. I ask how he is feeling and he smiles. He says that his head feels clearer.

In this example the supervisor, supervisee and the client all struggled with a prevailing feeling of helplessness as the balance between carrying an appropriate level of hope and an acceptance of a sense of hopelessness was grappled with. The inter-subjective field is often shot through with this sense of vulnerability in the work with asylum seekers and refugees. The extremity of life and death, loss, and displacement are commonplace and our interventions seem puny in the face of such severity of these life events. The work of supervision is particularly important in helping supervisees to carry the work without resorting to heroic striving, to sinking under the weight of the distress or to cutting off from the pain of their inevitable inability to 'make it better'.

One supervisee was extremely distressed by the helplessness of a very isolated asylum seeker client who went into labour with a baby conceived as the result of a rape by a soldier. His distress and sense of helplessness were such that he found himself, not only driving her to hospital, but driving her home after the birth as well. His compassion and commitment, as well as his distress about his helplessness, were well recognized by his supervisor but he was also helped to re-find his appropriate role as her counsellor.

Coping with a sense of hopelessness is often present in the work with very distressed clients but with asylum seekers and refugees the issues are writ large and so reveal dilemmas which might not always be seen. The desire to be 'helpful' rather than reflective can be very seductive.

The sense of being out of control can also be exacerbated by the necessity to use interpreters as asylum seekers and refugees have often been in the host country for a relatively short period of time and they frequently have language difficulties which necessitate this need. It is a complex situation and is largely beyond the scope of this chapter. It can be very helpful if supervisors are familiar with work with interpreters in order to assist the supervisee to think about the complexities of the work where three are present rather than two. Interpretation in most other situations is a simple matter of the interpreter rendering what is said as accurately as possible from one language to the other. Work with therapists or counsellors inevitably involves a familiarity between the three as all are party to the intimacy of that which is revealed and shared. Complex transferences and counter-transferences are built up between them which can be reflected on, often helpfully in supervision, if the work is to progress satisfactorily (Ryde 2006). Supervision, or at least support, of interpreters needs to be considered if they, too, are to be able to sustain the work.

The levels of distress are often such that it is important to have an opportunity to discharge it in supervision as it keeps the therapist open and alive to the client's experience, however distressing. Extending supervision, particularly supervision groups, to include rituals of saying goodbye has also been found to be useful at BCPC as clients can sometimes disappear without trace. They may have been sent back to their country of origin or may disappear into the population to escape that fate, for instance.

Given the complexity of this work it is often best for therapists to seek specialist supervision. The project at BCPC, for instance, provides special extra monthly group supervision with a specialist supervisor on top of the therapist's normal supervision (Ryde 2004). The benefit of sharing experiences in the group can point up the importance of bearing witness to atrocities, which matches the client's need, without going beyond well-held therapy boundaries.

Conclusion

Working with cultural difference is demanding. It is often fraught with difficult and even violent feelings, particularly where this difference has been ignored and denied over years. It is nevertheless of utmost importance to work with this dimension, particularly in an increasingly multicultural world where the norms of the 'white', western world tend to be taken as 'normal'.

Possibly because of power imbalances which are often denied or unrecognized, the whole area of difference, often subsumed under the heading of 'equal opportunities', has been very painful and fraught with conflict. These range from the extremes of race hatred leading to many deaths in minority groups, including ethnic and gay groups, to less extreme but very damaging injustices such as those in the workplace, education and the professions. In the face of these painful clashes, simple prescriptions have been sought for 'getting it right'. Many of these prescriptions, such as an insistence on using 'correct' words, have helped to draw attention to areas of inequality. However, there is a danger that merely prescribing correct behaviour can do nothing but drive real feelings underground so that lip service only is played to greater tolerance and full explorations are curtailed for fear of vilification. An open-hearted and non-defensive attitude can lead to a deeper understanding of the issues and real exploration of difference as we have seen above.

Supervisory sessions that accept that prejudiced feelings are inevitable, given our cultural heritage, may open up genuine explorations in which they can be challenged and changed. This open supervision does not put into question the basic worth of the supervisee who reveals prejudiced or culturally insensitive attitudes. They could indeed be praised for their courage in being prepared to own to difficult thoughts, feelings and beliefs. Having been voiced and explored, a genuine change of attitude is the most likely outcome, particularly if there is a real meeting across difference.

We end with a salutary story from the Sufi Middle-eastern wise fool, Nasrudin, who, as the story goes (Hawkins 2005), became a consultant. He decided to have a well-earned rest by taking a cruise.

> The first night of the voyage he was given a table with a Frenchman. At the beginning of the meal the Frenchman greeted him with 'Bon appetit'. Nasrudin thought that the Frenchman was politely introducing himself, so he responded by saying 'Mulla Nasrudin'. They had a pleasant meal.
>
> However, the next morning breakfast started with the same ritual, the Frenchman saying 'Bon appetit' and Nasrudin who now thought the Frenchman must be a little deaf said more loudly, 'Mulla Nasrudin'.
>
> At lunch the same thing happened and by now Nasrudin was getting a little irritated with what he thought must be a very dim-witted Frenchman. Luckily that day he got talking to a fellow passenger who spoke French and was, by extraordinary coincidence, a trans-cultural supervisor. He was able to enlighten Nasrudin and tell him that 'Bon appetit' was a polite French greeting that meant 'have a nice meal'.
>
> 'Ah! Thank you,' said the enlightened and relieved Nasrudin. All afternoon he practised his next intervention, walking up and down the deck of the boat. That evening he very proudly sat down at dinner, smiled and said to his new French friend, 'Bon appetit.'
>
> 'Mulla Nasrudin,' the Frenchman replied.

9 Supervisor training and development

Introduction
Assessing your learning needs
Setting up training courses
Core supervision for new supervisors
 Supervisory feedback skills
 Supervisory intervention skills
 Mapping supervision
Core supervision for student and practice supervisors
Course in team and group supervision
Therapeutic supervision courses for those who supervise in-depth counselling,
 psychotherapy or other therapeutic work
Advanced supervision course
 Use of video and inter-personal process recall
  Helping students attend to the phenomena of a session non-judgementally
  Increasing the sensitivity to non-verbal behaviour
  Being able to attend to how the wider patterns of a session or a whole relationship are
  reflected in the microcosm of a few minutes
  Becoming more aware of the parallel process
  Noticing our own previously unconscious reactivity and desensitizing ourselves to certain
  things that trigger us
  Noticing what interrupts us from being fully present
Training in ethical dilemmas
Training in transcultural supervision
Evaluation and accreditation
Conclusion

Introduction

This chapter is addressed both to those new or experienced supervisors who want to assess their own learning and development and plan what future training they want for themselves, and to those who are responsible for providing training in supervision. In the second part of this chapter we outline a variety of possible training courses to meet different supervisory training needs.

Assessing your learning needs

There are two attitudes that are often held by new supervisors:

- Now I have been made a supervisor I should know how to do it and should just get on and do the job.
- I do not know anything about supervision and the only way I am going to learn to be a proper supervisor is from a full supervision training course.

Both ways of thinking are unhelpful and prevent new supervisors from carefully assessing their own knowledge and abilities and what they need to learn beyond these. It prevents them from realizing that learning to be a competent supervisor can come from a great variety of sources and is a lifetime process. We believe that a good training course is an essential component of any supervisor's development, but it should be only one of several. For most supervisees there are a great variety of learning possibilities that can be used in different combinations to feed into each other.

A possible learning programme could look like Figure 9.1.

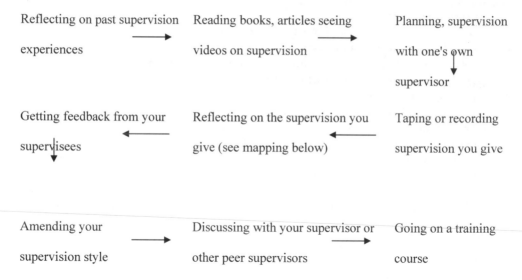

Figure 9.1   Supervision learning process

This learning cycle can flow in any of the directions and be reordered in any way that most suits the learning needs and opportunities of the supervisor. However, if you are to learn systematically it is useful to start the process by carrying out a self-appraisal and learning-needs assessment. Table 9.1 offers a possible format for such an assessment, but this is only a blueprint which you can amend and rewrite to fit your circumstances and needs. It is important to recognize that the craft of supervision has many dimensions and requires a range of competencies, capabilities and capacities. Hawkins and Smith (2006) define these different levels:

- *Competencies* we see as the ability to utilize a skill or use a tool.
- *Capability* is the ability to use the tool or skill, at the right time, in the right way and in the right place.

- *Capacity* is a human quality, rather than a skill and more to do with how you are, rather than what you do.

This self-assessment questionnaire affords you the opportunity of getting 360-degree feedback from supervisees, peers, tutor and supervisor. Each person is asked to rate each area of skill on a 1 to 5 scale. To create some common understanding of how to use this rating scale we offer the following descriptions:

1   professional learning need – don't know how to do this;
2   personal learning need – know how to but unable to make it happen;
3   sporadically competent – occasionally do it fine;
4   consistently competent – this has become part of natural way of doing things;
5   mastery – can role model for this – can teach it to others.

Table 9.1   Self-assessment questionnaire for supervisors

	Learning need		Competent		Expert
	1	2	3	4	5
1 Knowledge					
1.1 Understand the purpose of supervision					
1.2 Clear about the boundaries of supervision					
1.3 Understand the following elements:					
Qualitative					
Developmental					
Resourcing					
1.4 Know the various types of supervision					
contract					
2 Supervision management skills					
2.1 Can explain to supervisees the purpose of supervision					
2.2 Can negotiate a mutually agreed and clear contract					
2.3 Can maintain appropriate boundaries					
2.4 Can set a supervision climate that is:					
empathic					
genuine					
congruent					
trustworthy					
immediate					
2.5 Can maintain a balance between the qualitative, developmental and resourcing functions					
2.6 Can end a session on time and appropriately					
3 Supervision intervention skills					
3.1 Can utilise all stages of the CLEAR process (see Chapter 5)					
3.2 Can use the following types of intervention (see pp. 00)					

	Learning need		Competent		Expert
	1	2	3	4	5
prescriptive					
informative					
confrontative					
catalytic					
cathartic					
supportive					
3.3 Can give feedback in a way that is (see pp. 00):					
clear					
owned					
regular					
balanced					
specific					
3.4 Can usefully focus on (see Chapter 6):					
client content					
supervisee's interventions					
supervisee/client relationship					
supervisee's counter-transference					
supervision relationship					
own counter-transference					
wider context					
3.4 Can describe own way of working					
3.5 Can offer own experience appropriately					
3.6 Can develop self-supervision skills in supervisees					
4 Capacities or qualities					
4.1 Commitment to the role of supervisor					
4.2 Appropriate authority, presence and impact					
4.3 Can encourage, motivate and carry appropriate optimism					
4.4 Sensitive to supervisee's needs					
4.5 Aware of and able to adapt to individual differences due to:					
gender					
age					
cultural and ethnic background					
class					
sexual orientation					
personality					
professional training					
4.6 Sense of humour					
4.7 Ethical maturity					
5 Commitment to own ongoing development					
5.1 Have ensured own appropriate supervision					
5.2 Committed to updating own practitioner and supervisory skills and knowledge					

	Learning need		Competent		Expert
	1	2	3	4	5
5.3 Recognize own limits and identify my own strengths and weaknesses as supervisor					
5.4 Get regular feedback from:					
supervisees					
peers					
own supervisor/senior					
6 For group supervisors					
6.1 Have knowledge of group dynamics					
6.2 Can use the process of the group to aid the supervision process					
6.3 Can handle competitiveness in groups					
7 For senior organizational supervisors					
7.1 Can supervise inter-professional issues					
7.2 Can supervise organizational issues					
7.3 Have knowledge of stages in team and organizational development					
7.4 Can surface the underlying team or organizational culture					
7.5 Can facilitate organizational change					
7.6 Can create a learning culture in which supervision flourishes					

This form of assessment can be undertaken collaboratively, either by using it as a format for requesting feedback from supervisees, or by sharing one's own self-appraisal with one's own supervisor or work team, and receiving their feedback and appraisal of one's work.

Setting up training courses

In Chapter 5 on becoming a supervisor, we argued that it was important that all new supervisors not only obtain supervision on their supervision, but also receive some training for the new role of being a supervisor. For some people it might seem preferable that they receive training before they embark on giving any supervision, so that they are clear about what they are providing and how they are going to function, before they even start. The limitation of this approach is that, like all pre-training, trainees have no direct experience to reflect and work on within their training course, other than their experience of being supervised.

We recommend that all new supervisors receive a training course some time within the first year of their functioning as a supervisor. If the new supervisor is in a situation where they do not currently receive good supervision, which can act both as a model and a support for their new role, then the training should take place before they embark on the new role. However, in such cases it is grossly inadequate just to send them on a short supervisor training course and then expect them to function well as a supervisor. The most important part of the development of good supervisors comes, not from attending a training course, but from being well supported in planning and reflecting on the supervision that they give. If there is no possibility that new supervisors receive this form of support from the person responsible for supervising them, then the training course should set up an ongoing peer or led support group for new supervisors to meet and reflect on their supervisory practice.

Hawkins and Smith (2006) provide a summary of key principles on which to base the design of training and development:

1 Start with a focus on self-awareness, developed through experiential learning processes.
2 Develop the individuals' 'authority, presence and impact' through high degrees of feedback in small groups where the trainee undertakes supervising with their peers.
3 Teach basic skills and techniques in the most lively way possible, using demonstrations, illustrative stories, engagement and trainees reflecting on experiences from their lives. Provide plenty of opportunity to practice and receive feedback.
4 Teach theory only when experiential learning has already got underway.
5 Just-in-time learning: Learning is most effective when the learner has already recognized the need for that piece of learning and can apply the learning close to receiving it.
6 Real-time learning: Learning is greatly enhanced by the learners addressing real issues that are current and unresolved, rather than case studies from the past. They refer to this as real-play as opposed to role-play.
7 After initial training learners need a prolonged period of supervised practice before they return to create their own integration between self-awareness, skills, theory and their experience of practice.

Following these principles means that courses should ideally form a sandwich course, where the trainees have time mid-way to return to work and carry out some action learning on the supervision that they either give or receive. Then they will have the opportunity to return to the course and explore their experience and how they can handle certain situations differently.

Another way of ensuring that the course is practical is to make the courses substantially experiential, with much of the time given over to the trainees working together in giving, receiving and observing supervision, and then giving structured feedback to each other. On the courses that we run ourselves, much of the time is spent in different triads, with each member having the opportunity to be supervisor, supervisee and observer. Course members report that this is often the most valuable part of the course, with a great deal of learning being experienced in all three roles.

A different way of using triads in training is described by Spice and Spice (1976):

> Working in groups of three, beginning supervisors take turns functioning in three different roles: beginning supervisor, commentator, and facilitator. The

beginning supervisor presents samples (e.g., audiotape, videotape, case report) of an actual supervision, the commentator reviews the sample and then shares observations and encourages dialogue about the session, and then the facilitator comments on the present, here-and-now dialogue between the beginning supervisor and the commentator. Four processes are taught in the triadic model: a) presentation of supervision work, b) art of critical commentary, c) engagement of meaningful self-dialogue, and d) deepening of the here-and-now process.

(Quoted in Borders and Leddick 1987)

Harold Marchant, who has done much to develop supervision training in the areas of youth and community work, writes: 'Supervision involves knowledge, skills and techniques. Above all it involves attitudes and feelings of a supervisor in a relationship with another person' (Marchant, in Marken and Payne 1988).

It is thus important that supervision training includes not only the relevant knowledge, skills and training to equip a competent technical supervisor, but also concentrates on exploring the attitudes and assumptions of the trainees. It must also focus on 'exploring the concept of empathy and to working out its expression in the supervisory relationship' (Marchant, in Marken and Payne 1988: 40).

All supervisor training must, therefore, focus on how to build a relationship with a wide range of supervisees, that is built on trust, openness, awareness of difference and a sense of mutual exploration. In doing this the trainers need to be very aware of how the course itself is providing a role model and endeavour to provide a setting which is warm, open and trusting and where trainees feel able to explore both their experiences and inadequacies, despite their inevitable fears and vulnerabilities. This is a difficult task, for as Barbara Dearnley says:

> I have come to learn that looking in detail at supervisory practice is widely experienced as a very exposing affair, much more so than discussing one's own difficult cases. It is as if the public confirmation that one is sufficiently experienced to supervise leads to persecutory personal expectations that supervisors should say and do no wrong.
>
> (Dearnley 1985)

Being made a supervisor can decrease the space we give ourselves to be open to learning, for now we can believe that we should have the answers, be the experts, and should certainly not let on that we do not know what we are doing. Guy Claxton (1984) described the four beliefs that get in the way of adults' learning as being:

- I must be *competent*,
- I must be in *control*,
- I must be *consistent*,
- I must be *comfortable*.

All these four beliefs can easily be reinforced when a practitioner becomes a supervisor, and doubly reinforced when a supervisor starts training other supervisors!

A training course needs to set a climate that challenges these attitudes and creates a climate where making mistakes, trying out very different approaches and being vulnerable is valued. To set this climate the trainers have to model not being 'super-competent in-control experts', but experienced supervisors who are still open to and needing to learn and who are also open about their vulnerabilities.

Much of the material that needs to be included in courses is common to all types of trainee supervisors, but there are also different training needs depending on the context in which the trainee supervisor will be functioning. We propose five distinct types of courses as shown in Table 9.2.

Table 9.2   Types of supervision training courses

1   core supervision course for new supervisors;

2   core supervision for student and practice supervisors;

3   courses in team and group supervision for those who supervise teams or in group settings;

4   therapeutic supervision courses for those who supervise in-depth counselling or psychotherapy or other therapeutic work;

5   advanced supervision courses for those who have to supervise across teams and organizations or teach supervision or want to become advance practitioners.

We now look at what each of these courses might include, and we will illustrate this by describing some of the content of our own courses.

Core supervision for new supervisors

It is useful to begin the course by ascertaining what experience the course members have of both supervising and being supervised; for both kinds of experience will provide useful material to learn from and will also colour the attitudes and assumptions with which the course members begin their training.

In our early days of teaching supervision we naively used to expect course members to come on the course already believing that supervision was a good thing and eager to learn how to give it. We were soon disillusioned. We found many trainees who had spent years as social workers, doctors, occupational therapists, executive coaches or probation officers, who had never received any formal supervision. There were others whose experience of supervision was very negative. Supervision was a place where they had been made to feel very inadequate by over-critical supervisors. Others had been led to trust their supervisors and share their difficulties and sense of inadequacy, only to find that this had later been used against them by more senior management.

We discovered that it helped course members to be more open if we drew out all the bad experiences and negative attitudes to supervision at a very early stage of the course as this not only stopped them from covertly sabotaging the course, but was also useful learning material. As new supervisors they could explore how not to repeat the negative scenarios that their fellow course members had experienced.

We also learned from experience to avoid the process whereby we would be very evangelical about supervision and its benefits and the course members would have to carry the negative attitudes. On some courses we introduced a debate where some of the course members would argue for the effectiveness and the benefits of supervision and the others would argue its costs and negative side effects. Halfway through the debate we would ask them all to switch sides and carry on the heated exchange, but now arguing the opposite case. This ensured that the course was not divided into pro- and anti-supervision factions, and that both the costs and benefits of supervision were clearly recognized.

Following this it is important to explore what supervision is. There are many maps and models in Chapter 6 that can be used for this purpose. At this stage trainees should not be overloaded with too many different theories and maps, but given a clear and simple framework, such as the CLEAR model, which can help them identify the boundaries, process and roles involved in supervision.

This naturally leads on to the issue of contracting for supervision, and the attendant issues of confidentiality, responsibility and appropriate focus. We also find it necessary to explore the setting in which supervision is carried out. Where, when and how does supervision take place? Is it done in a cluttered office with the phone always ringing? Is it done across a desk? What is allowed to interrupt the supervision, or cause its postponement?

We also look at who takes responsibility for arranging the time for the supervision and seeing that it happens – the supervisor or the supervisee? Also how does the supervision start? We often find that the first two or three minutes of a supervision session set the stage and the atmosphere for the rest of the session. Early on in the course it is also important to introduce basic ethical guidelines for supervision as well as an awareness of the power relationship and the importance of an anti-discriminatory practice base (see Chapter 8).

The rest of the time on the first part of our course is divided between providing new supervisors with maps and models with which to reflect on their supervision and teaching and practising supervisory skills.

The first skill that we teach is the skill of giving good feedback, as this is not only essential to being competent supervisors, but also a skill they will be using throughout the training course as they work with each other.

Supervisory feedback skills

The process of telling another individual how they are experienced is known as feedback. Giving and receiving feedback is fraught with difficulty and anxiety because negative feedback restimulates memories of being rebuked as a child and positive feedback goes against injunctions 'not to have a big head'. Certainly most people give or experience feedback only when something is amiss. The feelings surrounding feedback often lead to its being badly given, so fears surrounding it are often reinforced. There are a few simple rules for giving and receiving feedback that help it to be a useful transaction which can lead to change.

Table 9.3 Giving feedback

Clear: Try to be clear about what the feedback is that you want to give. Being vague and faltering will increase the anxiety in the receiver and not be understood.

Owned: The feedback you give is your own perception and not an ultimate truth. It, therefore, says as much about you as it does about the person who receives it. It helps the receiver if this is stated or implied in the feedback (for example, 'When you ... I feel ...' rather than 'You are ...').

Regular: If the feedback is given regularly it is more likely to be useful. If this does not happen there is a danger that grievances are saved until they are delivered in one large package. Try to give the feedback as close to the event as possible and early enough for the person to do something about it (that is, do not wait until someone is leaving to tell them how they could have done the job better).

Balanced: It is good to balance negative and positive feedback and, if you find that the feedback you give to any individual is always either positive or negative, this probably means that your view is distorted in some way. This does not mean that each piece of critical feedback must always be accompanied by something positive, but rather a balance should be created over time.

Specific: Generalized feedback is hard to learn from. Phrases like, 'You are irritating' can only lead to hurt and anger. 'I feel irritated when you forget to record the telephone messages,' gives the receiver some information which he or she can choose to use or ignore.

Giving feedback
A mnemonic to help remember how to give good feedback is CORBS: Clear, Owned, Regular, Balanced and Specific (Table 9.3).

Receiving feedback
It is not necessary to be completely passive in the process of receiving feedback. It is possible to share the responsibility for the feedback received being well given. What is done with the feedback is nearly entirely the responsibility of the receiver.

- If the feedback is not given in the way suggested above you can ask for it to be more clear balanced, owned, regular and/or specific.
- Listen to the feedback all the way through without judging it or jumping to a defensive response, both of which can mean that the feedback is misunderstood.
- Try not to explain compulsively why you did something or even explain away the positive feedback. Try and hear others' feedback as *their* experiences of you. Often it is enough to hear the feedback and say, 'Thank you.'
- Ask for feedback you are not given but would like to hear.

Our own emphasis on feedback has been paralleled by that of Freeman (1985). His conclusions are summarized by Hess (1987):

> Freeman (1985) comprehensively outlined a number of important considerations for the supervisor delivering feedback. It should be a) systematic (objective,

accurate, consistent and reliable feedback that is less influenced by subjective variables); b) timely (feedback is delivered soon after an important event); c) clearly understood (both positive and negative feedback are based on explicit and specific performance criteria); and d) reciprocal (feedback is provided in two way interactions in which suggestions are made, not as the only way to approach a problem, but as only one of a number of potentially useful alternatives).

Supervisory intervention skills

The other major area of skill learning that needs to be included in any basic supervision training is to review the trainee's facilitation skills of the course members and help them adapt and develop them in an appropriate way for supervision. One useful tool in doing this is the Heron Model of six categories of intervention (Table 9.4). Heron (1975) developed a way of dividing all possible interventions in any facilitating or enabling process into six categories. They apply equally to one-to-one and group situations. Although they may not be exhaustive, their use is in helping us to become aware of the different interventions we use, those we are comfortable with, and those we avoid. Fol-

Table 9.4 Heron's six categories of intervention

Prescriptive	Give advice, be directive (e.g. You need to write a report on that. You need to stand up to your father).
Informative	Be didactic, instruct, inform (e.g. You will find similar reports in the filing cabinet in the office. This is how our recording system works).
Confrontative	Be challenging, give direct feedback (e.g. I notice when you talk about your last supervisor you always smile).
Cathartic	Release tension, abreaction (e.g. What is it you really want to say to your client?).
Catalytic	Be reflective, encourage self-directed problem-solving (e.g. Can you say some more about that? How can you do that?).

lowing on from that, we can, with practice, begin to widen our choices. The emphasis in definition is on the intended effect of the intervention on the client. There is no implication that any one category is more or less significant and important than any other.

These six types of intervention are only of any real value if they are rooted in care and concern for the client or supervisee. They are valueless when used degenerately or perversely (Heron 1975). Degenerate interventions happen when the practitioner is using them in an unskilled, compulsive or unsolicited way. They are usually rooted in lack of awareness whereas a perverted intervention is one which is primarily serving the needs of the intervener.

We have used this model widely in helping supervisors to look at their own style of intervention. We ask them to appraise themselves in terms of which category they predominantly use and with which category they feel least comfortable. We then have all trainee supervisors carrying out individual supervisions with a fellow trainee, while a third trainee records the pattern of interventions they use.

This makes it possible for trainees to decide to develop one of their less used intervention skills. For many new supervisors it provides an opportunity to consider how their intervention style needs to be different as a supervisor from what it was as a practitioner. A non-directive counsellor may find that their previous training and experience have led them dominantly to use catalytic interventions and that as a supervisor they have to incorporate more informative and confrontative interventions.

We have found that some supervisors switch styles completely and abandon many of their very useful counselling skills when they move into a managerial or supervisory role. These workers need help in revaluing their own practitioner skills, albeit within a new context and role.

This model can also be used by trainee supervisors in mapping their own supervision style. Some trainees have recorded their supervision sessions and then scored each of the interventions that they have used. Others have used the model for both the supervisees and themselves to reflect back on the session and in particular the supervisor's interventions; then to explore how each party would like the emphasis in intervention style to change.

Bond and Holland (1998, chapters 4, 5 and 6) give detailed guidelines on how to develop each of the Heron intervention styles.

Mapping supervision

The other main system for mapping supervision that we provide for trainee supervisors is a model that helps them chart the content focus of a session, how it shifts from management issues, to client issues, to areas of supporting the supervisee. The model also looks at who is responsible for the shift in focus. This is published elsewhere (Hawkins 1982).

As mentioned above, the main emphasis of any good supervision course should not be on teaching these or other skills and models. It is better to emphasize the use of these skills and maps as a language with which to reflect on the practice supervisions they give on the course and on the supervision that they then give back at work. This is why a central part of the courses is the trainees' return to work with an action-learning project, using one of the skills or maps as a research tool in order to find out more about their own supervision.

The course needs to reconvene in order to harvest the learning from these action-learning projects, so that course members are learning not only from their own experience, but also from that of their colleagues.

To harvest this learning both discursive case presentations and more action-based methods like group sculpting, role-play and enacted stakeholder role-plays can be used (see Chapters 10 and 11). This part of the course can be thought of as an extended group supervision of the course members' supervisory work.

Core supervision for student and practice supervisors

There are two types of student supervisors: those who are college-based, and those who are placement- or practice-based. A training course for both types of student supervisors has to include most, if not all, of the material recommended for new first-line supervisors, but the context and the emphasis of the course need to be slightly different.

Firstly, the college-based student supervisor is working within a different supervision contract, where the emphasis is on the developmental and supportive aspects of supervision and where the managerial aspects are being carried by the practice supervisor or manager. Even the practice supervisor will have a greater emphasis on the developmental side of supervision.

One of the difficulties for many college-based supervisors is that they are often more at home in a teacher role than a supervisory one. The danger here is that their supervision may consist of didactic tutorials, and the supervisees, instead of being enabled to reflect on their own experience, have theoretical references thrown at their 'inadequacies'. 'If only you had read X, then you would not have been so foolish,' is the attitude that the student experiences. This is similar to the 'game' that Kadushin (1968) calls: 'If you knew Dostoevsky like I know Dostoevsky.' He points out it can be played by either the supervisor or the supervisees (see Chapter 5).

The college-based supervisor needs to provide a climate that goes against the common educational culture of dependency and instead provide a setting in which supervisees are encouraged to be responsible for their own learning and can rely on the support, trust and openness of their supervisor.

At the former South-west London College counselling course where one of us taught and supervised counselling, the students were encouraged to work out their own contracts with both their group and individual supervisor. They were given a blueprint, based on the current staff thinking about supervision. An example is provided in table 9.5 overleaf. This is similar to the list of supervisor and supervisee responsibilities listed in Chapter 4.

The other major issue that needs to be focused on in a course for student supervisors is hinted at in the above contract where it says: 'to be aware of the organizational contracts which the supervisor and the students have with college, employers, clients and supervision group'. Most often the student supervisor is part of an extended triangle, with the student having two supervisors (one in the college and one in the placement) and two organizational contexts to work between. We have mentioned in Chapter 8 the dynamics that are created in triangular relationships, with the tendency to create splitting, with one becoming the 'good supervisor' and the other the 'bad supervisor'. Student supervisors need to learn how to negotiate clear contracts not only with their supervisees, but also with their co-supervisor in the practice setting, and also how to carry out three-way assessment and evaluation meetings with the supervisee and the co-supervisor.

Table 9.5   A blueprint of responsibilities

Supervisor responsibility

- to ensure a safe enough space for students to lay out practice issues in their own way;
- to help students explore and clarify thinking, feeling and fantasies which underlie their practice;
- to share experience, information and skill appropriately;
- to challenge practice which they judge is unethical, unwise or incompetent;
- to challenge personal or professional blind-spots which they may perceive in individuals or the group;
- to be aware of the organizational contracts which they and the students have with the college, employers, clients and supervision group.

Student responsibility

- to oneself;
- to identify practice issues with which they need help and to ask for time in the group to deal with these;
- to become increasingly able to share these issues freely;
- to identify what kind of responses they want;
- to become more aware of the organizational contracts the student is in, in the workplace, in the college, with clients, with the supervision group;
- to be open to others' feedback;
- to monitor tendencies to justify, explain, or defend;
- to develop the ability to discriminate what feedback is useful.

To others (when in group supervision):

- to share with other members all the responsibilities of the supervisor, in such a way that safety and challenge can both be possible in the group,
- to monitor tendencies to advise or compete.

(quoted in Proctor 1988a)

Course in team and group supervision

Courses need to be arranged in organizations for people such as district occupational therapists, principal care officers in social services, area youth officers or district psychologists who are required to supervise a number of different teams. Such a course would also be useful for experienced team leaders and for training managers who are increasingly finding that they are called upon to provide team consultancy services and not just to put on courses.

It is important that all the people who attend such a course are already trained and experienced supervisors. If they are not, they should be given some basic supervision training before attending this type of course.

As in the basic course it is useful to start by reviewing the knowledge, skills and abilities of the course members and then looking at what their learning needs are from this particular course. This process is also important as it acts as a model for the course members in how to negotiate a working contract with a group or team.

The course then needs to provide an opportunity to explore the differences between individual and team supervision and to encourage the course members to present the difficulties they have, which are specific to working with teams. Chapters 10 and 11 provide the basis for presenting some of the themes specific to supervising in groups and teams and the course also needs to include teaching on group dynamics, the developmental stages in the formation and growth of a team and some basic theory of team development.

Chapter 11, 'Exploring the dynamics of teams, groups and peer groups', also provides the outline of some of the models and techniques we teach to team supervisors, both for them to use with the teams they supervise and also to explore their work while they are on the course. Course members can actively involve each other in the dynamics of their supervised teams by using the other group members as a sculpt of a team they would like to explore. They then bring the sculpt to life and have other course members try out various ways of supervising the same enacted group (for a description of sculpting see Chapter 11).

Another useful strategy for teaching group supervision skills is as follows:

1   Divide the group into two parts – A and B.
2   First the groups meet for a while separately to explore their learning needs.
3   Then group A provides a consultant and a process observer for group B. Group B does the same for group A.
4   After a designated length of time the consultants and observers return to their groups to process all three types of experience – that of the consultant, the observer and the members who received consultancy.
5   The exercise can also include structured feedback from the group members to the visiting consultant.

This exercise can continue through several cycles or until every course member has had the opportunity to be in each role. Where possible the team-supervision course should also be taught as a sandwich course, so that course members can further explore some of their new perspectives in an action-learning stage, before returning to the course with more monitored experience which they can share with the other course members.

Therapeutic supervision courses for those who supervise in-depth counselling, psychotherapy or other therapeutic work

This course also has to ensure that its members have already acquired the skills, knowledge and techniques included in the basic supervision course. If not, such teaching would need to be included in this course.

Where this course needs to go further and deeper than the basic course is in understanding the ways of working with the interlocking psychodynamic processes of the therapy relationship and the supervision relationship. We use our own model of 'seven-eyed supervision' (see Chapter 7) to teach this area and have developed a series of different experiential exercises to train supervisors in each of the seven modes, as well as exercises in how to integrate the modes into their own personal style.

The course also needs to address the developmental model (see Chapter 6) and how the supervision style needs to change and adapt according to the developmental stage of both the supervisee and the supervision relationship.

Advanced supervision course

For this course members should already have the knowledge, techniques and skills equivalent to those taught on courses 1, 2 and 3. Our own experience of running an advanced supervision course over many years has led us to believe that the main focus should be on providing a learning space for supervisors to return to the knowledge and skills they have developed from earlier supervision training, having applied these skills in their own work setting. This means that the course is appropriately less structured and more student-determined than the earlier courses, with plenty of opportunity for supervisors to present difficult situations from their own supervision practice.

We have also discovered that a series of other inputs are useful when supervisors have reached this stage. These include:

- in-depth work with video recordings of supervision practice either pre-prepared at work or filmed on the course;
- the use of inter-personal process recall techniques (Kagan 1980) to reflect on the detailed dynamics of videoed or practice sessions;
- case study seminar on ethical dilemmas in supervision (see below);
- workshop on developing transcultural competence (see below and Chapter 8);
- seminar on dealing with issues concerning appraisal, evaluation and accreditation (see below);
- reflections of case material involving inter-agency dynamics (see Chapter 12);
- a seminar on ways of developing supervision policies in organizations and also how to assist it in bringing about organizational change at the levels of culture and ethos, strategy and structure (see Chapter 13 and 14).

Use of video and inter-personal process recall

Using video can add an extra dimension and richness to supervision training. In our own work we have built on the work of Kagan (1980) and others to develop ways of using video to develop not only supervisory skills, but also reflective skills. Kagan and his colleagues developed the use of video in training in the 1960s. They were in the habit of recording lectures of visiting speakers, which the speakers wanted to see and, whilst watching the recordings, 'would spontaneously and uncharacteristically comment on a range of covert experiences they had been having at the time' (Allen in Tudor and

Worrall 2004, chapter 9). Further research by Kagan and others showed that if you watch a video of a human interaction you have been part of within 24 or 36 hours, you have the same physical responses as you had while in the meeting, but with more space to reflect on what was happening, not only for you, but also the client and the relationship.

We started using video as a training method for supervision in the late 1970s. Despite initial resistance to the video stemming from, on the one hand fear of seeing oneself and being seen on video, and on the other hand a feeling of intimidation around technology, it rapidly became clear that it was like having another supervisor in the room. On the first training that we used the video we reviewed a session where there did not seem to be a strong relationship between the supervisor and the supervisee. However, on viewing the video it was very obvious throughout the session there had been much mirroring of body position such as angle of body and crossed arms; but most fascinating of all was what appeared to be a lively dialogue between their feet whilst their conversation was flat and unresponsive. On this occasion it was the camera person who noticed this – it was almost as if the narrow focus of the viewfinder focused their powers of observation.

We then developed ways of working with the video playback by building on Kagan's very useful reflective questions in the Inter-personal process recall (IPR) method (see Table 9.6).

Table 9.6 Inter-personal process recall: key questions

These questions are adapted from the work of Kagan and his IPR method. They can be used to help a supervisor or therapist review a video of their work.

1   What did you feel at this point?

2   What were you thinking?

3   What bodily sensations did you have?

4   What did/would you do?

5   What would you have rather done?

6   What problems or risks would there be if you did so?

7   What sort of person does this supervisee see you as?

8   Does this episode remind you of any past situations?

9   Do you have any images or associations in relation to this episode?

10 Are there any other feelings or thoughts that the situation provokes in you?

We have found his questions extremely useful when watching the videoed sessions, partly because people can tend to glaze over when watching the tape, either because of the hypnotic affect brought on by watching something on TV and/or because they were reticent about commenting. In fact, this dynamic is reflective of one of Kagan's premises that people perceive and understand much more of their communication with each other than one would suppose, but that they are afraid to act on their perceptions. The questions gave them permission and a structure with which to focus on the material and, by being encouraged to be more explicit, they discovered that this was also experienced as supportive by the supervisee.

Using video in training has a number of benefits:

1   helping students attend to the phenomena of a session non-judgementally;
2   increasing the sensitivity to non-verbal behaviour;
3   being able to attend to how the wider patterns of a session or a whole rela-
    tionship are reflected in the microcosm of a few minutes;
4   becoming more aware of the parallel process;
5   noticing our own previously unconscious reactivity and desensitizing ourselves
    to certain things that trigger us;
6   noticing what interrupts us from being fully present.

Helping students attend to the phenomena of a session non-judgementally
Using video is particularly useful as a teaching tool for Mode 1 – for observing phenomenology. We have learnt a great deal from working with William Emerson, an
American psychologist who has specialized in pre- and perinatal birth trauma. Of particular interest was Emerson's way of focusing the video camera on a person's face and its
asymmetry, and inviting us to make observations. What was fascinating was that what
might have been assumed to be intuitions about a person could be observed. This was
even when the person's face was 'at rest'. Then, by using freeze frame and slow motion, it
was possible to observe minute changes of expression that revealed a whole wealth of
detail behind the apparently simple statement or movement that the person was making.

Increasing the sensitivity to non-verbal behaviour
Replaying videotapes with the sound turned off, or in slow motion, greatly helps trainees
attend to small movements and changes they would not normally see. One can also
blank the screen and just listen to the non-verbal aspects of the voices; the tone, timbre,
volume, pitch and rhythm of the voices.

Being able to attend to how the wider patterns of a session or a whole relationship are reflected in the microcosm of a few minutes
Allen (in Worrall and Tudor 2004) also comments on a phenomenon that we too have
noticed, that you need only focus on a minute or two of the tape to see the major themes
of the work. 'Kagan always maintained that if there was an issue, a hesitancy, something
not being said, a defensiveness, anything going on in the relationship, then it would
come to the surface no matter where you stopped the tape and took a slice to recall' – the
macrocosm is in the microcosm. John Heron would say when teaching co-counselling
that if you invited a person to describe their breakfast that morning, there would be their
whole life!

> IPR is based on the idea that at any moment in time we are receiving and
> experiencing hundreds of feelings, thoughts, sensations, images and bodily
> reactions, of which we are not normally aware and which we do not have time to
> process in the moment but which subtly behave, react and interact. If we can
> find a safe way to bring this into conscious awareness, name it and examine it in
> a spirit of non-judgemental inquiry, then it can provide us with useful

information about our own interactions, our mode of behaving in certain situations, the way we perceive others and the way they may perceive us.

(Allen, in Worrall and Tudor 2004)

Becoming more aware of the parallel process

On another occasion there was a wonderful example of parallel process, which was not observed by anyone until the video was watched. On this occasion the supervisee had been talking about how uncomfortable they felt about what appeared to be some seductiveness on the part of their client. The supervisor struggled, not very successfully, to help them around this. On the video we were amazed to see the supervisee act in a seductive way as she adjusted her skirt and arranged herself on the chair. In fact it was so obvious and so surprising that we all burst out laughing. It was an example both of parallel process and how much the here and now offers us an opportunity to work directly with the material. The 'here and now' can be like the emperor's new clothes – we can avoid seeing the obvious. Without the video this would have remained out of awareness, at least in that particular session.

Noticing our own previously unconscious reactivity and desensitizing ourselves to certain things that trigger us

We also use video to help trainees confront their fears of what might happen in a supervision session. We ask them to share the worst things that a supervisee might say or do and capture these on video as 30-second role-plays. These then are played back to the whole group as 'trigger tapes', and all the participants are asked to record their responses to this very short video clip using the trigger tape questions (see Table 9.7).

Table 9.7 Trigger tape questions

- What did I notice?
- What did I hear?
- What did I feel whilst watching?
- What were my thoughts whilst watching?
- What would I do next?
- What effect do I think that would have?
- What alternative response(s) would I like to be able to make?
- What effect do I think that those interventions would have?

Noticing what interrupts us from being fully present

A second dynamic that Kagan observed was that of 'tuning out' – of not seeing or hearing the other person. This usually occurred when students were particularly concerned about the impression that they hoped to be making on the client. Kagan noticed after recall sessions that these two dynamics were considerably less. We have noticed examples of this on the advanced course. Participants are concerned about their abilities as supervisors, how they are going to be viewed by their peers and needing to be advanced enough to be on an advanced course. Making these thoughts and concerns explicit, greatly reduced their effect.

The IPR questions invite the supervisor to review what was happening to them at chosen points in the session; what they were feeling; what they were noticing in their body; and what thoughts they were having. These tie in with Mode 6 where the supervisor concentrates on his or her own responses to possible information about the client, the supervisee and the relationships involved. IPR can be a useful means for trainees to appreciate that their own process is as relevant in the relationship as the client's or, as in the case of supervision, the supervisor's and the supervisee's.

As we have said elsewhere in this book, our main stumbling block to being present, either as a supervisor or as a human being, is our fear. Kagan's work invites people to face their own personal nightmare by the use of 'trigger tapes' in which a person faces what they are most afraid of. On the course we invite each person to say the sentence they would least like to hear from a client or supervisee, and then work with them on that, via the video clip in which this is said, either by them or another member of the group. We view the tape first at normal speed and then in slow motion. Also, the IPR work, by inviting the person to trust their own inner process and to share it, helps them to practise different ways of behaving and being intimate. In that way it becomes a practice for life as well as a practice for supervision.

Watching and reflecting on videos of other supervisors is also a rich form of learning and can help trainees to practise utilizing a number of the other models mentioned in this book. In Table 9.8 we show the questions we use to help the reflection process.

Training in ethical dilemmas

In Chapter 5 we discussed the importance of developing one's own ethical principles as well as familiarizing oneself with the codes of ethics of one's professional association. We quoted Michael Carroll's four-stage model of ethical decision making. Carroll (1996) also includes a very comprehensive curriculum for training supervisors in ethical decision making. We provide an abbreviated version of this curriculum which we use on our courses as a framework for reviewing real ethical dilemmas, either brought by participants or supplied by ourselves from our past experience.

Training in transcultural supervision

Training in this area can utilize the material included in Chapter 8. Judy Ryde has developed a workshop for the Centre for Supervision and Team Development which begins by asking people to share something about their cultural background. Many white, western people tend to think of themselves as not 'having' a culture at all and that other cultures are measured by the way they differ from what appears to them to be 'normal'. It is important to address this by sensitizing members of the course to their own cultural norms, assumptions and values (Ryde 2005). This can be initially addressed, for example, by asking them to share the history of any of their names. This exercise is relevant both for 'whites' and 'non-whites'.

Table 9.8 Questions for reflecting on supervision

- What do you notice the supervisor focusing on?
- Why do you think they are doing this?
- What do you think the session achieved?
- Do you notice any resistance in (a) client; (b) therapist; (c) supervisor?
- What strategies did you notice being used by the supervisor?
- What did the supervisor ignore that you might have worked with?
- What did the supervisor work with that you might have ignored?
- Find a symbol for (a) the therapy relationship; (b) the supervisory relationship.

Using seven modes of supervision

- Which modes of supervision are they using? Which do they ignore?
- How do they switch from one mode to another?
- What do you think makes them switch, and how effective is the switch?
- What aspects of the following are present but not explored?

  paralleling,

  supervisee's counter-transference,

  supervisor counter-transference.

It is important that those who attend this course understand that they are bound to be rooted in their own cultural assumptions and then to learn to work across differences in culture. This becomes complex, particularly in the triangular supervision situation, as described in Chapter 8, and we have devised several exercises to explore these issues. Here is one:

- Person A says to person B, 'What I would like you to know about my cultural background is...'
- Person B says, 'What I heard was...'
- Person A clarifies.
- Person B says, 'How I would supervise you differently on the basis of what I have heard is...'
- Person A gives feedback on what they would find helpful of the suggestions made by B.
- Steps 1–4 are carried out with A and B reversing roles.
- Having explored their differences, A and B share ways in which they may be unawarely similar.

This can be followed by using vignettes from Chapter 8 and asking groups to answer the following three questions:

Table 9.9 A Checklist for ethical decision making in supervision training (based on Carroll 1996)

---

1 Creating ethical sensitivity

- creating one's own list of moral principles;
- reading ethical codes and related literature;
- case vignettes on ethical and transcultural issues;
- sharing critical incidents from members own experience.

2 Formulating a moral course of action

- Identify the ethical problem or dilemma.
- Identify the potential issues involved.
- Review the relevant ethical guidelines.
- Ascertain who else should be consulted.
- Consider possible and probable courses of action.
- Enumerate the consequences of the various options.
- Decide on the best course of action.

3 Implementing an ethical decision

- Anticipate the potential difficulties in implementing the decision.
- Explore the internal fears and resistances to taking the action.
- Set up the necessary support and strategies for dealing with the potential difficulties and resistances.

4 Living with the ambiguities of an ethical decision

- dealing with the anxiety and fears attending the decision;
- confronting one's internal and anticipated external critical judgements;
- accepting the limitations involved;
- formulating the learning from the experience that can be applied elsewhere.

- What cultural assumptions may be in operation in the behaviour of the therapist and client?
- How might they need to change their mind-sets and behaviour to work in a more transculturally competent manner?
- How would you supervise the therapist?

This can be followed by role-playing a supervision session with the therapist from the vignette.

Evaluation and accreditation

Since writing the first edition of this book the whole area of supervision training and accreditation has grown and become more fixed. In the 1980s there was no formal accreditation for being a supervisor, and little in the way of formal training. Most practitioners became supervisors as a result of having been in the profession long enough. While we welcome the growth in research, training and accreditation in the field of supervision we become increasingly concerned that the joy of continual learning can be overshadowed by the need to fulfil externally generated requirements, and the anxiety this evokes.

Accreditation begins with some form of appraisal. We believe that all appraisal processes should start with the individual appraising themselves and being challenged openly to face their own strengths and weaknesses. This should be followed by some form of structured 360-degree feedback which includes supervisees, fellow trainee supervisors, as well as trainers and more experienced supervisors. The reason for this is to support the supervisor in taking their own authority and to lessen the degree to which they become dependent or reactive to the authority of others. Another reason is that supervisory ability is always embedded in relationship and can never become a mechanical process,. Therefore assessment should also be within a relationship that ideally acknowledges the inter-subjective and power dimensions involved (see Chapter 8).

Earlier in this chapter we offered a format for carrying out a self-appraisal. The same form can be used by supervisees to appraise their supervisor, as well as by the supervisor's supervisor. It is then possible to review the different ratings given by all three parties and for the person being appraised to reflect on how they see their proficiencies and learning needs differently from others' perceptions.

Where accreditation is carried out by some official professional body, it is important that it avoids the twin dangers of ignoring *individual autonomy* on the one hand, and *institutionalized authority* on the other.

The danger of individual autonomy

Accreditation that just rubber stamps the individuals' own self and peer-assessment abrogates the responsibility of the elders of a profession of the need to initiate a new member into the community of practising professionals. This involves challenging their own self-perception, challenging peer collusion in their training group and ensuring that they have been exposed to training and experience that is of the necessary depth and breadth appropriate for the work they will supervise. The most important challenge is that the supervisor seeking accreditation is aware of their own shortcomings and personal biases, and can respond to feedback on these in an open and non-defensive manner that leads to further learning and development.

The danger of institutionalized authority

The other danger in accreditation is that the professional body becomes increasingly fixed in its professional requirements and that these become more and more based on quantifiable inputs in the training that the supervisor has undergone, rather than the qualities and abilities the supervisor has developed through both training and experience. The evaluation process needs to happen within a direct form of relationship and not by the examination of paperwork by a distant and unknown committee. There is also a tendency for professional bodies constantly to increase the standards required from those being evaluated. This can be justified as a wish to improve but it can also be driven by a socioeconomic process of professions restricting the gateway into an already crowded market niche. It can also be driven by a collective psychological process which searches for perfection rather than accepting our human ignorance and fallibility. In Chapter 1 we talked about 'good-enough' supervision, and accreditation must evaluate someone as a 'good-enough' supervisor, and as a person who is committed to continuing their learning and development.

Supervisor evaluation and accreditation needs to be carefully managed, as the accredited supervisor will often have to combine the role of supervisor with that of providing evaluation and contributions to the accreditation of their supervisees. It is important that they experience how this can be done both effectively and sensitively, where support and challenge are combined in healthy relationship.

Conclusion

In this chapter we have emphasized the importance of supervision training that is experiential, practical, involves action learning and is appropriate to the type of supervision that the course members give. However, supervision courses can never be a substitute for having good supervision oneself.

In teams, organizations or professions that do not have a healthy tradition and practice of supervision, it is unrealistic to try to solve this absence by randomly setting up supervisor training courses. Supervisor training will always be most effective when it is part of a strategic plan to create an organizational learning culture. How to go about creating the right sort of organization or team climate in which supervision can flourish is explored at length in Chapters 13 and 14. But first we look at the challenging area of supervising across and between organizations.

PART THREE
Group, team and peer-group supervision

10 Group, team and peer-group supervision

Introduction
Group supervision
    Advantages
    Disadvantages of group supervision
    Early stage contracting before the group starts
    Group supervision styles and foci
    Contracting
    Setting the climate
    Structuring the group
    Techniques
    Acknowledging the group dynamic
Team supervision
    Working group
    Team
Peer supervision
    How to form a peer supervision group
    Organizing a peer supervision meeting
Conclusion

Introduction

The emphasis so far in this book has been mainly on individual supervision. This is because it is practised more often than group supervision, and also because it enables us to address many of the key issues and processes in a simpler situation before moving on to the more complex setting of a group. However, many of the issues so far covered, such as contracting, modes of supervision, the importance of transcultural and anti-oppressive practice and ethics, also apply to supervision in groups and teams.

In this chapter we explore first the advantages and disadvantages of group supervision. We then look at the different styles of supervision groups and what role the facilitator plays in each. We go on to look at setting up supervision groups, contracting and setting the climate. This is followed by describing some techniques we have found particularly effective as they make good use of having several participants. Finally we explore issues involved with team and peer supervision.

Group supervision

Advantages

There are several reasons why you might choose to supervise in a group rather than individually. The first may be connected to economies of time, money or expertise. Clearly, if there is a shortage of people who can supervise, or their time is very limited, supervisors can probably see more supervisees by conducting supervision groups. However, ideally group supervision should come from a positive choice rather than a compromise forced upon the group and supervisor.

The second advantage is that unlike a one-to-one supervision the group provides a supportive atmosphere of peers in which new staff or trainees can share anxieties and realize that others are facing similar issues.

The third advantage is that group supervision gains from the supervisees' receiving reflections, feedback, sharing and inputs from their colleagues as well as the group supervisor. Thus potentially this setting is less dominated by the supervisor, with the concurrent dangers of over-influence and dependency. We look at this in greater detail in the section on different supervision styles and foci. A group can also, when working well, challenge the supervisor on their blind spots.

A fourth advantage is that a group can provide a way for the supervisor to test out their emotional or intuitive response to the material presented by checking if other group members have had the same response.

The fifth advantage is that a group can also provide a wider range of life experience and thus there is more likelihood of someone in the group's being able to empathize both with the supervisees and the client. A group provides a greater empathic range, not just at the level of gender, race or age range, but also of personality types.

The sixth advantage is that groups provide more opportunity to use action techniques as part of the supervision. We describe some of these later in the chapter.

The final advantage of group supervision is that, where possible, the supervision context should reflect the therapeutic context which is being supervised. Thus, if the supervisees run groups, learning can be gained from the supervision taking place in a group with other group leaders. This provides opportunities to learn from how the supervisor runs the group and also how the dynamics of the presented groups are mirrored in the supervision group (see section on paralleling in Chapter 7).

Disadvantages of group supervision

There are also some disadvantages to supervising in groups. Group supervision is less likely to mirror the dynamic of individual therapy as clearly as would individual supervision.

There are also group dynamics to be contended with. These can be a benefit if they are made conscious within the group and used as an adjunct to the supervisees increasing their self-awareness, through understanding their part in the group process. However, the group process can also be destructive and undermining of the supervisory process. Groups can establish very strong norms that are hard to challenge. These can sometimes be set up by the group leader, but wherever they come from they exert a power that an individual member might feel too intimidated to question. Sometimes there is a competitive spirit in the group which can be undermining when it is not made conscious. The dynamics of the supervisory group can also become a preoccupation. We have both been in supervision groups that have gradually become centrally concerned with their own dynamics almost to the exclusion of any interest in the clients of those present. We discuss group dynamics more in the next chapter.

The final disadvantage is that there can be less time for each person to receive supervision. The individual might, therefore, only get a turn every three meetings and, if these are held fortnightly, this could, in effect, result in direct supervision only every six weeks.

Early stage contracting before the group starts

How a group is first contracted with can set a tone for the whole process. In this early contracting it is also important to clarify intention and boundaries. It is possible that group members may know each other's clients; or they might all be working for the same organization, even though they are not a team and may have different statuses within the organization; or there may be professional rivalries or unfinished business between members. All these factors make it very important that group composition and objectives are clearly thought out. For example, one of us was called in to an organization where employees had little knowledge of supervision. In discussions with the contact person it became clear there was a covert agenda of listening to how awful the organization was. The link person wanted the group to be concerned with difficulties with senior management rather than with the client group. As with one-to-one supervision it is important to establish who the stakeholders are and to whom the supervisor is responsible. Given that there are many more people involved, the question of confidentiality is bound to be more complex.

Some questions that might be useful to reflect on are:

- How are size and membership to be determined?
- Who decides if it is to be an open or closed group?
- What messages are being given to group members about their membership and expected attendance? For example is it a requirement or can people choose?

We have found that groups generally elicit stronger feelings than one-to-one sessions which is why the group is potentially such a powerful force for change. Managing this powerful energy is a very important part of group supervision and before the group starts we think it is important that the supervisor reflects on how comfortable they are with groups. Some people are intimidated and are more comfortable in one-to-one situations. Understanding about the life of groups can be a great help in working towards seeing it as a resource rather than an unruly animal that has to be tamed and controlled. Helping to create safety is of paramount importance. Much will be communicated through the supervisor's non verbal communication, but we believe in trying to be as explicit as possible about options. The next section explains some options on leadership styles.

Group supervision styles and foci

Group members, unless they are very experienced, will mostly take their lead from the group supervisor and make interventions with a similar style and focus. It is thus very important that supervisors be aware of how they are modelling ways of responding to material that is shared. Similar to the typology of Inskipp and Proctor, we created a model of four quadrants (Figure 10.1).

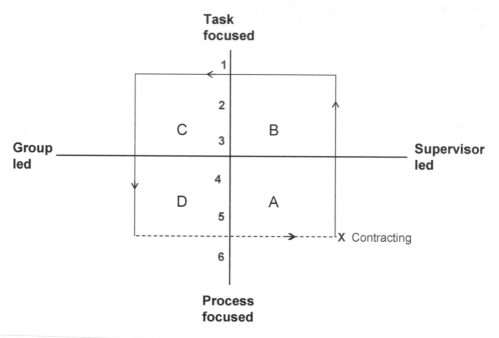

Figure 10.1   Model of group supervision styles

Figure 10.1 shows four quadrants, each representing a different style of group supervision. In quadrant A, the supervision group is more directively led by the group supervisor and has a strong focus on the group process. In quadrant B, the supervisor is still taking the central lead, but the focus is more on the content of the cases brought. In quadrant C, the group moves over to taking more leadership responsibility among the members, but with a focus on the cases brought. In quadrant D, the group take responsibility for focusing on their own process.

Each quadrant has its own shadow side which will come to the fore if the supervision group gets stuck in just this one style. Quadrant A groups can become a therapy group, attending to the personal needs of the members, but ignoring the client issues. Quadrant B groups can become a forum for group supervisors to show off their expertise and create dependency in the group members. Supervision that becomes stuck in Quadrant C, can become competitive peer advice giving, with group members trying to outdo each other with, 'If I were you' solutions. Quadrant D supervision groups can become over-collusive peer support groups and like groups in Quadrant A, inward looking and failing to attend to the task.

Good group supervision needs to be able to move flexibly through all these areas, depending on the needs of the group and the stage of group development. Most commonly a supervision group will begin in Quadrant A in its forming and contracting phase, move into quadrant B, as it begins to settle to its task, and then gradually incorporate Quadrants C and D, as the group becomes more mature and self-responsible. However, good supervision groups, once well-established will cycle through all four quadrants, and avoid getting stuck in the shadow side of one box.

This model can also be linked to our model of seven-eyed supervision (see Chapter 7). Each focus can be placed on the vertical axis, as in Figure 10.1.

We have included this typology here because we suggest that supervisors become aware of their styles so that they are able to explain to the group the various options and contract with them. For example, at the beginning of our group supervision training we demonstrate with a very supervisor-led style. The reason for this is that we find it conducive to safety. If we did not explain the reasons clearly beforehand, the group might think that was the only way to supervise.

A group supervisor needs to be able to manage a number of simultaneous processes, as supervision in a group is contained within a number of rings of context (see Figure 10.2 and also Inskipp and Proctor 1995: 86 who have a similar model).

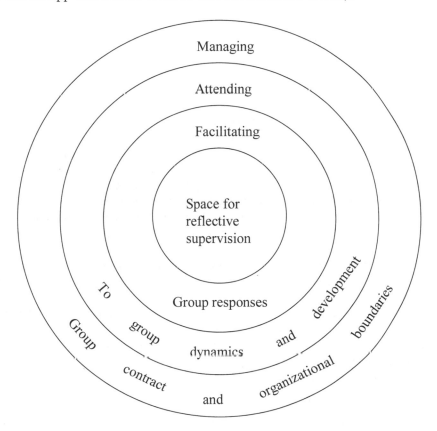

Figure 10.2 The concentric rings of group supervision process

The central skills of facilitating reflective supervision are similar to working one to one. However, to use the richness of the group to the full, the group supervisor must facilitate the responses of the group members and link these back to the case.

The third contextual ring is managing the group dynamics, and attending to the developmental stage and developmental needs of the group process. The outer ring ensures that the supervision happens within an appropriate contract and boundaries. The group contract, as discussed above, is something that is not a one-off event, but a process that must be regularly revisited. The contract may involve more people than the group members and supervisor, as the group supervision may be happening in the context of an organization, or members may be sponsored by a number of different organizations. The boundaries and relationship with these organizations becomes an important context that the supervisor must attend to for the supervision to feel appropriately contained.

We have found Proctor and Inskipp's (2000) classification of groups very useful in understanding the roles of leaders and participants. They distinguish four different kinds of supervision groups.

1   authoritative, where the group supervisor does one-to-one supervision in the group with members looking on;
2   participative supervision, where participants are invited to contribute to the supervision;
3   cooperative, where the facilitator takes responsibility for managing the group boundaries, but leaves the supervision to group members;
4   peer group supervision, where all members take joint responsibility for everything.

Obviously, as they themselves explain, these types are not discrete and can overlap. Sometimes a group will fluctuate, say, go from type 2 to 3 and back again. On occasions even with experienced groups, there are times when just one person supervising might be what is called for. This can happen when a particularly complex case is being presented, where having too many contributions can add to the confusion.

Proctor and Inskipp list the advantages and disadvantages of each type. For example, authoritative supervision groups can be an excellent master class but keeps people passive and does not use the skills in the group. Participative supervision groups can engage the members but can become competitive or bombard the supervisee. Cooperative supervision groups can dissolve into group process (as indeed all groups can) and exclude the client, but at its best is truly empowering for the members and group as a whole. This is also true for the peer group.

As with the setting up of any supervisory relationship, it is important to be aware of how experienced and skilled the supervisees are. An authoritative group with experienced practitioners could lead to resentment, but provide safety for less experienced supervisees. A cooperative group could lead to participants floundering if too much is expected of them, but really encourage others to take risks.

Contracting

The different styles of group also can be part of the contracting phase of the group and within this process the supervisor can be explicit about their own supervisory style. With many people coming perhaps from different professions, orientations or experience, it is highly likely that there will be many different expectations of the group and its purpose. Even if some rounds are what people are hoping for, it is useful to remember, particularly in group situations, that at the first meeting anxieties will be high. People will understand what has been agreed quite differently, so, as in one-to-one supervision it is always useful to revisit the contract. It is also useful to find out if members are receiving other supervision as it is not possible to cover all clients in a group setting because of time constraints. Who has the responsibility for the clients if there is another supervisor?

We explain that as well as bringing clients (the task), there is also a need for the group to be maintained in a way that makes it a safe, helpful place (quadrants A and D). How the group gives feedback in a way that is useful and relevant is very important and we will occasionally interrupt a piece of feedback if we feel it is not given for the benefit of the person who has just presented.

As with one-to-one supervision, any evaluation role needs to be explicit. We have found that this is one of the chief inhibitors in presenting material. We need to bear in mind also that as well as explicit evaluation, there is a constant implicit evaluation of group members of each other (see below).

Setting the climate

The next task is to set a safe climate for the supervisees to open up their work to others – a process that always has some fear and anxiety:

- 'Will I be found out?'
- 'Will everyone else find flaws that I am unaware of, not only in my work, but who I am as a person?'
- 'Will they think, "Why the hell does he think he can be a therapist with those attitudes or hang-ups?"'

In training groups we encourage supervisors to recognize that group members might have similar anxieties, and that acknowledging this will be of great help to their supervisees. Self-disclosure for members can feel safer if group leaders also share some of their own insecurities, anxieties and times when they do not know, rather than always having to be the one with the answers (see Jourard 1971). We are aiming for a climate that encourages a sharing of vulnerabilities and anxieties without group members being put down or turned into 'the group patient'. It is an easy escape route for group members to avoid their own insecurities by finding a group patient which allows them the chance to return to the much safer role of therapist!

Simple ground rules help to avoid destructive group processes, such as ensuring that all statements are owned and group members speak from their own experience. In this way group members avoid giving generalized good advice: 'If I were you, I would', and preaching: 'Therapists ought to be warm and accepting', etc. As mentioned in Chapter 9, another useful ground rule is to ensure that feedback from group members is owned, balanced and specific. It is important that the group supervisor ensures that there is a roughly equal amount of sharing between all group members, both in terms of quantity and level of self-disclosure.

However, as well as safety we want to encourage risk taking. In fact, the paradox is that unless there is some risk taking the group will feel quite unsafe and the supervisor needs to model being comfortable.

Finally, for any group to work the leader is dependent on goodwill. We make this explicit and say that, as we all have the same goals (the welfare of our clients and developing ourselves and our practice), we are here to help each other. One of our trainees called this 'Good Will Hunting,' after the film, which emphasizes that, however many rules we make, and however clear we are about the contract, we need to all be working together with goodwill.

Structuring the group

For the group supervisor there are a number of choices in how to structure the group session. Which one they choose will depend on the type and size of group as well as their own style and inclination. One of us sometimes starts group supervision sessions, which are part of a psychotherapy training, with a round where each group member states what issues they would like to bring to the group. This is followed by a negotiation between the competing requests to decide on the order and how much time each person should have.

A variant that we sometimes use with this approach is to follow the round by an exploration of whose issue most represents the current 'core concern' of the group. This can be done by asking group members to identify which issue, other than their own, they would learn most from exploring and then working with the issue that has the most interest. This ensures that the person who is the centre of the work is not just working for him or herself, but has the energy and interest of the group.

Other colleagues divide the group time equally between all those present so that they all know they will get some attention from each group. This becomes impractical if the group is too large and/or the time too short.

The group may arrange a schedule where each group member knows in advance that he or she will be the one presenting on a particular day. This makes it possible for some outline notes on the case to be circulated in advance. This moves the session more into a group case study with a greater emphasis on learning from an overview, rather than focusing on current concerns and difficulties. This structure may entail group members' having other supervision for their more immediate supervision needs.

Another option is to 'trust the process' and to wait to see what emerges and where the interest of the group moves. You can also start by checking out what has happened to issues that were explored at the previous meeting.

Techniques

Techniques for group supervision work best when the members of the group can usefully contribute and are actively engaged. Having so many resources and perspectives is one of the big advantages of groups as we have mentioned above.

Sharing question responses

A very simple technique is to let the person presenting a client talk for a set time, five minutes maximum. Each person in the group is then allowed to ask one question and the presenter is asked which question has engaged them most and they follow that line of inquiry.

Sharing responses

A more complex version of this is to ask each member to be aware of what is happening to them when someone is presenting a client. We explain that it is impossible to get this wrong. If they are having a feeling of, say, hunger or a feeling of restlessness that is important to share. Physical sensations like pains can yield very important information. If they are bored, or unaccountably feeling sad, or angry, or switching off, that is useful too. We ask for thoughts, images, feelings, body sensations or fantasies. Framing it in this way does a variety of things. It gives everyone an opportunity to contribute. It allows for different modalities of experiencing. It does not suggest that one response is better than another. It gives permission for 'off the wall' responses which cannot be wrong – they are just experiences and encourages members to start trusting their intuition.

The theory inherent in this idea is that we do to others what has been done to us. We talked about this earlier when describing parallel process about the client who said 'yes but' to his counsellor, who said 'yes but' to her supervisor, who said 'yes but' to her supervisor (Chapter 7, Mode 5). Another way of putting this is that when something has been too much for us to 'swallow' or 'stomach' we often 'vomit it up' later. It is usually these cases that are brought to supervision, where some aspect of the client has not been digested. By asking members to be aware of what they are experiencing when a case has been presented, we are offering an opportunity to catch the parallel process. With a group there are bound to be different responses, and the job of the supervisor is to help the person presenting to see if any of them are useful.

A vital ingredient in this process is to make sure all responses are given to the group leader so that the presenter can simply listen and not feel either overwhelmed or that they have to reply in order not to upset the person who has responded to them. The presenter just listens and then says which responses were ones that they think could take him or her further.

Here is an example from our work which illustrates the process at work:

> On a supervision course for therapeutic community members, a new staff member presented a client with whom she had been having difficulty. After an initial enthusiasm and opening up, the client was either missing her session or hardly communicating. As soon as the worker began to present her client, I found myself switching off. I just did not want to be bothered. However, I kept going for a few minutes asking seemingly appropriate questions until I could stand it no longer. I shared my feelings of disinterest hesitantly – they just did not seem to fit – and group members seemed to be so involved. In fact, it turned out that the group was split roughly half and half. One half was very involved and the other half had totally switched off too, but like me was trying to appear involved. The presenter was astonished to see how accurately her feelings for her client of both being very involved and identifying with her, and not wanting to

know about her, were being mirrored. The group really began to work well and deeply after that, because permission had been given, not only to share apparent negativity, but its relevance had been confirmed. This is one way in which the supervisor can check whether his counter-transference is coming from his own psyche or is a useful reaction triggered by the material presented.

Behind the back

Another variant of this is to ask the presenter to sit outside the group and listen while the group discusses what they have heard. We give the group permission to say whatever comes to mind and bounce ideas off each other. The supervisee is then invited back in and asked to say what they have found useful.

Practicum groups

Hawkins and Smith (2006) have developed a supervision approach called practicum groups, for training those who supervise coaches, mentors and organizational consultants, which can also be used for group supervision in other professions.

Each of the group members has a chance to be in each of the following roles: The supervisee who brings a real, current, challenging case situation; the supervisor, who aims in about 45 minutes to create a shift in how the supervisee is thinking, feeling and acting in relation to their case; the shadow supervisors who have responsibility for monitoring some aspect of the supervision process (for example, the seven modes, Heron categories of intervention (see Chapter 9), non-verbal communication etc.). At regular intervals the facilitator or supervisor can call time-outs in which the supervisee sits quietly while the shadow supervisors and facilitator supervise the supervisor on the supervision.

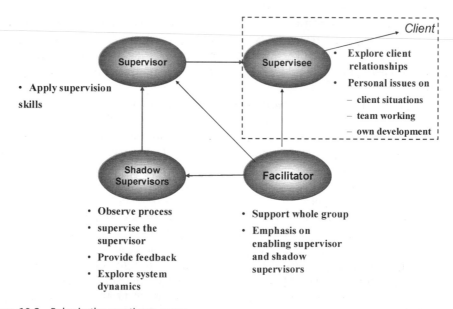

Figure 10.3 Roles in the practicum group

Hawkins and Smith (2006) write: 'In transformational supervision the intention is not for the person bringing the issue or case to leave with a new insight or a "must do action list"; but rather to have experienced a "felt shift" in the session, starting to think, feel and act differently about the situation they are concerned with. Our research shows that the chance of learning and change being transferred back into the live situation, is much higher when this felt shift occurs than when people leave with good intentions.'

In practicum groups we are working with a systemic understanding of 'parallel process'. By this we mean that the job of the shadow coach is to shift the coach, so they shift how they are relating to the consultant, so the consultant shifts, and changes how they are relating to the client, so we can be fairly confident the client system will shift beneficially.

'Systems approach' means that an intervention for change at any point of the system ripples through the whole, generating change on all levels – provided the initial point of intervention has been chosen for maximum effect or minimum resistance to change.

Tag supervision

One of the techniques we have used to great effect is tag supervision, which we use in conjunction with the seven modes (see Chapter 7). Someone elects to be supervisee and we place an empty chair opposite them. We then assign modes to each of the other members of the group. It works especially well in training groups because they tend to be larger and it is, therefore, possible for more than one person to play each mode. The supervisee starts with a sentence: e.g., 'I'd like to bring my client X who has an eating disorder.' The facilitator shouts out a number like 'four' and the person who has been assigned Mode 4 comes and sits in the empty chair and makes an intervention such as, 'Does this person remind you of anyone?' or 'What do you experience when you are with this person?' or any other Mode 4 intervention. This person can clap themselves out and anyone from the group can clap themselves in, or the supervisor can clap and suggest a mode. After initial hesitation we find that people want to rush in and try an intervention.

Tag supervision has proved useful in many ways. It provides an opportunity to practise the modes and watch others using them, and also to see how they fit together. Although this method may seem artificial or disjointed, we find that the resulting supervision is surprisingly thorough and insightful whilst giving group members a see-mingly light-hearted way of taking the risk of providing some of the supervision.

As well as presenting actual cases, we sometimes try a variation which involves asking people to describe the worst situation they could face, or have faced, as a supervisor. We ask them to come up with an opening sentence. A very common one is, 'I don't think this supervision is working. I want to change supervisor.' Another feared one is, 'I have to tell you I am having a relationship with my client.' Tag supervision is a useful way of exploring these fears and, in our experience, is a very powerful learning tool.

Acknowledging the group dynamic

Sometimes, for whatever reason, the group atmosphere does not feel safe or members are reluctant to contribute. Perhaps there is overt or covert conflict. It is essential that the group leader can ensure that group dynamics do not proceed unacknowledged and finds a way of bringing the dynamics into awareness so that they can be attended to and learnt from, without taking over as the major focus of the group. Using the awareness of the here-and-now dynamics is an essential part of the learning process but the distinction between a supervision group and a 'T' group, encounter group, or therapy group must be maintained. (For more details see Chapter 11.)

Team supervision

Team supervision is different from group supervision. It involves working with a group that has not come together just for the purposes of joint supervision, but have an interrelated work life outside the group. Thus, although many of the approaches to group supervision that we have outlined above are relevant, there are other factors that have to be managed.

There is a difference between teams that share work with the same clients, such as a mental health team in a psychiatric hospital, or the staff of a residential home, and teams which, although they work with similar approaches and in the same geographical area, have separate clients, such as a GP practice or a field social work team. A simple way of classifying the nature of teams is to use a sports analogy. In football teams all members play the same game, although with different special roles, at the same time, and are highly interdependent. In tennis teams the team members play the same game, but do so either individually or in pairs. In athletics teams the members take part in very different sports, at different times, but occasionally work together (relays), train together, combine their scores and support each other's morale.

Casey (1985) warns of the dangers of thinking that all work must be done in teams and provides a model for deciding when teamwork is necessary. Payne and Scott (1982) also provide guidance for considering what sort of supervision is appropriate for which sort of teams. Katzenbach and Smith (1993) make a very useful distinction between working groups and teams. The characteristics of each they describe below.

Working group

- strong clearly focused leadership;
- individual accountability;
- the group's purpose is the same as the broader organizational mission;
- individual work products;
- runs efficient meetings;
- measures its effectiveness indirectly by its influence on others (e.g. Financial performance of the business);
- discusses, decides and delegates.

Team

- shared leadership roles;
- individual and mutual accountability;
- specific team purposes that the team itself delivers;
- collective work products;

- encourages open-ended discussion and active problem solving meetings;
- measures performance directly by assessing collective work products;
- discusses, decides, and does real work together.

From this we can see that teams are where there is more shared activity and joint responsibility, where a work group may only share the fact that they report to the same boss.

Katzenbach and Smith (1993), go on to describe the characteristics of effective teams based on their research:

- shared and owned purpose and objectives;
- shared specific performance goals;
- shared approach;
- mutually accountable;
- complimentary skills and styles,
    - technical/functional,
    - problem solving/decision making styles,
    - interpersonal style and personality type.

Supervision in teams that know each other's clients has both advantages and disadvantages, as often in supervision you are attending not to the client 'out there' but to how the client has entered into the intra-psychic life of the supervisee.

> In a residential children's home where a staff member, Jane, was exploring her profound irritation with one of the difficult boys called Robert, the other members of the team all piled in with their ways of handling Robert. The supervisor had to work very hard to reopen the space for Jane to explore what it was that Robert triggered in her, who he reminded her of, and to help her generate more options for herself. He created this space by pointing out to the team that the Robert she was struggling with could almost be thought of as a different Robert from the Roberts they were each relating to. This was true on two accounts: first, Robert was a very fragmented and manipulative boy who would present quite differently to each staff member, but also every staff member was differently affected by him, depending on their own personality, history and ways of reacting.
>
> It was crucial in this case that Jane's space was protected or she would have quickly become the staff member seen as the one who couldn't cope with Robert and be covertly elected to carry the helpless aspects of Robert and of the team working with him. By letting the team flood her with good ideas for dealing with this boy, the supervision would have colluded to intensify the split within the team and hence in Robert. Certainly after having worked with the feelings of helplessness in Jane and helping her to understand and generate more creative options for herself, it was then possible to return to the team and explore their differing experiences and views of the boy, so that they could gradually put together the fragmented feelings that had been scattered throughout the team.

When conducting team supervision there are still issues about group selection. Firstly, it is necessary to decide where the boundary of the team is drawn. Do you include assistant staff, clerical staff or trainees? If it is an inter-professional team, issues of inclusion and exclusion are even more highly charged.

Secondly, good team supervision should alert the team to the danger of the tendency to fill vacancies with 'more people like us'. There is a need for teams to have some degree of homogeneity, but teams also need a balance in personality types, age, gender and skills. Belbin (1981) has carried out a classic study of what range of roles a team needs in order to be effective.

Team supervision supposes that there is one more entity than the team members needing supervision, as, besides the individuals in the supervision group, the team can be considered as an entity needing supervision itself. We consider the team as an entity to be more than the sum of its parts and to have a personality and, intra-psychic life of its own. This is termed by some writers as the team culture or the team dynamic. We will say more about this in Chapter 11. Team supervision is different from other forms of supervision in that it inevitably involves some form of team development.

Steve Fineman (1985) in his study of a social work department looked at five different teams. One of the teams was significantly more effective in maintaining a high morale and low levels of stress than the other four. One of the key factors in this success was the effective team supervision by the team leader:

> (the) mutual trust established, found links with the team leaders' activities in promoting support. Indeed his integrative meetings with staff on professional matters – which he took most seriously and sensitively judging from his and other reports – were probably critical ingredients in helping to set the supportive climate.
>
> (Fineman 1985: 106)

In the next chapter we illustrate ways of exploring and improving team dynamics, and in the organizational section we discuss how to access and change the culture of both organizations and teams.

Peer supervision

Many professionals on our courses complain that they cannot get good supervision as their immediate line senior has neither the time nor the ability to supervise them. We are often surprised that they have not even considered the possibility of setting up peer supervision for themselves. Many years ago, Peter ran a therapeutic community and his immediate line manager was the assistant director of a large mental health charity organization who had no direct experience of either therapeutic communities or supervision. This experience is similar to many of the situations we find with senior practitioners in various professions who are nominally supervised by senior managers with little or no clinical experience. In response to this situation Peter set up a series of peer supervisions. Firstly, he exchanged supervision with his deputy who was more experienced than he in the work with the clients. This worked very well for obtaining supervision for the work with clients, but did not solve the problems of Peter's receiving supervision on his leadership of the staff team.

Peter's second peer supervision was with the senior trainer within the organization who had spent many years working in a variety of therapeutic communities. Again this worked well for a time, but as both she and he were involved in the senior management meetings of the organization, mutual sharing of their struggles with the management structure became an over-dominant focus.

The third move Peter made was to use the facilities of a professional association, in this case the Association of Therapeutic Communities, to set up a peer supervision group for senior staff within therapeutic communities. He was surprised to find that many other senior practitioners in voluntary organizations, social services departments and the National Health Service shared the same shortage and need for supervision. This proved a rich and rewarding group with the opportunity to focus on whole community problems and dynamics. This group went on existing well after Peter and the other original members had left.

Later Peter had his own peer supervision setting for his psychotherapy work which was a peer triad with a consultant psychiatrist/psychotherapist and a clinical psychologist/psychotherapist. At each meeting one of the three members took his turn at being supervisor. Each of the other two received 40 minutes' supervision. At the end of each person's supervision the supervisee shared with the supervisor what he found helpful and difficult and then the supervisor shared his own reflections of the session. This was followed by the third member, who had been observing, giving feedback, both positive and negative, to the supervisor. This suited the need of those in the triad who received not only supervision on their psychotherapy but reflections and learning on how they supervised.

This illustrates how peer supervision can be either individually reciprocal or can take place in a group of workers with similar needs, approach and level of expertise. It also illustrates how it is possible to look for peer supervisors not only within your immediate workplace but also in similar workplaces within your own organization or with workers from different organizations. We have been involved in helping a number of staff set up their own peer supervision systems. These include heads of children's homes giving each other reciprocal supervision in one local authority; a group of principal officers meeting regularly for peer supervision in another local authority, and an inter-profession peer supervision system in a community mental health team.

One area that has actively encouraged the development of peer supervision has been humanistic psychotherapy. This is partly due to the professional commitment of the profession and bodies like the Association of Humanistic Psychology Practitioners (AHPP) and the Humanistic and Integrative section of the United Kingdom Council of Psychotherapy to continuous supervision throughout one's professional career and not only when one is in training. This is backed up by members having to reapply for membership every five years; and in their reapplication they have to state what supervision they are currently having.

Peer supervision clearly has many advantages, but there are also many pitfalls and traps. In the absence of a group leader there is a greater need for a firm and clear structure and it requires greater commitment from the group members.

Gaie Houston (1985) has written about some of the traps or games (as in transactional analysis) that we have known peer groups to fall into.

- *'Measuring cocks'*:   She describes a group where the various members become very competitive in their need to show each other how well they work. They often use phrases about their groups such as: 'Mine are so cooperative ... Mine say I have helped them a lot', 'It was such a powerful experience.' She goes on to write: 'An American consultant I know calls this activity "measuring cocks". All the statements in it add up to "Mine's Better Than Yours". Everyone feels tense, knowing that if one person wins and has the biggest or best, everyone else has lost' (Houston 1985).

- *'Ain't it awful?'*:   In this game the peer group sits around, reinforcing each other's sense of powerlessness. One variant of the game is to spend the time sharing how you must be mad to work for this 'authority' or 'hospital'. Another variant is for therapists or counsellors to spend their time showing how clients are hateful, vicious and manipulative beings who resist your best endeavours at every attempt. This can spill over into another game called 'Get the client'.

- *'We are all so wonderful'*:   Peer group members can avoid having their anxieties about being criticized or found out by heaping fulsome praise on other peer members as an unacknowledged payment for returning the favour. This becomes a covert form of a 'protection racket' and in the long term ensures that that the group is too fearful to let new members join or old members leave as this might threaten the unearthing of what is buried. John Heron refers to this as consensus collusion (Heron 1975).

- *'Who is the best supervisor?'*:   This is a straightforward but often undisclosed or acknowledged competition to fill the void left by not having a group supervisor. It can emerge through group members straining to make the cleverest or most helpful comments, or through distracting peripheral arguments on the efficacy of this or that approach. Peer groups often have no mechanism for dealing with their group dynamics and unfortunately group members who point out the processes that are going on may get caught up in the competition to be the 'supervisor'.

- *'Hunt the patient'*:   Groups, like families, can identify one member to be the patient and the focus for the inadequate or difficult feelings to which the others do not wish to own. Having an identified patient also allows the other group members to retreat into the safe and known role of therapist and collectively to try to treat the elected patient. A probation officer might be elected to carry all the fear of violence for the peer group. While the other members 'help' this member explore their fears, they also protect themselves from facing the similar fears within themselves.

These games are not the sole prerogative of peer groups, but there is more risk that the group may fall into some of them as there is no outside facilitator whose job (or one of them) is to watch the process. Some of these games will be explored further in Chapter 11.

How to form a peer supervision group

It is clear from the above that peer supervision has many pitfalls, but if properly organized it also has many advantages. In workshops that we run we are often asked for advice in the starting and running of peer groups and we generally give the following recommendations:

- Try to form a group that has shared values but a range of approaches. It is important that you can dialogue together within a reasonably shared language and belief system but, if you all have the same training and style of working, the group can become rather collusive and lack a more distant perspective.
- The group needs to be no more than seven people. It must also ensure that it has enough time to meet the needs of all its members. It is no good having a peer supervision group of seven people, all of whom have a large number of clients for whom they want supervision, unless the group meets very regularly for at least two or three hours.
- Be clear about commitment. It is not helpful for the group members to commit themselves because they think they ought to and then fail to meet the commitment. Members must be encouraged to share their resistance to meeting for supervision and, if possible, to share how they might avoid or otherwise sabotage the supervision group. For example, one member may warn the group that he or she is likely to get too busy with more pressing engagements, while another member may say that his pattern is to get bad headaches.
- Make a clear contract. It needs to be clear about frequency and place of meetings, time boundaries, confidentiality, how time will be allocated and how the process is to be managed. You might need to be clear how you will handle one group member's knowing the clients that other members bring for supervision; will the person leave the group while that client is being discussed, will the worker be expected to get supervision on that person elsewhere, or with an experienced group will the group find a way that uses psychodynamic processes such as projection, transference and counter-transference and parallel process to explore and illuminate the work with the client as well as dealing with the apparent dilemma of confidentiality.
- Be clear about the different expectations. Some members may expect a greater focus on their personal process than others are comfortable with. Some members may expect all their client work to be covered by the group, while others may also have individual supervision elsewhere. Some members may expect a greater amount of advice on what to do next, while others may expect to use role-play or other experiential techniques. Try to discover if there are any hidden group agendas. We came across one peer group that consisted of two separate sub-groups that were working out their relationships.
- Be clear about role expectations. Who is going to maintain the time boundaries or deal with any interruptions? Who is going to organize the rooms? Is there going to be one person each time who carries the main responsibility for facilitating or will this emerge out of the group process?
- Build some time into each meeting (it need only be five or ten minutes), to give

feedback on how the supervision process has been for each person. This can include appreciations and any resentments.
- Plan to have a review session every three months when all the members receive feedback on their role in the group, the dynamics of the group are looked at and the contract is renegotiated. Many of the exercises and approaches that are mentioned in Chapter 11 exploring the dynamics of teams and groups can be adopted by a peer group in its own review.

There are several other books that give useful hints on establishing peer groups for therapeutic work and, although they have a different focus from peer supervision groups, they often throw up similar dynamics.

Organizing a peer supervision meeting

Many of the suggestions made above about structuring group supervision also apply to peer-group supervision:

- Set ground rules (for example, that member give direct, balanced and owned feedback; avoid patronizing advice; time is equally shared).
- Either start each session by discovering each others' needs or have a set rotational system for allocating time.
- Encourage all the members to be clear about what they need from the group in relation to what they are sharing. Do they need just to be listened to; given feedback; facilitated in exploring their unaware responses to the client; or helped in exploring where to go next, choosing between various options, etc. It is often useful if you do not know what the person wants to ask – 'What has led you to bring this particular issue today?' or 'What is it you need in relation to this case?'
- Decide about informal time. Often, if you have no social or informal time scheduled, the need to catch up with each other's news, to gossip, and to make personal contact can interrupt the other tasks of the group. Some peer groups schedule a short social time at the beginning and/or end of the supervision group.

Conclusion

Groups clearly have many advantages over individual supervision in the range of possible learning opportunities and different perspectives that they can provide. They also have many potential pitfalls. Those leading supervision groups need to be aware of and work with the group dynamic and this necessitates that they have some training in group leadership and dynamics. Peer groups also need to have a system for attending to their own process so that it stays healthily supporting the task of supervision rather than diverting or sabotaging it.

The mode of supervision should reflect what is being supervised, so some form of group supervision is ideally suited for those being supervised on their work with groups. Group supervision is also useful in expanding the range of perspectives that one draws upon in reflecting on one's individual work, but we would recommend that, in the case of in-depth individual counselling and psychotherapy, group supervision should be an adjunct to, rather than a replacement for individual supervision. The exception to this is that peer or group supervision can be quite adequate for senior practitioners who have developed not only their own individual competence but also an integrated form of self-supervision (see Chapter 4).

11 Exploring the dynamics of groups, teams and peer groups

Introduction
Group stages
Group dynamics
Facilitating group or team reviews
    Contracting
    Giving feedback
    Estrangement exercise
    Exploring the group dynamics
    Sculpting the group
    Exploring the wider context in which the group exists
Conclusion

Introduction

In the previous chapter we touched on some of the dynamics that may occur in supervision groups. In this chapter we examine these dynamics a little further and propose some structures for working with them. Whether your supervision group is led, peer or part of a working team, its effectiveness will depend to a large extent on the ability of its members to be aware of, and process, the group dynamics that prevail. We, therefore, believe that all those who consider supervising in groups should have some training in this field and we outline some of the factors that we see occurring most often. This should include understanding the basic stages that groups go through and how to facilitate the group development in the various stages.

Group stages

Margaret Rioch has written extensively on the interface between supervision and group dynamics. In her *Dialogues for Therapists* (Rioch et al. 1976) she charts a complete series of group supervisions (which she terms seminars) with therapists in training. After each seminar she comments on the group dynamics and concludes that, 'It is also clear that the group interaction was an important part of the process, sometimes furthering, sometimes interfering, with the learning.'

Most of the theories and our own experience would suggest that groups most often progress through a number of discernible phases. These should not be seen as predetermined or inevitable. Most often groups start by dealing with their own boundaries, membership and the group rules and expectations. Schutz (1973) calls this 'inclusion'; Tuckman (1965) 'the stages of Forming and Norming'. This is the contracting stage in group supervision, where issues of confidentiality, commitment to the group, how time will be allocated and what will be focused on and what will be excluded need to be decided and clarified.

Table 11.1 Group/team stages: comparative models

Tuckman: Group stages	Schutz: Key dynamic themes	Bion: Basic assumptions	Scott Peck: Community stages
Forming	Inclusion/exclusion	Dependency	Pseudo community
Storming	Authority	Fight/flight	Chaos
Norming	Affection	Pairing	Emptying
Performing		Work group	Community
Mourning			

This period of clarifying the basic structure of the supervision group is often followed by a period of testing out power and authority within the group. This can take the form of rivalrous competitiveness: 'Who does the best work?', 'Who most cares about their clients?', 'Who has the most difficult cases?', 'Who makes the most penetrating insightful comments?', etc. Or it may take the form of testing out the authority of the supervisor by challenging their approach, trying to show that one can supervise other group members better than they can, or inappropriately applying their recommendations to show that they do not work. This is called the stage of 'Fight/flight' by Bion (1961); 'Authority' by Schutz (1973) and 'Storming' by Tuckman (1965).

It is only when these stages have been successfully handled that the group can settle to its most productive work, with a climate of respect for each individual, and without either dependency or rivalry in its relationship to the supervisor. Groups often return to this stage from time to time so an understanding of the dynamics involved is essential throughout the life of the group.

Group dynamics

Rioch's description of the seminars she ran shows how these stages of group development certainly cannot be ignored when supervising in a group. Understanding the theories of group development and having insight into the group dynamics are not enough. The group supervisor must also know how to confront the group process and facilitate positive group behaviour.

Rioch et al. (1976) illustrate in detail the importance of confronting the issues of both competition and authority in the supervision group. After a long discussion amongst participants in her seminar Rioch asks: 'Could it be that the seminar is skirting around the question of who is the best therapist here? That is no doubt a hot potato, and what is even more hot is the question of who is the worst therapist.'

Looking at the issue of competition and group process she writes:

> The issue of competition can contribute to the work of the group if everyone tries to do the best he can. It may also interfere if people become too afraid of being rejected or envied ... In this seminar, as in most groups, there was a strong competitive element. The instructor is trying to point out that this was going on even as people were overtly discussing other issues. Although it was not the primary task of the group to learn about its own processes, it was often desirable to observe what the group was doing, particularly when its processes interfered with the primary task of learning to be useful to clients. The problem in the seminar was to use the students' competition, resistance and transference to the instructor in the service of the task of helping clients.

She also usefully points out that supervisors are also part of the process:

> It may also be helpful to teachers and supervisors to remember that they are subject to the same group pressures that are influencing their students. In other words, teachers and supervisors are competitive, resistant and reluctant to expose their failures, incompetencies, and insecurities. It is important that they should model for their students, not so much perfection which is impossible, but a willingness to learn from their imperfections.

Receiving authority projections and being comfortable with them are part of both the supervisor's and the helper's role:

> The instructor, who was reasonably well-liked on a conscious level by seminar members, readily took on the role of an old 'witch' in the unconscious fantasies of seminar members when they felt, as they sometimes did, like abused children in a fairy tale. Hansel and Gretel were scarcely in any position to be therapeutic to their clients. Neither did they harbour warm feelings toward the old witch whom they shoved into the oven in the happy ending.
>
> (Rioch, Coulter and Weinberger 1976)

After a discussion during which members of the group hint that it would be better and freer without the leader, one of the members says: 'The real problem is not how nice it would be without her, but how to live with her. And not only with her, but with all the other authorities too.' Rioch sums up some of the ambivalence that we think is very often present in a supervision group, especially of trainees, when she says:

> As mature young people engaged in serious study, the students consciously wanted to use the instructor as a teacher and resource person, not as an adversary to be overthrown or a parent to take care of them. But less consciously, as in all groups, the elements of adolescent rebellion and childish dependency were present and active.

Another pitfall is to engage in therapy (described earlier as 'hunt the patient'). The problem case or member is dealt with perhaps sympathetically but certainly in a way that is subtly putting down. The purpose of this game is that once more the group members can allay these anxieties and inadequacies and move into the more comfortable helping role.

Finally, it is possible to look at the dynamics of supervision presentation in terms of how you might consider a dream. When Robin runs dream groups, he does not pay attention only to the actual dream, but to when and how it is told within the group life. For example, if someone tells him a dream in which the dreamer is struggling to get somewhere, and is angry that no one is helping him, he holds the hypothesis that the dreamer could be feeling this way in the group as well as in the dream. The way the dream is told can also give clues. A dream in which the person could make no headway was reflected in the group as the group struggled for different ways of working with the dream and were blocked with 'yes buts'. Similarly a supervision case can be a statement to the group and a reflection of how the supervisee feels in the group expressed through the client.

> An example of this occurred with a trainee who was having a very hard time staying on one of our courses. She presented a client who was near to despair and was wondering if it was too late for her to work with this client. The group offered helpful suggestions but nothing seemed to help until the supervisor suggested that maybe she was afraid that things had got too bad on the course, and that it was too late for her, the counsellor, to put things right. This was a tremendous relief, as she realized how she was trying to communicate her despair to group members via the client.

Another time there was extreme tension and lack of progress in a supervision group and someone volunteered to present a case. It seemed a trifle masochistic as the group was not in a supportive place. We suggested that she make sure that she did want to present. Despite her reassuring us that the group tension did not bother her, we decided to pay attention to group process rather than just blindly work with the material presented. It turned out that she was working in an establishment where she felt other staff members were using her to do their work. The parallels with what was happening in the group became obvious. It also transpired that she was the one in her family who always tried to sort things out, so this issue of working for others was operating on three levels – family, work and here and now in the group. By commenting on the group process we were able to make sure she did not get stranded in the here and now and were able to facilitate the group as well as the individual.

Facilitating group or team reviews

We have noticed that supervisees are more stressed because of their difficult relationships with colleagues, than they are by their work with clients'. Scaife and Walsch (2001) wrote, 'In our experience the range of emotions aroused at work in relation to clients is at least equalled if not exceeded by those evoked by colleagues!' Although at times it can be useful to attend to collegial relationships in individual supervision, it is far more effectively addressed when all parties are present. If there is no suitable meeting where these issue can be addressed, the focus of the supervisor needs to be on the support the supervisee needs to focus on:

- how they are like the colleague with whom they are having difficulty;
- how this might be parallel process;
- what support might be needed to be able to bring the issues back to the person involved;
- or what support they might need to help set up team meetings where these type of issues can be addressed.

To recycle the material without doing any of these would either become gossip or keep the supervisee in 'victim' role or both. In team supervision it is easier more fully to explore how much this collegial conflict needs to be addressed at the interpersonal level, or as a symptom of the team dynamic, or organizational conflict, or as a collective paralleling of client dynamics.

Supervising teams has much in common with being a team coach or acting as a team development consultant (Hawkins and Smith 2006). In all these roles it is important that we challenge some of the limiting mind-sets about teams and their development. Hawkins and Smith (2006) summarizes these beliefs and potential antidotes, which we quote here:

Table 11.2 Ten limiting mind-sets in working with team development: a provocation

Limiting mind-sets	Antidote
1 Team building only needs to happen when the team first forms.	The best teams engage in life-long learning and development.
2 Team development only needs to happen when things are getting difficult.	If the first time you address relationship issues is in the divorce court you have left it too late!
3 The performance of the team is the sum total of the team members performance.	A team can perform at more than the sum of its parts or less than the sum of its parts. It is important to focus on the team added value.
4 Team development is about relating better to each other.	Team development is also about how the team relates to all its stakeholders and is aligned to the wider organizations mission.
5 Team development is about the team having better meetings.	Team performance happens when the team, or sub-parts of it, engage with the team's stakeholders. The team meeting by itself is the training ground, not the match.
6 Team development only happens off-site in away-days	Team development can be assisted by off-site away-days but the core development happens in the heat of working together.

Limiting mind-sets	Antidote
7 Team development is about the team trusting each other.	Absolute trust between human beings is an unrealizable goal, particularly in work teams. A more useful goal is the team trusting each other enough to disclose their mistrust.
8 Conflict in teams is a bad thing.	Too much or too little conflict is unhelpful in a team. Great teams can creatively work through the conflictual needs in their wider system.
9 'We are not a team unless we work at the same things together.'	A team is defined by having a shared enterprise that cannot be done by the members working out of connection with each other.
10 Team development is an end in itself.	Team development is only valuable when it is linked to improving the team's business performance.

In our roles as consultant and supervisors we have been called in to help groups, teams or peer groups explore their dynamics and to facilitate them in finding better ways of functioning. This has ranged from a simple one-off meeting, to in-depth three-day team-development session, to an ongoing role as a team coach. Whatever the length and whether it is a team, group or peer group, some of the issues we would explore and how we would explore them would be the same.

Contracting

We begin by clearly contracting with the group members as to what they want to achieve from the group or team development activity and specifically what would success look like. Sometimes we ask the team to work together to finish the following three statements:

- This event would be a success for us as a team if . . .
- This event would be a success for our organization if . . .
- This event would be a success for our clients if . . .

We can then ask what they need both from each other and from us as consultant or facilitator of the team in order to achieve that success.

Successful contracting involves both starting with the end in mind and the ability to ask intentionally naive questions, such as:

- What is the purpose of your meetings?
- What do you expect from one another?
- Why have you called me in as a consultant? And why now?
- How would you know if this consultancy had been successful for you?
- What specifically would be happening differently?

Clear contracting is not only important for the success of the consultancy but it also models the way members of the team or group can contract among themselves, both about how they meet generally, but also how each person can be proactive in negotiating with the group his or her supervision needs.

Giving feedback

Before looking at what the group or team can become, it is necessary to start by finding out more about what it already is. One way to do this is for each person to receive feedback from all the other group or team members on what they have appreciated and found difficult about his or her contribution to the group.

Then each person can say what they have most appreciated and found most difficult about the group as a whole. This provides the beginnings of three lists: what the group values and needs to build on; and what it wants to change; and what is missing and needs to be introduced.

Estrangement exercise

This provides another means of exploring the issues in the team or group that need to be addressed. In this exercise each member takes on the role of a person totally different from themselves, who might attend an international conference on supervision. This person could be from a foreign country, be of a different gender, be a member of the press, etc. It is important to choose somebody who will see things very differently, but whose perspective it is possible to take up.

When the group members have taken up their roles and given themselves names, they are asked to close their eyes and relax. They are then led through a fantasy of arriving at the international conference, meeting people, hearing talks, etc. Then they find they are going on a visit to a supervision group to see how it operates. The group they visit happens to be the group they belong to in their everyday personas. In the fantasy they are directed to attend to what they notice when they first arrive, how they are received and by whom, how the group gets under way, who initiates, what the starting rituals are, what other roles are taken up, who is most verbal, who least verbal, what is the non-verbal behaviour and what is it indicating, what do they feel as they watch the group proceed, how does it end and what happens after the ending.

Still in the fantasy they say goodbye to the group and return to the conference where there is a message awaiting them, asking them to write to the group they have just visited and give them feedback. This is requested to be in the form of:

- What did you think was most positive about the group that needed to be built on?
- What do you think was most problematic that needs to be changed?
- What is one new thing that you think the group should introduce?

Still in role, people come out of the fantasy journey and actually write their letter from their assumed role to their own group. Having signed off and de-roled, they then read either their own or each others letters to the group and the issues are collected under the three different headings.

This can provide an agenda for exploring changes in how the group functions, leading to a recontracting stage. But it is also possible to go deeper in exploring the unconscious dynamics.

Exploring the group dynamics

Some useful statements that can be used in exploring the deeper dynamics of groups are:

- The unwritten rules of this group are...
- What I find it hard to admit about my work in this team is...
- What I think we avoid talking about here is...
- What I hold back on saying about other people here is...
- The hidden agendas that this group carries are...
- We are at our best when...
- What interrupts us from being at our best is...

Sculpting the group

This is an approach taken from sociodrama but which we have adapted and developed for exploring the underlying dynamics of teams and groups.

- *Stage 1*   The group is asked to find objects or symbols that represent what is at the heart or core of the group. These are placed in the centre of the room.
- *Stage 2*   Without discussing it, the group members are asked to stand up and move around until they can find a place that symbolically represents where they are in the group (i.e. how far are they from the centre, who are they close to and who are they distant from?). Then they are asked to take up a statuesque pose that typifies how they are in the group. This often takes several minutes as each person's move is affected by the moves of the others.
- *Stage 3*   Each person is invited to make a statement beginning: 'In this position in the group I feel...'
- *Stage 4*   All the members are given the opportunity to explore how they would like to move to a different position in the group and what such a move would entail for them and for others. For example, one person who has sculpted himself on the outside of the group might say that he would ideally like to be right in the middle of the group. Having verbalized this desire, he would be invited to find his own way of moving into the centre and seeing what that shift felt like for him and for the others in the middle.
- *Stage 5*   Members are requested to reframe the group by being asked – If this group were a family what sort of family would it be? Who would be in what role? Who would be the identified patient? And so on. Or if this group were a television programme which programme would it be? Again, who would be in what role and what would be the transactions?

It is also possible for the groups to try out their own frames. There are countless possibilities – meals, animals, countries, modes of transport, myths, Shakespearean plays etc.

- *Stage 6*   Then a chair is introduced as the 'Creative consultant's chair'. Each person is invited to go and sit in it and to make a statement: 'If I were the creative consultant to this group I would . . .' This gives the opportunity for each person to leave their own role-bound perspective and to see the whole system and to make a comment from outside.

Exploring the wider context in which the group exists

As in individual supervision, where Mode 7 focuses on the wider, social and organizational context in which the work operates, it is also important to focus on the context that surrounds the boundary of the team. All teams and groups exist within a wider context which they are both affected by and affecting. Thus a social work team exists in the context of the clients it works with, the whole organization of which it is a part, the other agencies it works alongside, the ratepayers and the council that controls its activities.

A peer supervision group of psychotherapists may have a different context. The sorts of people they affect and are affected by may include their clients, their families and friends, their own therapists and any individual supervisors they also see.

This wider system can also be sculpted through what we call an 'enacted role set'.

- *Stage 1*   The group or team brainstorms all the significant roles that are affected by and/or affect the group. It then selects the most important roles and relationships that need to be explored.
- *Stage 2*   One person takes on the role of each of these aspects of the wider system (e.g. one person represents all the clients, one person the partners of the group members).
- *Stage 3*   The group is symbolically placed in the middle of the room and the various roles place and sculpt themselves in relation to the group.
- *Stage 4*   Each role makes three statements:
  What I offer this group is . . .
  What I expect from this group is . . .
  What I see happening in this group is . . .
- *Stage 5*   It is then possible to explore dramatically a dialogue between the group and the people and roles that it relates to.

Having completed this exercise the group can look at how it would like to change the relationships with those with whom it interrelates. Here is an example:

> A community work team were exploring how they could improve their team's functioning. They did this in a two-day team development workshop. The first day they worked on their internal dynamics, support and supervision arrangements and had given each other a lot of feedback. On the second day they wanted to explore how they could change their relationship with the wider network. They began by brainstorming to establish who were the significant

others in the wider network who had a stake in how they operated. From this list they chose to explore the relationship to the following stakeholders.

- the senior management team,
- the director of the community leisure department to whom they were responsible,
- the community leisure committee,
- the ratepayer,
- the personnel department of the council,
- the social work department,
- the education department.

All of these roles were taken on by the team members who sculpted themselves in a position in relation to the other stakeholders, and to a chair that represented their community work team. Each person in role then used the three statements:

- What I offer this team is...
- What I expect from this team is...
- What I see happening in this team is...

There was much laughter, amusement and surprise, as they found they were able to say many challenging things about their own team, when speaking from the role of the other stakeholders.

They were also able to explore dramatically the relationship with some of these stakeholders by creating a dialogue in which one team member would speak for the team and another would respond in the role, for example, of the education department.

Conclusion

Whether you work in a team, or have supervision in a group or peer group, it is important that regular attention is paid to the dynamics that are operating within the process. In supervision groups, as in any other group, it is important to create a balance between focusing on the task, the individuals within the group and the group maintenance activities. The task needs will centre on attending to the improvement of the work done with clients by the group members. The individual needs include development, support, reassurance, approval, acceptance, etc. The group maintenance needs include issues of competitiveness, rivalry, authority, inclusion/exclusion, sub-grouping, etc.

Where there are good group or team supervisions, they will try to see that all three types of needs are attended to and are in some degree of alignment with each other. However, the team leader is not only someone who can attend to the dynamics, but is also part of the dynamics that are operating. The team or group supervisors are inevitably limited in the amount they can be aware of in such a complex system. Thus there is a necessity to build some structures whereby the whole group is able to share responsibility for focusing, not only on the task needs, but also on the individual and group maintenance needs.

Some structures can become a regular part of group supervision meetings, such as spending ten minutes at the end of each group, with each group member saying, 'What I have most appreciated about this session has been ... What I have found most difficult about this session has been . . .' Other structures may take place at greater intervals, such as an agreement to have a review of how the group is functioning every three months, with structured feedback to the group facilitator and to each member.

Teams that work regularly and intensively together need also to take regular time away from the pressures of the front-line work, to stand back and look at how they are functioning, both individually and collectively, and how they relate to the wider system which they operate. This may take the form of an away-day, or a team-development workshop, or sessions with an outside consultant, or may be part of a larger organizational change and development programme.

Whichever way a team or group decides to manage their own dynamics, it is important to remember that the time to start focusing on what is happening in the process is when things are going well and not to wait until the group or team is in a crisis. When the levels of conflict, hurt and fear rise it becomes much more difficult to see what is happening and to risk making changes. However, for some teams it is only when they hit a crisis that they create the motivation to face what is happening and sometimes 'crises create the heat in which new learning can be forged' (Hawkins 1986).

PART FOUR
An organizational and inter-organizational approach

12 Supervising networks

Introduction
The bucket theory of containment and displacement
The story of Andrew and his multiple therapeutic agencies
The story of Brenda and spreading the anxiety
The story of Carol and sexual abuse
The story of sexual abuse in Cleveland
Conclusion

Introduction

In Chapter 11 we advocated the need for supervision at all levels – the individual, the team, the department and the organization. We also recommended that each level is supervised as a whole entity (e.g. the department is supervised with regard to how it functions as a department). This supervision is essential if each level, whether it be in a social work department, hospital or school, is going to provide a measure of containment, holding and understanding for what happens within it.

The bucket theory of containment and displacement

We sometimes describe the containment process in a way that one organization called 'the bucket theory'. All helping organizations are, by their very nature, importing distress, disturbance, fragmentation and need. This is usually met by individual workers, who, if they are empathically relating to the client's distress, will experience parallel distress and sometimes disturbance and fragmentation within themselves. How much of this they will be able to contain and work through will depend on the size of their emotional container (or bucket), and will relate to their personality, their emotional maturity and professional development, the amount of pressure and stress they are currently under at work and at home and, most important, the quality and regularity of the supervision they receive.

What is not contained at this level will lead to decreased functioning in the worker and can also lead to fragmentation in the team. This comes about as those who are stressed quite often act out this stress on their colleagues. They can get irritable with the secretary, angry with their boss and non-cooperative with their colleagues. Fights can develop about who is responsible for what, and arguments over duty rotas. Team meetings begin to start later and later and become more fractious.

In Chapter 10 on 'Group, team and peer-group supervision', we talked about the need for the team to take stock of how they were functioning, individually and as a whole unit. Good team supervision increases the ability of the team to contain pressure, stress and disturbance. What the team does not contain can once again spill further out into the department or organization. Communication channels are often the first to suffer, with projections increasing both from the team on to management and other teams, but also on to the teams from other parts of the organization.

The team can become either the identified patient or the scapegoat for the organization – their problem child (see the section on the pathologizing culture in Chapter 13). Being either the identified patient or the scapegoat means that the team has not only its own problems but may have the disturbance from elsewhere in the organization projected onto it.

The organization needs good regular supervision and time to stand back and reflect on its own health and functioning. This is essential particularly in times of cuts in resources, but it is often ignored. The result is that consultant psychiatrists or directors of services stop working cooperatively and start to fight each other for diminishing resources, and basic grade workers retreat back into the enclaves of their own teams.

Some of this organizational supervision needs to be done by the leader within the organization. Mao Tse-tung (1957) said the job of a leader is to give back to the people clearly what the people give to the leader confusedly. However, few leaders of caring or people organizations receive good training in the skills required for supervisory overview and leadership of the organizational processes. Being a leader requires different and additional skills from being a good manager.

Also, no matter how good the leadership and 'helicopter skills' of consultant psychiatrists, directors of social services or heads of schools, they will always be part of the organizational system they are trying to support and supervise. This will mean that they will also be part of the problems of that system, and unconsciously trapped within the perspective of their particular organizational culture. Furthermore, they will also be trapped within a 'tops' perspective on the system, which is inevitably partial (Oshry 1996).

What the organization does not contain, process and understand can then spill over the boundaries of the whole organization and be played out between professions and organizations. This is not only enormously costly to all the helping professions, but very hard to supervise. Even so, some form of outside consultancy supervision is nearly always necessary.

It is also important to recognize that stress does not only flow from clients through front-line workers into the wider organizational system, but also the unresolved societal issues will create stress upon helping organizations which, if not processed and integrated, will create stress on front-line workers and their clients. An example of this is of society wanting to pay lower taxes and yet at the same time wanting higher quality health and social care and thus creating a demand that helping organizations achieve more with fewer resources.

The job of leadership and indeed supervision is to mediate and integrate the stressful processes that flow up and down the organization and to minimize the amount that is passed on unprocessed.

Here are three case studies of a client's process being enacted between a variety of professional agencies. We wish to explore how supervision both within and between these agencies could address the complex issues involved; how it could help the staff to work together in the interests of the client, rather than enact the client's process through inter-professional rivalries.

To avoid breaching confidence, significant details of the cases have been changed and material from more than one case has been combined. However, the cases are in essence both true and typical of inter-organizational working as we experience it, working across a large number of different agencies.

The story of Andrew and his multiple therapeutic agencies

The first case illustrates the way clients involve a whole network of helping professionals, often with different expectations. We include it in order to illustrate how, in many situations, clients are involved with a number of helping professionals, each of whom has a personal investment in and perspective of the client. In such cases the supervisor cannot afford to focus only on the supervisee and his or her relationship with the client, but must also focus outwards on the network of professionals and how they are enacting the various aspects of the client.

The client, whom we will call Andrew, had spent several years in a special hospital for the criminally insane for burning down supermarkets. He had been sent to a halfway house therapeutic community, in order to be gradually rehabilitated back into the community. Any reoffence would mean his immediate recall to the special hospital.

The counsellor in the therapeutic community has not only to relate to the expressed needs of the client (Andrew) but also to cope with the pressures and demands of the personal and professional network with which Andrew is involved.

The hospital is anxious that the therapeutic community ensures Andrew has no opportunity to reoffend. The local probation officer, who is greatly overworked, whose team is understaffed and who is thus under a great deal of pressure, wants the community to keep Andrew 'off her back'. Andrew has taken to phoning her every time he is at all upset or lonely in the community – a bit like the way a new boy at boarding school might phone his mother.

Andrew's parents want the community to help Andrew to return to their very religious and Victorian values, the deviation from which they see as the start of his problems. They insist that the local priest calls regularly.

The local authority, which is paying the fees for Andrew to be at the therapeutic community, wants to know when he will be starting work and thus reducing their financial burden.

Andrew himself is ambivalent. Part of him wants to open up and explore himself in the groups and counselling; but part of him wants the staff by magic to remove his seething anger or to give him the early parenting that he never received. He presents as very cool and together, with no problems at all. All his anxieties and fears he feeds into the other professionals outside the therapeutic community. The counsellor cannot understand why the others are all getting so worried and needs to be helped by the supervisor to see how Andrew's process is being acted out on a network level. The supervisor also has the responsibility to work with the network to help them understand, not only how they are part of the therapeutic team, but that their behaviour is also likely to be a symptom of Andrew's process.

In any situation where there is more than one helping professional involved, it is important that the network meet and decide both who is the key worker, and whose task it is to manage and supervise the helping network (this ideally should be the supervisor of the key worker).

The story of Brenda and spreading the anxiety

Brenda, a London girl in her early 20s, is seeing a counsellor who is based at a GP practice. Her father had died the previous year and the mother, who has always suffered from mild depression, was unable to give her much support. The girl is unable to cope at college, and the GP has given her a low dose of antidepressants and referred her to the resident female counsellor. The counsellor works slowly and steadily with the client seeing her fortnightly for hourly sessions. The client is quite defensive and only slowly opens up. If there is a very emotional session, the client tends to miss the following appointment.

After a year's work, Brenda is still having difficulty and overeating, although she has been back at college for six months. She develops lower back pain which again necessitates her missing college. The counsellor mentions an osteopath that she herself goes to see. The client goes to the osteopath and at first is delighted. The treatment seems to ease the pain and makes her feel a lot better about herself. Then suddenly a session with the male osteopath inadvertently awakens feelings about sexual interference by a man and, as a consequence, she stops seeing both the osteopath and the counsellor.

Brenda's depression gets worse and the GP, who is now anxious, refers her to the local psychiatric outpatients' department, where a young registrar decides to take her on for psychotherapy, without any prior consultation with the counsellor.

Clearly the client's process is being played out, not within a contained therapeutic situation, but through multiple transference onto four different professionals. The professionals are not only failing to work together to bring about some integration of the various fragments of the client's process, but are also enacting some of the typical inter-professional rivalries endemic within and between each of their roles.

Any situation, where splitting and multiple transference are ensuring that no one helper can work with the whole process, requires the difficult supervision process of a case conference. In this case the case conference needs to involve the GP counsellor, the GP, the osteopath, the psychiatric registrar and perhaps even the tutor from the college. To make this happen would require overcoming several major hurdles:

- The client is working unconsciously to keep the various professionals apart.
- It is unlikely that all these busy professionals would be willing to give the time for this case conference concerning a client who is not in a major crisis (yet).
- The different professional trainings militate against inter-professional work. Orthodox and complementary medical practitioners mostly distrust each other and avoid working together. Some medical training teaches doctors to treat other staff as 'ancillary paramedics'.
- There would be issues of who convenes such a meeting and who would provide the supervisory overview. If no one provides this overview, there would be a

distinct danger that the case conference would just enact the client's process, rather than come to a better understanding and a new way of working with it.

Clearly supervision could have helped this situation. The place where it could have created the most change would have been in the supervision of the psychiatric registrar. This was unlikely to have been helpful, however, as he had been attending a weekly supervision group with the consultant psychiatrist where he would present a case only once every six weeks, and this focused on the one-to-one relationship. His supervision tended to ignore the wider social network where most of this client's process was being enacted.

It is probable that the psychiatric consultant was in the best position to call a case conference but, instead of the psychiatric service taking over the therapeutic work, its skills and resources could have been used to relocate and help support the therapeutic work back in the community, with the front-line workers.

The GP team needed supervision to explore why they tended to refer patients to the psychiatric services in reaction to a deterioration in a client's mental state and before first exploring the case with their own counsellors and health visitors who were also involved. Often the GPs referred clients to the counsellor who they felt were burdening them with their neuroses, but, if the same client later came to the surgery in a way that was disturbed or disturbing, the GPs would tend to refer to the psychiatric hospital without first checking what was happening in the counselling. This would happen despite the fact that the counsellor was better trained therapeutically than the junior registrars who would normally see clients at the hospital.

Supervision can increase the amount that the other involved professionals learn from this experience. The counsellor could have been better supervised in exploring her unconscious motivation in referring the client to her own male osteopath.

The osteopath also needed supervision that would help him to be alert to signals from women clients who had a history of sexual abuse, how to work with such clients in an appropriate, sensitive and therapeutic way and when to refer on to a female colleague.

The story of Carol and sexual abuse

Carol, a sixth-form student at a boarding school in the Midlands, came to the psychiatric hospital, near her home in the home counties. She had been anorexic for two years. She had a sister of 15 and twin half-brothers aged 3. Her own father had left home when she was 12 and she still idolized him.

Carol initially confided to her school teacher that she had been interfered with sexually by two men – both unknown. This was shared with the hospital. Carol was first seen by the male consultant, but then referred by him to a female nurse-therapist who was part of his team, and whom he supervised. There was soon evidence of splitting and multiple transference with the teacher becoming the 'bad person' and the therapist the 'good and helpful' adult. This splitting later spread to the two involved organizations. Carol had gone to hospital at Christmas as an inpatient, rather than going home. She told the school that she wished to do so again at Easter and they told her that, if she did, she would not be allowed back at the school. Despite this she was admitted to hospital and received twice weekly psychodynamic psychotherapy from the same nurse-therapist.

During the next three months, without any behavioural techniques being used, she put on over a stone in weight. As she did so, she became progressively more distressed and unhappy and required medical treatment with an antidepressant to help her sleep and to help her feel less distressed.

It came to light in the therapy that Carol had been sexually abused by the stepfather. It was thought that this abuse was comparatively mild, but the precaution was taken of informing the family GP in case the younger twins were at risk. The GP was confident that the twins were well and that there was no sign of abuse, physical or sexual.

It was thought that the abuse by the stepfather was not serious enough to warrant further action and the breaking of the patient's confidentiality. As a precaution the supervisor contacted the Medical Defence Union and asked under what circumstances confidentiality could be broken and was informed that, if a serious crime had been committed by someone, then it was appropriate to break confidentiality. The local health authority regulations suggested that a wide variety of people should be informed at the slightest suggestion of a child being at risk of abuse. This includes the chief medical officer, social services, the police and the general practitioners involved.

Carol then informed the psychotherapist that the abuse had been severe and had involved full sexual intercourse for about two years. The therapist and supervisor later discovered that she had informed the therapist the day before her sister was due to return home (that is, she was unconsciously protecting her sister). When asked about her sister she at first said that her sister was not at risk, but then explained that the sister was not at risk as long as she herself was at home to protect her.

After receiving the information, the supervisor arranged to contact the mother and stepfather to confront them with the information. He felt that he was now responsible to protect the at-risk sister, but was still in a dilemma about whether or not to contact social services. His previous experience of involving social services and the police in such situations had not been good, for it had led to increased distress within the family, but rarely to any resolution of the family situation, or acceptance of responsibility by either the perpetrator or the mother.

The supervisor and therapist were also anxious about breaking confidentiality. The client had been informed that all information shared in the therapy was confidential, but that on occasions the psychotherapist would need to discuss the case with her supervisor. The therapist and supervisor were both beginning to feel distressed, anxious and angry themselves.

The supervisor rang the relevant social-service team leader to discuss the situation in theory without mentioning names but, after a short discussion, made a unilateral decision to make an official warning of possible child abuse.

The supervisor explored the situation in his own supervision. What had made him change his mind, and why was he carrying all the responsibility for the patient, the patient's sister and the therapist? He explored how he felt, feeling not only totally responsible for the whole system, but also helpless and vulnerable. He described how he identified both with the patient (he himself had experienced a lot of distress as a boy) and with the perpetrator (being male, a father and someone whose job gave him power over people).

The case was extremely intrusive and produced distress in the supervisor and therapist, even when they were not at work. They half-shared their feelings in an inter-disciplinary staff meeting, but this led them to feel unsupported and as if they were receiving all the disowned anger and hostility of the other staff.

Through supervision the psychiatrist was helped gradually to express the great mixture of feelings that he was carrying in relation to this case. Only when these had been supportively listened to by the supervisor, could the psychiatrist be challenged about why he was taking on board feelings and responsibilities that did not belong to him. The psychiatrist became aware of how he tended to use omnipotence as a defence and how this was not only a personal trait, but also something that was part of the culture of medical training.

The psychiatrist also began to explore his failure to challenge the therapist to con-front the situation with the patient. Instead, he had enacted once again the conflict as being taken one stage further away from the family where it belonged and being carried by others. Firstly, the abused daughter was forced to take the conflict which belonged to her stepfather. Then the teacher and therapist start to carry the conflict for the girl. Then the psychiatrist took away the responsibility. The psychiatrist's supervisor could have been next in line, had they not recognized the process as it was happening and started to put the responsibility firmly back where it belonged.

The nurse-therapist needed support from the psychiatrist in order to point out to the patient how she was unconsciously worried about her sister being abused. Also to help Carol recognize how she was feeling responsible, while understandably not wanting to accuse her stepfather, but also secretly wanting to punish him, not only for the abuse, but for being the intruder in the family position that rightfully belonged to her real father.

By allowing the psychiatrist to take over, the therapist was leaving the process to become once more, between a young girl and an older man in authority, thus replicating the role of opting out and turning a blind eye as the mother had done.

The patient and the therapist needed then to be active participants in deciding how to manage the dilemma. Even if the patient opted out from any responsibility to confront the situation, she needed to be constantly informed of what the therapist and the psy-chiatrist were doing.

Then, instead of the family being handed over to either the social services or the police to deal with, the social services should have been brought in to meet with Carol and the therapist (with the psychiatrist as supervisor to the case conference) to work as a team on how to tackle the situation. If it became clear that the stepfather had carried out a criminal act, then the police would have to be added to this therapeutic team.

Throughout this process, it is important that the distress and vulnerability do not get separated from those carrying the responsibility and potency. The two must be kept together in order to avoid splitting and to make contained therapeutic work possible.

The story of sexual abuse in Cleveland

The Butler-Sloss report (1988) that followed the inquiry into how cases of suspected sexual abuse were handled in Cleveland recommended much greater cooperation between the health service, social services, police and GPs. One of the difficulties in putting this important and valid recommendation into practice is that of providing good supervision in these multidisciplinary settings. As we have illustrated in the two cases above, it is not enough for there to be good supervision within the respective disciplines; there must also be supervision of the whole therapeutic network.

One simple model which can help us to understand such cases, and how they can get played out between agencies, is the triangle of persecutor, victim and rescuer. In this model, not only does each of the roles get caught within the system, but also the roles can suddenly shift around. Let us illustrate this from the Cleveland situation (Butler-Sloss 1988; see also Campbell 1988).

The situation began with two doctors believing they had diagnosed sexual abuse in over a hundred cases. They recommended to the social services that these children be taken into care. At this stage the triangle appears as Figure 12.1.

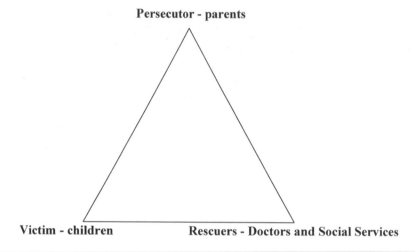

Persecutor - parents

Victim - children   **Rescuers - Doctors and Social Services**

Figure 12.1   The persecutor/victim/rescuer triangle (Stage 1)

There soon developed a massive outcry from the parents and disbelief by the media that sexual abuse could be so widespread. The local MP and a number of local and national papers started a crusade to rescue the victimized families (Figure 12.2).

But as in many such triangles the rescuers turned on the persecutors, calling for their dismissal and painting them as villains who were evil, rather than as dedicated professionals trying to do their jobs. The female doctor involved was portrayed by some popular newspapers as almost a witch, intent on breaking up innocent families. (The triangle is shown in Figure 12.3).

Like all such processes, this could have continued for a long time. The only way to stop the process is for one of the elected rescuers not to turn to persecuting the previous persecutors, but to understand the process as a whole. In this respect Butler-Sloss and her team produced a remarkably effective report, and avoided being drawn into the triangle with the hasty throwing of blame, and instead bringing good supervisory understanding of the whole situation, in which there were no 'goodies and baddies', but in which well-intentioned people on all sides made mistakes or were misguided.

One of the key pieces of learning that has come out of the very painful and costly

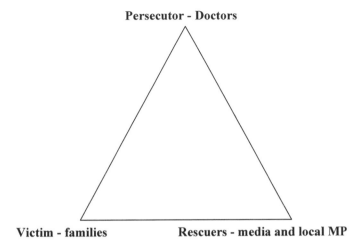

Figure 12.2   The persecutor/victim/rescuer triangle (Stage 2)

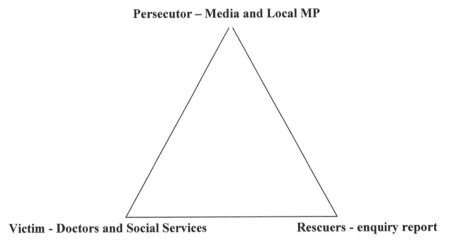

Figure 12.3   The persecutor/victim/rescuer triangle (Stage 3)

Cleveland situation is that all staff, even if they are senior paediatricians or social service directors need some form of regular supervision, which helps them to question their own work in a supportive way, so that they do not retreat into omnipotent conviction on the one hand, or turn a blind eye on the other. Let it not be forgotten that the professionals in the Cleveland case discovered incidents of child abuse that other professionals may well have ignored.

Conclusion

The report rightly called for much better cooperation between all the helping agencies. What still has to be further developed is the need for senior staff in social work, hospitals, general practice, the police force, etc., to be trained, not only in good supervision practice, but also in how to supervise complex, interdisciplinary situations.

We have argued elsewhere in this book that all first-line supervisors should receive training in supervision (see Chapter 9). We would also strongly advocate that those who supervise from more senior positions within an organization should also be given the opportunity to go on an advanced supervision skills training that focuses particularly on working with complex organizational and inter-professional situations.

13 Towards a learning culture: the organizational context of supervision

Introduction
What is culture?
Levels of culture
Organizational cultural dynamics that lead to degenerate supervision
    Hunt the personal pathology
    Strive for bureaucratic efficiency
    Watch your back
    Driven by crisis
    The addictive organization
Shifting the cultural pattern
Creating a learning developmental culture
Appreciative Inquiry in Schools
Supervision and the learning organization and learning profession
Review of generative learning in supervision
Conclusion

Introduction

In the 'seven-eyed' process model of supervision (Chapter 7), Mode 7 involves focusing on the context in which the supervision happens. One of the core contexts is the culture of the organization in which the therapeutic work and the supervision happens. In Chapter 4 we showed how the culture of the organization can not only influence and frame the supervision, but can even block effective supervision from happening. In Chapter 8 we explored the wider societal cultures which impact on both the work with clients and supervisees.

In this chapter we illustrate different types of cultures that are prevalent in helping organizations and how these affect supervision. In Chapter 14 we explore how to bring about change in organizations to produce a culture that is more conducive to staff learning and supervision.

What is culture?

In Chapter 8 we defined culture as: 'The different explicit and implicit assumptions and values that influence the behaviour and social artifacts of different groups' (Herskovitz 1948).

The understanding of culture derived from anthropology has been more recently used to understand the deeper context of organizations. Hawkins and Maclean (1991) quote the definitions of various writers who have studied organizational cultures:

> ...how things are done around here. (Ouchi and Johnson 1978)

> ...values and expectations which organization members come to share. (Van Maanen and Schein 1979)

> ...the social glue that holds the organization together. (Baker 1980)

> ...the way of thinking, speaking and interacting that characterize a certain group. (Braten 1983)

> ...the taken for granted and shared meanings that people assign to their social surroundings. (Wilkens 1983)

> ...the collection of traditions, values, policies, beliefs and attitudes that constitute a pervasive context for everything we do and think in an organization. (McLean and Marshall 1983)

McLean and Marshall (1986) explore how culture is carried, not only in the high-profile symbols of an organization such as logos, prestige events and training programmes, but also in the low-profile symbols.

Essentially, everything in an organization is symbolic; patterns of meaning in the culture mirrored in multiple forms of expression – in language, relationships, paperwork (or its lack), physical settings – how meetings are called and conducted, who sits next to whom, who interrupts, what time different topics are given, what lines of reasoning prevail, and so on.

Thus the organization's culture of supervision can be seen in the high-profile symbol of its policy about supervision, but can be seen more accurately in its low-profile symbols: where supervision takes place, who supervises, how regular the sessions are, what importance is given to them and what priority they have when time pressures necessitate something being cancelled.

There may be a split between the high and low cultures which is similar to the distinction that Argyris and Schon (1978) make concerning 'espoused theory' and 'theory in action'. Some social services departments have a policy with grand phrases about the key importance of supervision and ongoing development and support of staff; yet supervision is the first thing to be cancelled when there are staff shortages.

Other writers have referred to the organizational culture as representing the unconscious of the organization, as it is embedded in the ways of experiencing what happens; thus they see culture as less to do with what is done and more to do with how it is viewed, heard and experienced.

Levels of culture

Hawkins (1995, 1997) has built on this work, as well as the writings of Geertz and Schein, to develop a model of five levels of organizational culture, with each level being fundamentally influenced by the levels beneath it.

- *artefacts*:   the rituals, symbols, art, buildings, mission statements, policies etc.;
- *behaviour*:   the patterns of relating and behaving; the cultural norms;
- *mind-sets*:   the ways of seeing the world and framing experience;
- *emotional ground*:   the patterns of feeling that shape the making of meaning;
- *motivational roots*:   the fundamental aspirations that drive choices.

Like Schein (1985) we have utilized the water lily to illustrate the model.

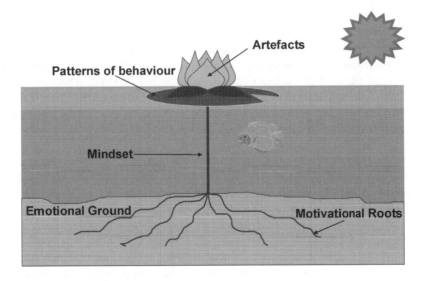

Figure 13.1   The five levels of organizational culture

The water lily illustrates that what is most noticeable about culture is the 'artefacts', the building, logo, mission statement, annual report etc., which equates with the flower of the lily. Just above the surface of the water the leaves of the water lily represent the typical behaviours of the culture. If the artefacts demonstrate the espoused values of the organization, the behaviours show the values in action. Many organizations have run into difficulties when there has been a rift between their rhetoric (what they say) and the reality (what they do).

Beneath the surface are the 'mind-sets', which hold in place the belief systems of a culture. These in turn grow out of the 'emotional ground' or climate of the organization. The 'motivational roots' are about the alignment of individual purpose and motivations with those of the collective organization.

Organizational cultural dynamics that lead to degenerate supervision

In working as organizational consultants to a number of health services, social work departments, probation teams, counselling and psychotherapy organizations and voluntary organizations, we have come to recognize certain distinct and typical cultural patterns that exist across all the helping professions.

We have called these cultural dynamics:

- **hunt the personal pathology**,
- **strive for bureaucratic efficiency**,
- **watch your back**,
- **driven by crisis**,
- **the addictive organization**.

We do not want to create another typology or classification of organizational cultures, as there are already many in existence (Harrison 1995; Handy 1976). Rather, we would see these patterns as recognizable system dynamics within the dominant organizational culture. Indeed, an organization may contain a number of these patterns at the same time. Each of these cultural patterns will create different motivation, emotional feeling, attitude, behaviours and policy around supervision. Each, in time, will lead to degenerate and even perverse forms of supervision.

Hunt the personal pathology

This culture is based on seeing all problems as located in the personal pathology of individuals. It is highly influenced by psychodynamic case-work theories, but with little understanding of either group dynamics or how systems function.

If there is a problem in one department's not functioning, the first thing that managers with this cultural mind-set do is to look for the problem person. This is often the head of the department. The belief is that, if we can cure the sick individual, the department will be healthy. If the sick individual does not seem to respond to treatment, then we look for a way of removing him or her.

This approach can happen at all levels of the organization and can degenerate very quickly into scapegoating. The residential home for children will report that all their troubles would be solved if only they could find a way of moving young Tommy somewhere else. However, when and if they do move Tommy to another home, then Sally becomes the problem child, and so on.

We have also worked with teams where the team has located all its problems in one member. 'If only Jack would take early retirement,' they all sigh. This attitude ensures that they are impotent in addressing the collective team problems as one cannot solve a problem that one does not first own.

In one large voluntary organization individual homes were elected one at a time to be 'the problem child' of the organization. The unspoken belief was that, if this home could be sorted out, then the whole organization would be problem free!

In this culture supervision can become problem-centred and aimed at treating pathology. This can create a subtle form of paranoia in the supervisees who fear that, if they do not keep the focus on the pathology of their clients, they themselves may become 'a suitable case for treatment'. On one of our supervision training courses, one head of an old people's home went back to his home to introduce supervision as his mid-course project. He announced in the staff meeting that he was going to introduce supervision and that he was going to start with James. James immediately exclaimed: 'Why pick on me – what have I done wrong?'

In this culture we also find that staff will sometimes say: 'I do not need supervision this week as I do not have any problems.' Team leaders will tell us that they give supervision on an ad hoc basis 'when problems arise'. This culture creates the belief that, if you go for supervision, you must have a problem or, more perniciously, there must be something wrong with you. This attitude is intensified by the policy of giving students the most regular supervision, the new staff the next largest amount, and senior staff no supervision at all. The message in this low-profile symbol is very clear, 'If you want to get on in this culture, demonstrate that you do not need supervision' and 'Supervision is only for the untrained, inexperienced, inadequate or needy.'

Supervision caught in this cultural pattern can degenerate into pseudo-therapy or, 'let us both analyse the client'. More importantly this approach precludes seeing supervision as a proactive process where its focus can be an 'appreciative inquiry' approach where the starting point is strengths and what is working well. In other words supervision can be part of modelling a health-based initiative instead of a problem-based one. Cooperrider and Srivastva (1987) write about appreciative inquiry and how 'organizations change in the direction in which they inquire.'

Strive for bureaucratic efficiency

This form of organization has been extensively written about by Isobel Menzies (1970) in her classic paper on nursing cultures in hospitals entitled *The Functioning of Social Systems as a Defence against Anxiety*. This form of organization is high on task orientation and low on personal relatedness. There are policies and rules to cover all eventualities and all meetings have tight agendas.

In this culture supervision is mostly concerned with checking up that all the tasks have been done correctly. We have worked with team leaders who have arrived at supervision with their staff with an agenda which is like a mechanic's checklist. When they have ticked off all the items, the supervision is finished. They may say as they walk out of the door: 'Oh by the way, how are you?' but possibly they will not stay to hear the answer. The managerial or qualitative function of supervision dominates.

For the supervisees the supervision is one of reporting back what they have and have not achieved. Again the culture is problem-centred but this time the ethos is that of mechanics rather than sickness and treatment. There is little space for understanding in the rush for tidy answers.

Watch your back

This form of organizational culture becomes prevalent where the climate is either very politicized or highly competitive. Some departments are riven with internal power battles between sub-groups. Sometimes this has been on political or racial grounds, but sometimes it is more to do with cliques and who is on whose side. In this atmosphere much energy goes in ensuring that the other side does not have all the information for fear that they may use what they know against you. Meanwhile, you make sure that you use everything you can to expose the other group.

Charles Handy (1976) in his book *Understanding Organizations* points out: 'In all organizations there are individuals and groups competing for influence or resources, there are differences of opinion and of values, conflicts of priorities and of goals. There are pressure groups and lobbies, cliques and cabals, rivalries and contests, clashes of personality and bonds of alliance.' Often in the helping professions power and rivalry are denied and then become even more powerful as shadow forces that are not recognized (see Chapter 2).

This form of culture can also develop in a very hierarchical organization where the climate guarantees that those who 'keep their noses clean' will get promotion. This leads staff to ensure that they cover up any difficulties, inadequacies or problems they are having, as it would be detrimental to share these.

> I have regular meetings with my supervisor, but always steer clear of my problems in coping with my report work. Can I trust her? I need her backing for my career progress, but will she use this sort of thing as evidence against me? There are some painful areas that are never discussed but need discussing so much. It is an awful dilemma for me.
>
> (Fineman 1985: 52)

What happens to supervision in this culture depends on who your supervisor is. If you are supervised by one of your own power sub-group, it becomes conspiratorial and falls into discussing 'how awful the other sides are'. If it is with someone who is 'one of them' or a manager you do not trust, then it is centred on covering up, putting a good gloss on the work you have done and making sure you are seen in a good light.

Driven by crisis

In one of our courses, where we were teaching the archetypal roles of helping (see Chapter 5), one of the course members suggested Superman as an archetypal role that some supervisors play. We were doubtful about this until our very next course, when there was a very quiet head of a children's home who sat taking notes in the corner. He was dressed more traditionally than the other course members, with a tie and jacket. Added to this, his glasses and studiousness made him seem more like a librarian than a social worker! In the middle of the second day a message arrived for him to say that there was a problem at his home. He jumped up in the middle of the session and seemed to grow before our very eyes. 'I must *go* – there is a crisis in my home,' he exclaimed loudly, as he swept out of the room. It was clear that this head of home became much more alive when there was a good crisis for him to handle and we are sure that his clients duly obliged by producing regular crises for him to respond to.

We have visited other hospitals and departments where the staff never have uninterrupted time to meet, as one of them is always responding to the latest crisis. In this type of organization there is never time to reflect properly on the work or the plan ahead, the focus is always on the intensity of the moment. As in the following story, clients pick up this culture and realize that, if you want to get attention around here, you must produce a crisis.

When we first worked in a half-way house for the adult mentally ill, cutting one's wrists seemed to be contagious. Even those who had no previous record of wrist-cutting seemed to be starting to do it. The staff were always rushing to the local casualty department, holding hastily bandaged arms. Eventually we managed to stem the flood of crises long enough to hold a staff meeting to reflect on this. We realized that those who cut their wrists were getting far more attention than the other residents. We, as a staff group, were perpetuating this particular crisis culture. The staff made it clear to the community that in future the staff would not visit clients in the hospital who had overdosed or cut their wrists and would instead give more attention to the clients who avoided such behaviour. Immediately the number of crises dropped dramatically.

In other organizations staff have told us that the only way to get time with the director is to have a crisis in your section, then the director who is always too busy to see you sends out an urgent summons for you to see him. In another voluntary organization the assistant director would fly in by plane or helicopter and give supervision in the nearest cafe, pub or in the car, before flying back to 'base'.

In this culture supervision is rarely a high priority and will get cancelled regularly, always for very important reasons. When it does happen, it often creates the atmosphere of being in a tremendous rush and having to solve problems in a hurry before the next wave or onslaught bears down upon us.

The addictive organization

Since writing the first edition both of us have been involved in working extensively with addiction treatment centres and also with the concept of the addictive organization. In 1991 we wrote a review (Hawkins and Shohet 1991) of the book by Ann Wilson Schaef and Diane Fassel entitled *The Addictive Organization* (Schaef and Fassel 1990) in which we described the four major forms of addiction in organizations as:

- Ones in which the key person in an organization is an addict. We have known directors and chief executives who have been alcohol dependent or workaholics, whose whole life was absorbed in their professional life.
- Where there are a number of people in the organization replicating their addictive or co-dependent patterns. In another book (Schaef 1992) she quotes the shocking statistic that in one study of nurses in the USA 83 per cent were found to be the eldest children of an alcoholic parent.

- Where the organization itself is an addictive substance, eliciting high degrees of dependency and workaholism from its members. This can be fuelled by the covert messages that say if you want to get on here, you do not take lunch breaks or leave until late in the evening.
- The organization as addict, where the organizational system functions in a parallel way to an addictive personality. The organization becomes unable to face its own truth and confront its own difficulties and starts to rationalize and defend dishonest and abusive behaviour.

One of the key notions in the field of addiction that is used by Schaef and Fassel is that of co-dependence. These are the partners, family or work colleagues who service, accommodate and protect the addict and their addiction. In the case of the addictive organization the entire workforce can be either acting addictively or colluding as a co-dependent.

In our article we invite the reader to reflect on an organization they either work for or supervise, and to answer the following questions:

- What are the family secrets in the organization – the things that most people know about, but which cannot be talked about publicly or openly? Why are they not being commented on?
- Whose behaviour cannot be commented on or confronted?
- What are the lost ideals and motivating visions that once inspired those working in the organization?
- How many of the following rules that make up the dysfunctional family system (Subby 1984) apply to the organization:
    - It is not OK to talk about problems.
    - Feelings should not be expressed openly.
    - Communication is best if indirect, with one person acting as a messenger between two others.
    - Be strong, good, right and perfect.
    - Make us proud.
    - Don't be selfish.
    - Do as I say, not as I do.
    - It is not OK to play or be playful.
    - Don't rock the boat.

If the organization has a culture of addiction, then it is important to interrupt the denial and dishonesty before attempting any other mode of development. Schaef and Fassel are sharply critical of many of the approaches to organizational development that facilitate the client organization in being more skilful in staying addicted. They criticize:

- stress management programmes that help individual managers to have techniques to keep their workaholism even longer and more intensively;
- programmes in worker participation which become subtle ways of staying in control;

- mission statements that become a 'fix': 'It can reassure us that we are important and do important work.'

Shifting the cultural pattern

The first step in shifting the cultural pattern is to become aware of the culture. This is not as easy as it sounds, for in the words of the Chinese proverb: 'The last one to know about the sea is the fish.' Our favourite definition of organizational culture is, 'what you stop noticing when you have worked somewhere for over three months'. Newcomers and visitors can often offer insightful feedback on your culture. There are also a number of exercises devised by the Bath Consultancy Group for accessing your own culture:

- by looking at typical patterns of behaviour;
- heroes, villains and fools stories;
- common metaphors;
- staging the unofficial induction programme;
- listing the unwritten rules etc.

(Hawkins 1994c)

Using such exercises a group can produce a detailed description of their own culture, at all the five levels mentioned above.

Just surfacing the culture can lead to some degree of change. Individuals and organizations may suddenly realize that they do not have to carry on with the same beliefs and ways of working that have become institutionalized. Their new awareness leads to greater choice.

Having surfaced an awareness of their culture, an organization can move on to exploring how they wish this culture to shift. One way of starting this process is known as 'three-way sorting' (Hawkins 1994c). The team or organization may have generated a great amount of data about their culture from carrying out the above exercises; they are then asked to create three new lists.

- What needs to be safeguarded, nurtured and held on to as the organization moves on?
- What can be discarded, is no longer appropriate and has outlived its usefulness? What is the excess baggage that is slowing down change?
- What needs to be incorporated, acquired, done differently?

This exercise represents the first step towards creating a cultural shift. To really change the culture in a sustainable way is a much longer and more difficult process, which is beyond the focus of this book, and we have written about this elsewhere (Hawkins 1995, 1997). However, we propose that all helping professions need to move away from the above forms of dysfunction and towards a more embedded learning and developmental culture.

Creating a learning developmental culture

Supervision flourishes most in a learning development culture. It is built on a belief system that a great deal of the work in all helping professions is about creating the milieu and relationships in which clients learn about themselves and their environment, in a way that leaves them with more options than they arrived with. Further, it believes that helping professionals are best able to facilitate others to learn if they are supported in constantly learning and developing themselves. An organization that is learning and developing from the top of the organization to the bottom is far more likely to be meeting the needs of the clients, because it is also meeting the needs of staff. One of the authors has written extensively about the learning culture elsewhere (Hawkins 1979, 1980, 1986, 1991, 1994a, 1994b) but we summarize the key attributes of such a culture and how they affect supervision.

- Learning and development are seen as continuous lifelong processes. Thus, in such a culture the most experienced and the most senior staff ensure that they have ongoing supervision or consultancy and do not see supervision as just for the untrained and inexperienced. The actions of the senior managers speak louder than their policy statements and it is important that they conspicuously exemplify the learning culture by, among other things, having supervision themselves.
- A learning culture emphasizes the potential that all the different work situations have for learning, both individually and collectively. Learning is not just something that happens in the classroom or on a training programme, but is built into the very fabric of work.
- Problems and crises are seen as important opportunities for learning and development, both individually and organizationally. Major crises are seen as growth points and the culture is one where it is safe to take risks, for failures are seen as events to be learnt from, not as evidence for the prosecution of individuals.
- Good practice emerges neither from an action culture that is always dealing with the latest problems and crises, nor from a theorizing culture that is withdrawing from the real issues to draw up theoretical policy papers. Good practice comes from staff, teams and departments that are well-balanced in all parts of the learning cycle, that goes from *action, to reflection, to new thinking, to planning* and then back to *action* (see Chapter 3).
- This means that supervision needs to avoid rushing for quick solutions, but also to avoid getting lost in abstract theorizing. Rather, it must start with reflecting on the concrete experience and try to make sense of this in a way that allows the experience to challenge one's own way of seeing and thinking about the world. But supervision must not stay at the point of new insight, but should use this new insight to generate new options, evaluate these options and choose what new strategy to put into operation. This new action then needs to be reviewed in the following supervision so that the learning cycle does not become a one-circuit process (see Chapter 3).

- Learning becomes an important value in its own right. Supervisors carry the attitude, 'How can I help these supervisees to maximize their learning in this situation so that they can help the client learn too?'; rather than the attitude, 'How can I ensure that the supervisees make no mistakes and do it the way I think is right?'
- Individuals and teams take time out to reflect on their effectiveness, learning and development. A learning culture includes team development sessions or 'away-days' (see Brown 1984, and Chapter 11). There are also 360-degree staff appraisals that go well beyond the senior grading the staff member on performance. They should involve a cooperative process where staff members appraise their own development, their own strengths and weaknesses and then receive feedback on and refinement of their own appraisal from both their peers, their senior and those that report to them.
- A good appraisal system will focus not just on performance, but also what the staff member has learnt, how they have developed and how their learning and development can best proceed and be nurtured in the forthcoming period.
- There should be a high level of ongoing feedback, both from peers and between levels within the organization. Also feedback should be encouraged from those with whom the work team or organization relate: customers, other helping organizations, professional networks, politicians, etc.
- Time and attention should be given to the transition of individuals: how new staff are welcomed and inducted into the team and organization: how they are helped to go through leaving and changes in status within the organization. Time should be given to this in both team and individual supervision.
- Roles should be regularly reviewed and negotiated. They should be allocated not just on the basis of efficiency, but also on the potential that each role provides as a learning opportunity for its incumbent. This should include the role of supervisor, which would not just be allocated automatically to the senior person in the hierarchy.
- In such a culture the learning does not reside just in individuals, who may up and leave, but it is ensured that the learning happens at the team and organizational levels and is both recorded and lived in the developing culture.

Appreciative Inquiry in Schools: an example of culture change

One of us (Robin) has been using appreciative inquiry as a way of helping to create a learning culture. He was asked by Teacher Support Network to write a book on supervision in schools, and wanted to discover more about school cultures. His belief was that, for supervision to be really effective, it had to be embedded in a culture that encouraged openness and was not a predominantly fear-based culture (Shohet forthcoming). From what he knew about schools, the culture was not ready to embrace supervision, exhibiting many of the symptoms of the negative cultures described above. What all these cultures have in common is a high level of fear. Appreciative inquiry, which focuses on what is working well already and offers a way of building on successes, naturally reduces fear. It encourages people to talk to each other about what has gone well, what they value and to imagine the future built on the best of the past. Participants are invited to tell stories about each others' successes. We call it positive gossip, a far cry from the fear-based gossip which can cripple an organization, and is nearer to the original meaning – God's sip.

As part of his research for the book, he focused on a large comprehensive school in East London. (For a fuller description see *Self and Society* vol. 33, No. 7, April–May 2005 ed. Shohet.) The school had received a poor government inspection report a few years previously and had been put on special measures. The staff knew how entrenched they had been in a culture that did not serve them or the children, and had already made steps to change that culture thanks to an inspirational head. They were very receptive to an appreciative inquiry approach and understood that to make the school work, the pupils had to be engaged in the running of the school. One of the principles of appreciative inquiry is to include as many of the stakeholders from across the system as possible, so right from the beginning pupils were engaged and were able to share what was good about the school for them. It was surprising for the staff to hear how much, underneath the difficult behaviour, the pupils valued them. It was also moving to watch how the trust between the two groups, staff and students, developed as time went on.

Another principle of appreciative inquiry is to ask positive questions. We like to ask: 'What is working well?' and, 'How can we build on what is going well?' This is a very different approach from asking: 'What are the problems in this organization and how can we fix them?' The students at the school took to this approach immediately and frequently challenged the staff: 'Miss, that isn't an appreciative comment. Say it in a different way.'

A key feature of the project was bringing in values assessments (see Barrett, R. 2006). This approach asks participants to choose their top ten from a list of about 100 values, that in their opinion, most exemplify the current culture, and the top ten they would like to see in the desired culture. This can be done online and very quickly provides the basis for a collective diagnosis of a system's culture (see next section for other ways). We were able to use this to provide 'hard' evidence to sceptics on which areas of the school and which sub-groups in the school would benefit most from an appreciative approach. It became clear from the results that the middle managers felt very undervalued. Without them any attempt at change would have foundered. Once they were on board, the project took off. Over time we have learnt to value the voices of those who are the most resistant in the system, as these voices can tell us something about the culture that others may not have noticed. The way the questions were asked enabled us to look together at what kind of a culture everyone in the school wanted, even those who appeared resistant to change and to such processes of inquiry.

Appreciative inquiries can be carried out on any topic and we have suggested in Chapter 6 that it might be a good idea to undertake such an inquiry on supervision. Bringing the positive into the room is quite challenging. It asks us to be open and vulnerable and share what is important to us. It challenges us to ask questions carefully, as the types of questions affect outcomes. Questions about what is working well result in a very different focus from asking about the problems. Blame, a feature of many organizations, can create a feeling of safety in the short term. It puts the problem out there, makes the blamer feel superior, and avoids their having to take responsibility. Long term, however, it is corrosive. It contributes to a fear culture. Appreciation leads to a very different one, closer to both love and compassion, which arises naturally from people who are given permission to tell their own and other people's stories of success. This subject will be developed further in a chapter in a forthcoming book *Passionate Supervision* (Shohet forthcoming).

Using the appreciative approach can be taken into any system or structure. One of us was interested in looking at different ways of accrediting psychotherapists and counsellors. At a conference looking at the dynamics of accreditation, he suggested a structure that involved everyone going into the middle and saying how love came into their work. Participants greatly appreciated the space to talk in a way that they had not done before. They shared how vulnerable they felt talking about what really mattered to them, but were really glad to have had the opportunity.

The value of appreciative inquiry in helping to change cultures in schools is now being recognized and at the time of writing Teacher Support Scotland has obtained funds for a pilot study to bring it to seven Scottish schools. If successful it could develop into a countrywide initiative. We believe this will make it far easier to introduce supervision, as supervision will be part of a culture of loving one's work and wanting to improve it, rather than experienced as being controlled by other's who do not trust you.

Supervision and the learning organization and learning profession

Where organizations have confronted the cultural patterns that lead to degenerate supervision and have developed a healthier learning and development culture, there is likely to be effective individual learning and development. However, this is not enough, for there is still a danger that despite the learning of all the individuals, the organization itself will have stopped learning and developing.

Supervision can also provide a key process in helping a living profession or organization to breathe and learn. For too long we have reduced the concept of supervision to a cultural socialization process where the elders of the professional community shape the practice, behaviours, understanding, perceptions, feelings and motivations of the apprentices and noviciates.

All the approaches discussed in the cultural patterns above have learning flowing from the supervisor to the supervisee. The learning is about conforming to the preformed professional norms and precepts – the culture's written and unwritten rules. While recognizing that both quality control and inducting newcomers into the professional collective wisdom are important aspects of supervision, if supervision is reduced to just these two aspects, as is often the case, we create a self-reinforcing profession which ceases to learn and develop. Eventually the profession becomes ossified, operating more and more within well-worn grooves of practice.

David Bohm, who was an outstanding professor of nuclear physics and eloquent follower of the spiritual teacher Krishnamurti, spoke about the challenge of creating self-renewing cultures in organizations, professions and societies:

> Therefore the key question is: is it possible to have a constantly creative culture? As soon as you set up a culture its meanings become repetitive and they begin to get in the way. Nevertheless we need a culture.

> Nobody has solved the problem of how the vision can be constantly renewed. It becomes more static, more of a habit. The thing becomes ... a disposition which gradually gets fixed. It gets transmitted from one generation to the other as a disposition, and the people who pick it up don't understand it in the same way as the people who had it, because they are merely imitating the disposition and not understanding the meaning from which it came. They may understand part of it, but not as well as those who came before. Each time it is made a little weaker.
>
> It's this repetition through generations which reinforces the habit to go along with the old ways of thinking and all the old social relationships and the old culture. Especially now this problem has to be solved if the civilizations are to survive. In the old days you could say 'well, a civilization could die and another one start up' but now with modern technology we may destroy the whole thing. The problem has become more urgent.
>
> (Bohm 1989: 73)

Supervision has a key challenge to move beyond the three central functions as defined by Kadushin:

- managerial (quality control),
- educative (development of the supervisee),
- supportive (ensuring the supervisee is able to process their experience, rather than be overwhelmed by it).

If we are to create learning professions that constantly renew their cultures, then supervision needs to become the learning lungs that assist the professional body in its learning, development and cultural evolution. This entails not only focusing on both the supervisee and supervisor learning, but providing a dialogical container in which new learning can emerge in the space between the supervisor and supervisee. Supervision needs to be practised in a way that allows learning to emerge in the interaction between the three unique areas of experience that are brought into relationship:

- the client situation and context,
- the supervisee's experience and understanding,
- the supervisor's experience and understanding.

Too often we have seen supervision reduced to the exchange of pre-existent 'thoughts' and knowledge. The supervisee tells their supervisor what they already have thought and know about their client, and the supervisor shares their pre-existent knowledge about similar clients or processes.

Review of generative learning in supervision

One useful test to review whether a supervision session has provided new generative learning is to ask four questions at the end of the session:

1   What have we learnt that neither of us knew before we came into supervision?
2   What have we learnt that neither of us could have arrived at alone?
3   What new capability have we generated in this session?
4   What new resolve have we each acquired?

The answer to these four questions will show the possible outputs of the dialogical learning that is generated in the space of our thinking and feeling together, rather than what has transpired from the exchange of pre-existent thoughts and 'felts'. David Bohm at a seminar in 1990, defined the difference between thoughts and thinking as follows:

> Thinking implies the present tense – some activity going on which may include critical sensitivity to what can go wrong. Also there may be new ideas, and perhaps occasionally perception of some kind inside. 'Thought' is the past participle of that. We have the idea that after we have been thinking something it just evaporates. But thinking doesn't disappear. It goes somehow into the brain and leaves something – a trace – which becomes thought ... thought is the response from memory – from the past, from what has been done.
>
> (Bohm 1994)

For a learning profession it is not enough to shift supervision from an exchange of thoughts to dialogical and generative thinking. We also have to consider how the learning that emerges from these supervisory dialogues can flow into the learning and cultural evolution of the wider profession. How do the learning lungs provide the necessary oxygen to the lifeblood of the organization?

We believe that any organization or professional working in the helping professions needs to create learning pathways, which can be used for harvesting emergent learning from supervision sessions, and taking this learning into new collective practice and standards.

Such learning pathways can include:

- supervision case reviews and action learning sets;
- supervisor seminars for the exchange of learning;
- conferences on new practice;
- new papers, articles and guidelines on professional practice using case material, appropriately disguised, from supervision;
- an appreciative inquiry approach in which the focus is on what is working and building on that rather than on what is not working and how to solve the problems. (Cooperider et al. 2000)

Conclusion

In this chapter we have tried to show how supervision is not just an event, but an ongoing process which should permeate the culture of any effective helping organization. Nearly all organizational cultures have a mix of several of the organizational dysfunctions that we have illustrated and caricatured. We have yet to meet an organization that fully lives up to the ideals of the learning and developmental culture. Some organizations do go a long way along the road in creating such an environment. One example which, alas, no longer functions in the same way, is Dingleton Hospital in Scotland. How it functioned and gradually became more of a learning culture can be read in Jones (1982).

In Chapter 14 we will explore how you can go about developing supervision in your own or another's organization. Developing supervision policy and practice should include attending to the organizational culture and helping it to evolve, away from some of the patterns illustrated in this chapter, towards being a learning and development culture. In such a culture, learning and development are an intrinsic part of every aspect of the workplace. Ultimately, we believe that clients of all helping professions, learn, develop and heal best in places where the staff and the whole organization are both continuously learning.

14 Developing supervision policy and practice in organizations

Introduction
Step 1: Create an appreciative inquiry into what supervision is already happening
Step 2: Awaken the interest in developing supervision practice and policy
Step 3: Initiate some experiments
Step 4: Deal with resistances to change
Step 5: Develop supervision policies
Step 6: Develop ongoing learning and development for supervisors, supervisees and the organization
Step 7: An ongoing audit and review process
Conclusion

Introduction

In Chapter 13 we explored the different types of organizational cultures in the helping professions and advocated the need to move to a learning-development culture. We believe that supervision is at the core of such an organizational culture. At many training courses and conferences we have been asked by dedicated staff from many different professions: 'How do I go about developing supervision practice in my organization?' This has never been an easy question to answer for several reasons:

- Every organization is different and has different needs.
- It depends on where you are starting from.
- Organizational change is a complex process and it is dangerous to follow (or preach) a simple recipe, or buy somebody else's solution.

However, having worked with a great variety of organizations that have been attempting to develop their supervision policy and practice, and listened to and read about many more, we have been able to discern a pattern or map for managing such development. Hopefully, this map will avoid the simple recipe but will point out several of the traps and pitfalls along the way. It is important to remember the maxim that the map is not the territory.

We suggest that there are seven stages in the organizational development process for introducing or upgrading the supervision policy and practice, which are:

1 creating an appreciative inquiry into what supervision is already happening;
2 awakening the interest in developing supervision practice and policy;

3   initiating some experiments;
4   dealing with resistance to change;
5   developing the supervision policies;
6   developing ongoing learning and development processes for supervisors and supervisees;
7   having an ongoing audit and review process.

These stages are not just a lineal process, but also a continuous cycle of development.

Step 1: Create an appreciative inquiry into what supervision is already happening

Many change efforts create unnecessary resistance, such as starting with the attitude that what is already happening is inadequate and that change must be imported from outside. This approach fails to honour the dedicated efforts of those who are already working to provide supervision in the organization.

When we first worked in this field nearly 30 years ago, it was possible to come across organizations where supervision was an unheard of concept. This is no longer the case in most professions and most countries. Change needs to start by appreciating what is already happening and what individuals and teams have already achieved. These pioneers can then become partners and collaborators in developing the supervision practice of the organization. (To read more about appreciative inquiry approaches to change see Cooperrider et al. 2000.)

Step 2: Awaken the interest in developing supervision practice and policy

We mentioned earlier the maxim that you cannot solve a problem that you do not own, and in organizational change it is no good trying to change an organization, department or team that does not recognize the need to change. The impetus for change must come from within. If staff do not own the problem, they are not going to own the solution. External agents, be they more senior managers, supervisors or external consultants, can help the organization or department to bring to the surface its own perceived strengths and problems; its unutilized capacities and resources; the environmental changes that are acting upon it and its dissatisfaction with the status quo. What they cannot do is create the commitment to change – that must come from within.

The two most effective ways of encouraging a commitment to the need for supervision, are to demonstrate the cost in not having supervision and to create a vision that demonstrates the benefits of good supervision.

The costs of the lack of supervision can be found in a number of diverse sources:

- poor or outdated practice,
- client complaints,
- staff morale,

- staff attitude surveys,
- staff turnover rates,
- practice audits,
- comparisons with best practice in the field.

It is also necessary to obtain commitment to the change process from those who have power or authority in relation to the department or organization, which wants to change. Change in one part of an organization has an effect on the other parts and can create resistance in those above or to the side, which may lead to the change effort being sabotaged. Before embarking on any change programme, it is important to map out all the interested parties (those who will be affected by the change process) and consider how they can be brought on board.

Bob Garratt, who works with change in global organizations, suggests (1987) asking three questions to ensure that the political support is maximized for the change effort from the wider network:

- *Who knows?* Who has the information about the problem? Not opinions, views, half-truths, official policies, but hard facts, which will determine the dimensions of the problem.
- *Who cares?* Who has the emotional investment in getting change made? Again, this is not who talks about the problem but who is involved in and committed to the outcome.
- *Who can?* Who has the power to reorder resources so that changes occur? Who, when faced with facts, commitment and energy, has the power to say 'Yes'?

When working with organizations to develop their supervision practice we have often been asked whether it is better to have 'top-down' or 'bottom-up' change. Our answer is both and in addition you need 'middle-out' change!

The fastest change happens when:

- those at the top create both the climate and framework in which others can get on and make the change happen;
- those at the bottom move from moaning about the absence to being more professional and articulating the need for supervision;
- those in middle management take on the responsibility to orchestrate the change process.

Step 3: Initiate some experiments

Most organizations not only have pockets of good practice (see Step 1) but also small groups of people who have the desire and commitment to take things forward. Rather than drive change from the centre or top of the organization it is often more effective to support and build on the creative energy of those in the middle. Finding one unit or division that wants to go ahead and try out new practice or have its senior staff undertake an external training programme, can often generate interest well beyond its own boundaries.

There is a danger that one unit will become too elitist and special, which can lead to them being both envied and discounted. This can be avoided by having two or three units, each engaging with their own experiments into supervision approaches, or ensuring that the unit is constantly including others in its experiment and inquiry process.

Step 4: Deal with resistances to change

However, even in an organization that achieves a large amount of the above preconditions, change can still create resistance. The difference is that in such an organization the resistance to the change would have a much better chance of being successfully worked through.

Resistance to change and unwillingness to engage in new behaviour are fuelled by a number of factors:

- fear of the unknown,
- lack of information,
- misinformation,
- historical factors,
- threat to core skills and competence,
- threat to status,
- threat to power base,
- no perceived benefits,
- low trust in the organization,
- poor relationships,
- fear of failure,
- fear of looking stupid,
- reluctance to experiment,
- custom bound,
- reluctance to let go,
- strong peer group norms.

(Plant 1987)

Kurt Lewin (1952) adapted from physics into the field of human relations the law that says: 'Every force creates its equal and opposite force.' He developed the concept of force-field analysis, that the more you push for change the more resistance you create. This is clearly seen in the following example taken from an inter-group negotiation:

> Group A bring three arguments to support their case. Group B bring three arguments to support theirs. Group A, instead of looking for common ground, make the mistake of adding three more reasons why they are right. Group B immediately doubles the number of reasons for its viewpoint and at the same

time raises its voice. Group A raises its decibel level by almost the same amount and starts ridiculing the case of group B who, surprise, surprise, replies in kind.

Creating any form of change, be it in an individual worker or a whole organization results in resistance; pushing harder for the change just creates more resistance. Lewin suggests, instead, stopping and attending to what is creating the impasse. Draw a line down the page and on one side put all the forces that are supporting the change. On the other side show all the forces that are resisting the change. Then in order to shift the status quo, find ways of attending to the resistances in a way that would meet the underlying needs that are fuelling them. If the resistance can be honoured and redirected, the change will happen without having to use greater effort.

Here is an example of a force-field analysis of a situation in which a new team leader is trying to introduce supervision into a team where it has previously not existed.

Table 14.1   Introducing individual supervision into a team

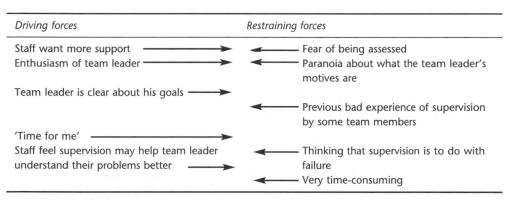

Driving forces	Restraining forces
Staff want more support ⟶	⟵ Fear of being assessed
Enthusiasm of team leader ⟶	⟵ Paranoia about what the team leader's motives are
Team leader is clear about his goals ⟶	
	⟵ Previous bad experience of supervision by some team members
'Time for me' ⟶	
Staff feel supervision may help team leader understand their problems better ⟶	⟵ Thinking that supervision is to do with failure
	⟵ Very time-consuming

In this situation an increase in the enthusiasm of the team leader about supervision, or even his trying to convince team members about how good it would be for them, would tend only to increase their paranoia about what he was trying to get them to do. Alternatively, it might give them the sense that they really must be in a bad way for him to be so insistent that they need supervision. The wise team leader would instead look at ways of honouring and redirecting their resistances. Perhaps he would give them time to talk about their previous bad experiences of supervision or would engage them in planning the best and most time-efficient supervision system for this particular team.

In dealing with resistance it is also useful to realize that resistance often changes over time and can go through various stages. Fink, Beak and Taddeo (1971) postulate four phases through which groups or organizations will pass in response to change:

- shock,
- defensive retreat,
- acknowledgement,
- adaption and change.

In shock, interpersonal relations become fragmented, decision making becomes paralysed and communication confused. This leads to *defensive retreat:* individuals become self-protective, teams retreat into their own enclaves and become inward-looking, decision making becomes more autocratic and communication more ritualized. In the *acknowledgement* phase individuals and teams begin to own that there are things that need changing and more support and confrontation is present. When the fourth stage of *adaptation and change* is reached, relations become more interdependent, there is more communication between individuals and across team boundaries, there is more willingness to explore and experiment with other ways of operating, and communication becomes more direct and open.

Thus it can be counter-productive to give people our marvellous scenarios for their future. They need to be involved in the thinking through and planning of the changes so that they have the opportunity to react, to understand the need for change and then adapt to the future necessities. It is very easy to think that, because we have worked through the issues and come up with a good solution, other people need only to accept the rightness of the solution and do not need to go through the thinking process for themselves.

Step 5: Develop supervision policies

All organizations need a clear statement of policy on supervision. Kemshall (1995) suggests that such a policy needs to state clearly:

1 purpose and function of supervision;
2 how supervision contributes to the agency's overall aims;
3 minimum standards for the content and conduct of supervision;
4 minimum requirements for supervision contracts, to include frequency and agenda setting;
5 a statement on anti-discriminatory practice;
6 how supervision will be recorded and status of supervision notes;
7 explicit statement of the relationship between supervision and appraisal;
8 rights and responsibilities of both supervisee and supervisor;
9 methods for resolving disagreements and/or breakdowns in the process;
10 the type of confidentiality expected and guaranteed;
11 a clear statement of how 'poor performance' will be dealt with and 'good performance' acknowledged.

To these we would add:

- what supervision should focus on;
- what priority supervision should be given in relation to other tasks.

Liz Pitman (personal communication 1999) has developed this approach in helping a number of organizations develop their own supervision policy, in a way that matches good practice to the reality of local resources and conditions. Organizational policies on supervision can then be used as the basis for a formal contract between the supervisor and supervisee. A sample contract is provided by Tony Morrison (1993).

Step 6: Develop ongoing learning and development for supervisors and supervisees and the organization

In Chapter 9 we have outlined the general broad curriculum that we believe is necessary for supervision training. However, we would also warn against the mind-set that separates learning and doing; that sees learning as happening off-the-job on training courses and practice happening at work. While we believe every helping organization should establish an ongoing training programme for supervisors along the lines outlined, we also believe that the best learning on how to supervise emerges from actual supervision.

The first step to becoming a skilled supervisor is to receive good supervision. Without this fundamental step the supervisor lacks both a good role model and also a solid inner experience of how beneficial supervision can be in one's professional life. The second step is, over time, to have supervision from more than one supervisor, so that one develops a range of role models, from which one can develop one's own style.

This fundamental learning is difficult in an organization that has not yet established a tradition of good supervision practice with experienced supervisors. Therefore, in the early stages of developing better practice a number of strategies can be utilized:

- using external supervision for senior practitioners;
- specifically recruiting new staff from agencies where supervision has been more established;
- arranging peer supervision between those staff who first undertake supervision training.

To receive good supervision also entails learning the skills of being a good proactive supervisee. It is also a mistake to believe that supervision training should only be focused on the supervisor. Workshops and conferences, for all staff, on how to get what you need from supervision can also provide an impetus in raising the level of supervision practice.

The final trap in planning supervision training is to believe that there is a programme that you can finish and then tick off that aspect of your development as completed. Supervision learning is continuous and needs updating, as do books on supervision! The nature of the training changes and senior supervision practitioners need less structured input and more space to reflect on what is emerging in their supervision practice and explore new emergent challenges. These may include supervising people from different cultures (see Chapter 8), different professions, different orientations, new ethical issues encountered, or changes in professional practice.

It is also important to build into the organization mechanisms whereby the organization can learn from what emerges in supervision. In Chapter 13 we listed a number of processes that can be embedded in an organization to create learning pathways, from the front-line experience shared in supervision to collective knowledge and wisdom, both about supervision and effective practice.

Step 7: An ongoing audit and review process

In the same way that an individual supervisor's development is a continuous process, so is the development of supervision practice and policy in both organizations and professions. Each year the organization should undertake some form of review of its supervision practice. A full review every year may not be possible, in which case a full review can be undertaken every three years with an interim review every year as part of the organization planning and review process.

The review and audit should include:

- where and what, and how much supervision is happening;
- staff satisfaction with the quality of supervision;
- an assessment of the impact of supervision on practice;
- the number of supervisors that have undertaken training, and to what level;
- illustrations of best practice within the organization;
- comparison to best practice in the profession;
- an anti-oppressive audit.

An audit is only as good as the change in practice that it produces. A full audit and review should produce changes to policy, training, practice guidelines and actual practice. As far as possible supervision needs to be built into the ongoing fabric of the organization through such mechanisms as:

- induction programmes,
- recruitment and promotion criteria,
- staff appraisals,
- job descriptions,
- staff competence frameworks,
- general audits and reviews of practice.

Conclusion

Introducing supervision into an organization can easily falter after the initial enthusiasm. We have had several experiences of successfully running supervision training with high commitment from those attending, only to see their enthusiasm turn to frustration, as others in the organization have not responded in the way they expected or hoped.

Supervision is likely to be established in a more sustainable way if the whole organizational process is carefully designed and monitored. This needs to include anticipating the potential personal, cultural and organizational resistances that are likely to be encountered and finding ways of engaging the needs behind the opposition.

The seven-stage cycle of developing supervision practice and policies is relevant for any organizational change process and can also be useful when supervising staff who are engaged in leading change.

15 Conclusion: keeping our hearts and minds open

> Until recently there was a GP in Glasgow whose patients would queue up for over three hours to see any other doctor but him. His lack of caring and sensitivity and his boredom with patients he had 'looked after' for years, eventually alienated them. Until, that is, his grandson was found to have leukaemia and slowly, through his own hurt and pain and anger, he was able to touch his patients again. Why is it that often, the very people we expect to understand the anguish of pain, illness and maybe death, often turn their professional, and for that matter human, backs until perhaps such time as they themselves have similar traumas?
>
> ('Society tomorrow', *Guardian*, 1 October 1986)

In many helping professions, from social work to alternative health practitioners, from doctors to teachers, and from nurses to marriage guidance counsellors, the hardest work, and yet also the simplest, is to meet the clients in their pain and helplessness. Some professionals, like the doctor mentioned in the *Guardian* quotation above, are in flight from their own pain and, therefore, have to construct enormous barriers between themselves and the pain of their clients. Other professionals take care of their own distress through projecting it into their clients and needing to make their clients better.

When the client gets too close, the doctor may reach for his prescription pad, the social worker may give advice, the probation officer plan a contract, and each in his or her own way is trying to take the pain away. Sometimes this is necessary as the pain and hurt in the client have become unmanageable for them and they need temporary relief before returning to face that wound within themselves. However, professionals can reach too quickly for ways of making it better, for their own needs, for it is they rather than the clients who cannot bear to sit with the pain and distress. We often remind supervisees that their clients have often lived with their pain for many, many years and the clients' ability to tolerate the pain is probably much greater than theirs.

There are many therapists who have shown the way to 'stay with' what is happening. Winnicott writes: 'If only we (therapists) can wait (and resist a personal need to interpret) the patient arrives at understanding creatively' (Winnicott 1971).

There is so much pain and hurt in the world that, if we get caught into believing we have to make it all better heroically, we are setting ourselves up to be overwhelmed and to burn out quickly. However, if we react to this reality with professional defensiveness, we may treat the symptoms but we fail to meet and support the human beings who are communicating through these symptoms. The middle ground entails being on the path of facing our own shadow, our own fear, hurt, distress and helplessness, and taking responsibility for ensuring that we practise what we preach. This means managing our own support and resourcing system, finding friends and colleagues who will not just reassure us but also challenge our defences, moving out of the 'drama triangle' into the 'beneficial triangle' and finding a supervisor or supervision group who will not collude in trying to see who can be most potent with ways of curing the client, but instead, will attend to how we are stuck in relating to the full truth of those with whom we work.

Often we have experienced working in supervision with a supervisee who is very stuck in knowing what to do next with the client. In the supervision supervisees may start by looking for better answers and techniques for managing the client out there, but the real shift comes when they start to look at their own responses to the client. They might find that they are afraid of that aspect of themselves that the client represents; that the client reminds them of someone in their own lives, restimulates a past distress within them, or produces a strong counter-reaction to their problems.

When this has been explored, supervisees will often report at their next session, with some surprise, that they did not need to use any of the new strategies for managing the client, for 'it was as if the client had heard the supervision and had arrived at the next session much freer'. Some people may term this 'absent healing', but at a much simpler level we believe that the client very quickly responds to an awareness that the helper is now ready to hear what the client needs to share.

Jampolsky (1979) tells a story where his own readiness through self-supervision made a direct and immediate impact on a client:

> The episode took place in 1951 at Stanford Lane Hospital, which was then located in San Francisco.
>
> The situation was one in which I felt trapped and immobilized by fear. I was feeling emotional pain, and thought I was threatened with potential physical pain. The past was certainly colouring my perception of the present...
>
> I was called in at 2 a.m. one Sunday morning to see a patient on the locked psychiatric ward who had suddenly gone berserk. The patient, whom I had not seen before, had been admitted the previous afternoon with a diagnosis of acute schizophrenia. About ten minutes before I saw him, he had removed the wooden moulding from around the door. I looked through the small window in the door, and saw a man six feet four inches tall weighing 280 pounds. He was running around the room nude, carrying this large piece of wood with nails sticking out, and talking gibberish. I really didn't know what to do. There were two male nurses, both of whom seemed scarcely five feet tall, who said, 'We will be right behind you, Doc.' I didn't find that reassuring.
>
> As I continued to look through the window, I began to recognize how scared the patient was, and then it began to trickle into my consciousness how scared I was. All of a sudden it occurred to me that he and I had a common bond that might allow for unity – namely, that we were both scared.
>
> Not knowing what else to do, I yelled through the thick door, 'My name is Dr Jampolsky and I want to come in and help you, but I'm scared. I'm scared that I might get hurt, and I'm scared you might get hurt, and I can't help wondering if you aren't scared too.' With this, he stopped his gibberish, turned around and said, 'You're goddam right I'm scared.'

> I continued yelling to him, telling him how scared I was, and he was yelling back how scared he was. In a sense we became therapists to each other. As we talked our fear disappeared and our voices calmed down. He then allowed me to walk in alone, talk with him and give him some oral medication and leave.

Jampolsky has more recently written a book on the importance of forgiveness of both self and other, in all therapeutic work (Jampolsky 1999).

In this book we have started with examining motives for wanting to help others. We see this as the beginning of self-supervision, the ability and the desire to question one's practice. We have, in the first instance, concentrated on some of the less straightforward motives – not because we believe that people are fundamentally devious, but because a thorough examination of motives can help us to be more honest with ourselves and, therefore, our clients.

From this examination of motives and the need for commitment to continual emotional growth we explored, in Chapter 3, how to stay learning and flourishing at work and then in Chapter 4, ways of taking charge of our own needs for support and supervision. We emphasized that there were skills that could be learnt in being an effective supervisee that formed part of being an effective supervisor.

In the second section of this book (Chapters 5–9) we introduced many of the issues involved in being a supervisor. The maps and models that are available in understanding the process and framework of supervision; the boundaries of the relationship; some of the skills needed for effective supervision and ways of establishing training courses for different types of supervisors. Throughout this exploration we have not confined ourselves to one approach, but rather presented the various choices and issues that each supervisor needs to consider in the process of establishing a personal style of supervising. The style chosen needs to be appropriate to the profession, the organization within which the supervision takes place, the level of development and the needs of the supervisees, and also the personality of the supervisor.

In the third section of the book (Chapters 10–11) we explored supervision in groups, peer groups and work teams. We examined the advantages and disadvantages of these forms of supervision and also ways of working with the group dynamics and team development.

However, supervision does not take place in isolation and we devoted the fourth part of the book (Chapters 12–14) to looking at the organizational context in which supervision takes place. We outlined ways of looking at the 'culture' of organizations and some of the typical cultural dysfunctions that prevail within helping organizations. We looked at the importance of establishing a learning culture to provide the climate that supports and sustains supervision, not just in formal sessions, but also as an integral part of the working context. We also outlined ways of introducing supervision policies and practice into an organization and managing change processes.

In writing this book we have stressed the need to integrate both the emotional and the rational, the personal and the organizational, and the developmental, resourcing and qualitative aspects of supervision. This integration inevitably provides a creative tension that has to be constantly understood and worked with.

Our ways of working have both followed and developed the process-centred approach to supervision which was first suggested by Ekstein and Wallerstein (1972) in which the emphasis is on the interaction between client, worker and supervisor. In this approach we avoid the polarization of focusing solely on the client or the supervisee; instead we focus on how the relationship between the supervisee and the client emerges in the supervision session, both in the content brought by the supervisee and in the process that emerges between supervisee and supervisor.

Throughout the book we are aware that we have been acting on certain assumptions – namely that supervision is worthwhile. We have occasionally cited evidence that job satisfaction is related to receiving good supervision, quoted cases where shifts have occurred through supervision, and included both theory and personal accounts. But ultimately as Rioch et al. (1976) suggest:

> There is no way to escape the fact that in (helping others) we are not really able to count the cost or measure the results ... The truth is that we are performing an act of faith – faith in our clients, and the workers we supervise. It does not really matter that this is occasionally misplaced or that we fail more than once in spite of experience or skill. Like other kinds of faith, this one persists although it is based on things unseen and unheard. Essentially, it is faith in the value of truth, not so much truth with a capital 'T' that would reveal to us the nature of ultimate reality, but truth as the opposite of the small daily self deceptions or the large paranoid delusions that destroy people's respect for themselves and each other.

This commitment to truth, we believe, is more important than all techniques and theoretical approaches. Eventually there comes a time when we have to act from some deep place within ourselves – perhaps induced by a crisis or a client who tests us out or who is very similar to us. At these times it may be that the right course of action is something which goes against all our previous convictions. 'There were rules in the monastery, but the master always warned against the tyranny of the law. "Obedience keeps the rules," he would say, "but Love knows when to break them"' (De Mello 1985).

Hawkins and Smith (2006) who have described at length the skills and capacities needed for those who supervise coaches and mentors, stress that the most important quality is 'fearless compassion', the courage to both speak the truth and yet do so with respect and compassion for the other. A moving example of this is illustrated by Archbishop Desmond Tutu who chaired the Truth and Reconciliation Tribunals after the changes in South Africa in the 1990s. In March 2006 the BBC screened three films called *Facing the Truth* of Desmond Tutu 'supervising' the first meetings between Protestants and Catholics in Northern Ireland, where one party had murdered the partner of the other. In these meetings Tutu was constantly exemplifying fearless compassion. His whole being was simply love and respect. He appreciated that the people were in the same room telling their stories. He had no agenda – he did not require change or outcomes, but that people spoke their truth. He was fully present to the painful truths in both parties and in their relationship.

Good supervision, like love, we believe, cannot be taught. The understanding, maps and techniques that we provide in this book cannot and, perhaps should not, protect supervisees and supervisor alike from times of self-questioning and doubt. At these times it is the quality of the relationship that has already been established between them that holds and supports the supervisee in times of crisis and doubt. How we personally relate to our supervisors and supervisees is far more important than mere skills, for all techniques need to be embedded in a good relationship. We agree with Hunt (1986) when she says: 'It seems that whatever approach or method is used, in the end it is the quality of the relationship between supervisor and supervisee that determines whether supervision is effective or not'.

This relationship provides the container for the helper and forms part of the therapeutic triad we referred to in Chapter 1. It is a relationship that, like any other, will have its difficulties. But without it we believe the work with clients is incomplete.

As Dr Margaret Tonnesmann (1979) emphasized in her lecture at the fourth annual conference to commemorate the work of Donald Winnicott:

> The human encounter in the helping profession is inherently stressful. The stress aroused can be accommodated and used for the understanding of our patients and clients. But our emotional responsiveness will wither if the human encounter cannot be contained within the institutions in which we work. Defensive manoeuvres will then become operative and these will prevent healing, even if cure can be maintained by scientific methods, technical skills and organizational competence. By contrast, if we can maintain contact with the emotional reality of our clients and ourselves then the human encounter can facilitate not only a healing experience, but also an enriching experience for them and for us.

A good supervisory relationship is the best way we know to ensure that we keep our hearts and minds open to ourselves and our clients.

Glossary

Action learning A form of learning in which the learning is deliberately based on learning from experience and not just theories. Action learning sets first used by Reg Revans involve staff working in small groups to explore real work problems, issues and challenges.

Anti-discrimination practices which draw attention to and work against discriminatory behaviour and policies towards minority groups.

Anti-oppressive practices which encourage behaviour that attends to addressing past and current oppressive experiences based on race, gender, sexual orientation, age, disability etc.

Appraisal A meeting of a senior with a junior staff member to systematically evaluate their work and plan future developments. 360-degree appraisal involves feedback from clients, peers and subordinates.

Behaviourist A school of psychology and psychotherapy which seeks to understand human behaviour. Behaviour therapists work to help change unwanted patterns of behaviour usually by trying to change conditioned responses. There is no attempt to understanding meaning behind these patterns.

Burn-out The psychological state reached by an individual in the undertaking of their work in which they are unable to continue through stress, illness and fatigue. Typically an individual who is 'burnt out' is out of balance with what they give out to others and receive for themselves.

Co-counselling A type of reciprocal counselling invented by Harvey Jackins in which two people undertake to take it in turns to be client and counsellor. Emotional expression and discharge are understood to be helpful and techniques to encourage this are learnt by those who undertake this method.

Congruence A state of being in which the emotional, bodily and verbal response are in alignment with each other and, therefore, are not contradictory. A congruent response is therefore, felt to be authentic.

Contract An agreement made between supervisor and supervisee concerning the boundaries of their work together (see Chapter 6).

Counter-transference The responses of the counsellor or psychotherapist to their patient/client, both conscious and unconscious. A fuller description of different types of counter-transference can be found in Chapter 7: Mode 4.

Culture The different explicit and implicit assumptions and values that influence the behaviour and social artifacts of different groups (Herskovitz 1948). Organizational culture is the specific culture imbedded in an organization.

Drama therapy A type of therapy which involves dramatic enactment and active exercises designed to explore and express conflicts and issues experienced by participants.

Dynamics The tendency towards certain movement of patterned behaviour or mood states within the psyche (which is referred to in the term *psychodynamics*) or between people, as in group dynamics.

Empathy An understanding (usually a felt understanding) of the other, from the other's point of view.

Ethnic A cultural construct which describes different geographical or 'racial' groupings.

Ethnocentric Having a world view confined by one's own cultural frame of reference.

Ethnorelative Having a world view which takes into account and can adapt to different cultural perspectives.

Force field analysis The analysis of the patterned behaviour within a given situation or 'field' to show the balance of changing and resisting forces. First used by Kurt Lewin.

Game A habitual and patterned way of relating in which two individuals play mutually relating roles. First used in transactional analysis (Berne).

Guided fantasy An exercise in which a facilitator encourages others to imaginatively immerse themselves in a situation, following it in their minds as it unfolds.

Humanistic psychology This was invented to become a 'third way' – not psychoanalytic or behavioural – within psychology to have human values at its core. In therapeutic work the client's potential is uncovered during a process which stays close to the client's direct experience. A coming together of mind, body and spirit is valued.

Intergroup That which happens dynamically between groups.

Interpretation A term coined by Freud to describe an intervention made by an analyst to a patient, which typically brings into consciousness unconscious material.

Intrapsychic That which is found within the internal world of the individual.

Introjection A psychic mechanism in which an experience with another is taken into the self but not properly integrated into the psyche.

Libido This word is coined by Freud to describe energy (usually sexual in nature) within the psyche of an individual.

Maximize Facilitate the greatest potential of any given situation.

Metavision A view taken from outside the frame of reference of any given situation so as to understand it within its wider context.

Multicultural A situation or perspective in which many cultures are represented.

Nursing triad The mother and baby who 'nurse' are joined by the father who watches over and protects the two.

Oedipus theory A theory developed by Freud and named after the Greek myth. It descibes a desire experienced by children at the age of about 5 within their relationship to their parents. In fantasy and usually unconsciously the child wishes, like Oedipus in the myth, to kill his father and marry his mother. This may be regressively re-experienced in later life.

Organizational learning Learning evidenced by changes in organizations. This involves not just the sum of learning by individuals within the organization but learning which leads to changes within the whole organization and its culture.

Parallel process A process which happens in one situation or relationship is repeated in another.

Personal construct theory A theory which explores the way in which experience is organized between interrelating opposites.

Phenomenology A philosophical theory which is concerned with experienced phenomena.

Process The developing and unfolding dynamic within an individual or group.

Projection A term used to describe a state in which an individual denies or cuts off from an (usually painful or unacceptable) emotional response and seems to find it within someone else.

Psyche The Latin word for 'mind', usually used to mean the whole of the self-thinking emotional, spiritual and unconscious aspects as well as a conscious, thinking mind.

Psychoanalytic A school of psychotherapy which originates in the work of Sigmund Freud. A central tenet of psychoanalysis is that the psychoanalyst or psychotherapist works to understand and uncover unconscious material, which is typically discovered within the transference and counter-transference relationship.

Psychodynamic All forms of pychological and psychotherapeutic approaches which are informed by psychoanalytic thought.

Race A cultural concept to describe apparently different groups based on body types, colour of skin, facial features etc., which tend to occur in different geographical areas.

Racism A phenomenon in which prejudiced attitudes are carried by the dominant culture of 'race' to other cultures or 'races'. Institutionalized racism occurs when an organization or society is imbued with racist assumptions.

Restimulation A bodily and/or emotionally felt memory of past events (often but not necessarily unconscious), brought about by a similar event happening in the present.

Rogerian Ways of understanding or behaving which are guided by the theories of Carl Rogers. He advocated a *client-centred* approach that privileged the client's experience in guiding the therapist in understanding and working with them.

Role-play An improvized enactment of a situation by taking on roles and trying them out.

Scapegoat Originally a 'scapegoat' was literally a goat which stood in for a person as a sacrifice to the gods or God as if they carried the negative characteristics which made the sacrifice necessary. Similarly within the dynamics of a group an individual may symbolically carry certain negative traits or experiences for the group and be cast out or vilified by them as a defensive way of denying these in themselves.

Sculpting A technique first used in psychodrama in which a situation or dynamic is explored pictorially by placing members of the group to make a symbolic representation.

Shadow A term coined by Jung to denote the part of the personality that is denied and/ or split off. The shadow is understood to be an inevitable part of the personality and a corresponding counterpart to 'positive' aspects. In psychotherapy it is generally acknowledged that the shadow needs to be understood and come to terms with, rather than cast out, so that it does not have an unconscious influence and appear in the guise of destructive patterns.

Sociodrama A form of group work in which societal issues are largely explored through dramatic enactment and other action techniques. First used by Moreno.

Splitting A defence mechanism first described by Melanie Klein in which the psyche is split in such a way that one part is unaware of the other.

Stress A state of fatigue, ill health and (often) depression caused by distressing, strenuous and emotionally overwhelming pursuits. Typically the individual is out of balance between what is given out and what is restorative and recreational for themselves.

Supervision 'a quintessential interpersonal interaction with the general goal that one person, the supervisor, meets with another, the supervisee, in an effort to make the latter more effective in helping people' (Hess 1980). Group supervision happens within a group with a supervisor present. Team supervision is supervision of a whole team working together. Peer supervision happens within a group between peers who supervise each other in a reciprocal way. Unconscious supervision is an unconscious communication from patient/client to therapist, which corrects or affirms what is happening within the work.

Symbiotic A psychological state in which two people become emotionally merged as if they were the same person.

Therapeutic community An intentional community which exists to enhance the mental and emotional health of those who live within it, particularly patients/clients who have come there for that specific purpose.

Therapeutic triad The client, therapist and supervisor. A reference in made in this term to the nursing triad (see above). The supervisor is, therefore, in the role of the father.

Transactional analysis A psychotherapeutic theory and method founded by Eric Berne in which the psyche is understood to be divided into the three ego states of parent, adult and child and in which interactions are analysed, understood and changed to be more positive and life-enhancing.

Transcultural competence The ability to work effectively across cultural differences.

Transference Seeing a present situation/relationship through the emotional lens of a past situation/relationship. It is often used to describe the relationship that is developed by patients/clients in relation to their therapist, especially within psychoanalytic and psychodynamic schools. Multiple transference occurs in groups when a group member relates to several group members with different transferences.

Unconscious A state of mind which is not available to conscious thought. Unconscious communication is, therefore, that which is not mediated through thought and thus often non-verbal.

Appendix 1: British Association for Counselling and Psychotherapy: Criteria for Supervisors

Counselling supervisor accreditation criteria

Introduction
Candidates can be accredited as a Counselling Supervisor of Individuals *or* groups *or* both.

Standard route

Criteria
The Criteria for Accreditation of Counselling Supervisors through the 'standard route' requires that:

The candidate

1 Has current individual BACP membership.
2 Demonstrates practice which adheres to the Association's Ethical Framework for Good Practice in Counselling and Psychotherapy and undertakes to continue working within this framework.

Counselling experience

3 Is a BACP Accredited Counsellor or equivalent (as defined from time to time by BACP).
4 Has undertaken not less than 600 contact hours over three years with clients.
5 Has demonstrated in counselling supervision a capacity for safe and effective counselling practice.
6 Can show evidence of continuing professional development.

Supervisor experience

7.1 EITHER
Has satisfactorily completed a substantial structured training programme in supervision.
OR
Can show evidence that a programme of learning has been followed with a supervisor which ensures that the BACP Ethical Framework for Good Practice in Counselling and Psychotherapy is applied in his/her practice.

OR
Has achieved a nationally recognized standard of competence in counselling supervision.

7.2   Is currently practising as a counselling supervisor.
7.3   Has had a minimum of two years' practice as a counselling supervisor.
7.4   Has had regular supervision of the work in 7.3. from an experienced counselling supervisor.
7.5   Has completed a minimum of 180 contact hours with supervisees over a maximum of three years immediately prior to application.
8   Can provide evidence of a range of experience (i.e. work with trainees and experienced counsellors; counselling supervisory relationships begun, maintained and ended).
9   Can provide evidence of the way in which he/she uses his/her authority as a counselling supervisor to promote the safety of the client.
10   Can provide evidence of an identified theoretical framework in his/her practice.
11.1 Can demonstrate an awareness of the values, beliefs and assumptions which underpin his/her work.
11.2 Can provide evidence of a capacity for self-regulation.

Experienced Route

Criteria
The criteria for Accreditation of Counselling Supervisors through the 'Experienced Route' require that:

The candidate

1   Has current individual BACP membership.
2   Demonstrates practice which adheres to the Association's Ethical Framework for Good Practice in Counselling and Psychotherapy and undertakes to continue working within this framework.

Counselling experience

3.1   Is or has been either: a BACP Accredited Counsellor or can produce evidence to demonstrate previous eligibility for BACP Counsellor Accreditation; a BACP Fellow; a COSCA Accredited Counsellor; a United Kingdom Council for Psychotherapy Registrant; a British Psychological Society Chartered Counselling Psychologist or a British Confederation of Psychotherapists Registrant.
3.2   Has undertaken not less than 600 contact hours of counselling practice with clients.
3.3   Has demonstrated in counselling supervision a capacity for safe and effective practice.
4   Is in supervised practice as a counsellor at a minimum of 50 counselling hours per year.

Supervisor experience

5.1   Has worked for seven years as a counselling supervisor.

5.2   Is currently practising as a counselling supervisor.

5.3   Has completed a minimum of 180 contact hours with supervisees over a maximum of three years.

6   Can provide evidence of a range of experience (i.e. work with trainees and experienced counsellors; counselling supervisory relationships begun, maintained and ended).

7   Can provide evidence of the way in which he/she uses his/her authority as a counselling supervisor to promote the safety of the client.

8   Can provide evidence of an identified theoretical framework in his/her practice.

9   Can demonstrate an awareness of the values, beliefs and assumptions which underpin his/her work.

10   Can provide evidence of a capacity for self-regulation.

Resources

National organizations for supervision
British Association Supervision Practice and Research, 132 Princess Avenue, London W3 8LT
National organizations for counselling and psychotherapy
British Association for Counselling, BACP House, 35–37 Albert Street, Rugby, Warks, CV21 2SG.   0870 443 5252
United Kingdom Council for Psychotherapy, 2nd Floor, Edward House, 2 Wakley Street, London EC1V 7LT.   020 7014 9955
Organizations that offer training in supervision of counsellors and psychotherapists *(For a fuller list see Gilbert and Evans, (2000)*
Centre for Supervision & Team Development – www.cstd.co.uk
Cascade Training Associates (Brigid Proctor and Francesca Inskipp), Cascade Training Associates, 27 Gardener Street, Portslade, East Sussex, BN41 1SX.   01273 411654   *Audiotapes* Francesca Inskipp and Brigid Proctor *Tape 1   Skills for Supervisees* *Tapes 2 & 3   Skills for Supervisors.* from: Alexia Publications, 2 Market Terrace, St Leonards, E. Sussex TN38 ODB.
Francesca Inskipp and Brigid Proctor *The Art, Craft and Tasks of Counselling Supervision (2nd edn 2001).* Pt 1 Making the Most of Supervision. Workbook and 2 tapes for supervisees/ors Pt 2 Becoming a Supervisor. Workbook and 4 tapes for supervisors.

from: Cascade Publications, 4 Ducks Walk, Twickenham, Middx, TW1 2DD.
Metanoia Institute, 13 North Common Road, Ealing, London, W5 2QB.   020 8579 2505
Minster Centre, 20 Lonsdale Road, Queen's Park, London, NW6 6RD.   020 7644 6240
Northern Guild of Psychotherapy and Counselling, 77 Acklam Road, Stockton on Tees, Cleveland, TS17 7BD   01642 649004 (Joan McCormack)
Roehampton Institute, Department of Psychology, Digby Stuart College Roehampton Lane, Roehampton, London, SW15 5PH   020 8392 3213
The Sherwood Psychotherapy Training Institute, Thiskney House, 2 St James Terrace, Nottingham, NG1 6FW   0115 844 7904 (Hilary Drysdale)
Spectrum Therapy, 7 Endymion Road, Finsbury Park, London, N4 1EE. 020 8341 2277
The Tavistock Clinic, 120 Belsize Lane, London, NW3 5BA.   020 7435 7111
University of Leicester, Institute of Lifelong Learning, Vaughan College, St Nicholas Circle, Leicester, LE1 4LB.   0116 252 2455
wpf Training Department, 23 Kensington Square, London, W8 5HN. 020 7361 4846

In-house supervision training in the helping professions

Centre for Supervision and Team Development, www.cstd.co.uk info@cstd.co.uk
The Centre for Crisis Management and Education, Roselyn House, 93 Old Newton Road, Newbury, Berkshire, RG14 7DE.   01635–30644
GO education – The Group and Education Consultancy, 7 Cheverton Road, London, N19 3BB.
Impact Training and Consultation Ltd, Beverley House, Old Chelsea Lane, Failand, Bristol BS8 3UQ.   01275 394 774

For training in supervision for the other helping professions contact the appropriate professional organization:

Association for Professional Executive Coaching and Supervision (www.apecs.org)

British Association of Occupational Therapists, 106–114 Borough High Street, London, SE1 1LB.   020 7357 6480
British Association of Social Workers, 16 Kent Street, Birmingham, B5 6RD. 0121 622 3911
British Psychological Society, St Andrews House, 48 Princess Road East, Leicester, LE1 7DR.   0116 254 9568 (Dawn Schubert)
Central Council for Education and Training in Social Work, Central Office, Derbyshire House, St Chad's Street, London, WC1H 8AD.   0171 278 2455
CIPD Chartered Institute of Personnel and Development (www.cipd.co.uk)
E.M.C.C. European Mentoring and Coaching Council (www.emccouncil.org)
The Royal College of Speech Therapists, 7 Bath Place, Rivington Street, London, EC2A 3DR.   020 7613 3855
Council for Education and Training in Youth and Community Work, 17–23 Albion Street, Leicester, LEI 6GD.   0116 285 6789
National Association of Probation Officers, 4 Chivalry Road, Battersea, London SW11 1HT.   020 7223 4887
Royal College of Nursing, 20 Cavendish Square, London W1G 0RN. 020 7647 3700
Royal College of Psychiatrists, 17 Belgrave Square, London SWIX 8PG.   020 7235 2351

Feedback Request

We would welcome any feedback on this book and any suggestions of contributions for further editions or future publications. These should be sent to:

> Robin Shohet and Peter Hawkins
> Centre for Supervision and Team Development
> 19B Mcgregor Road
> London W.11 1DE
>
> info@cstd.co.uk
> www.cstd.co.uk

Bibliography

Ahmad, B. (1990) *Advanced Award for Supervisors: Implications for Black Supervisors*. London: CCETSW.

Albott, W. (1984) Supervisory characteristics and other sources of supervision variance. *The Clinical Supervisor*, 2(4), 27–41.

Aldridge, L. (1982) *Construction of a Scale for the Rating of Supervisors of Psychology*. Auburn University, USA.

American Association for Counseling and Development (1989) *Standards for Counseling Supervisors*: AACD.

Argyris, C. (1982) *Reasoning, Learning and Action: Individual and Organizational*. San Francisco: Jossey-Bass.

Argyris, C. and Schon, D. (1978) *Organizational Learning*. Reading MA: Addison-Wesley.

Arundale, J. (1993) *Psychotherapy Supervision: Impact, Practice and Expectations*. University of London.

Association for Counselor Education and Supervision (1989) *Standards for Counseling Supervisors*. Alexandria, VA: ACES.

Association for Counselor Education and Supervision (1993) *Ethical Guidelines for Counseling Supervisors*. Alexandria, VA: ACES.

Badaines, J. (1985) Supervision: methods and issues. Self and Society: *Journal of Humanistic Psychology*, XIII(2), 77–81.

Bandler, R. and Grinder, G. (1979) *Frogs Into Princes: Neuro Linguistic Programming*. Utah: Real People Press.

Bartell, P. A. and Rubin, L. J. (1990) Dangerous liaisons: sexual intimacies in supervision. *Professional Psychology: Research and Practice*, 21(6), 442–50.

Bateson, G. and Bateson, M. C. (1987) *Angels Fear: an Investigation into the Meaning of the Sacred*. London: Rider.

Bath Consultancy Group. *Expanding Your Range of Emotional Expression and Communication Skills*.

Beebe, D. and Jaffe, J., et al. (2002) A dyadic systems view of communication, in N. Skolnick and H. Warshow (eds) *Relational Perspectives in Psychoanalysis*. New Jersey: The Analytic Press.

Belbin, M. (1981) *Management Teams: Why they Succeed or Fail*. London: Heinemann.

Bennett, M. J. (1993) Towards ethnorelatativism: a developmental model of intercultural sensitivity, in R. M. Paige (ed.) *Education for the Intercultural Experience (2nd edn)*. Yarmouth, ME: Intercultural Press.

Bennis, W. and Nanus, B. (1985) *Leaders: The Strategies for Taking Charge*. New York: Harper & Row.

Bernard, J. M. (1994) Multicultural supervision: a reaction to Leong and Wagner, Cook, Priest and Fukuyama. *Counselor Education and Supervision*, 34, 159–71.

Bernard, J. M. (1994a) Ethical and legal dimensions of supervision, in L. D. Borders (ed.) *Supervision: Exploring the Effective Components*. Greensboro: University of North Carolina.

Bernard, J. M. (1994b) Multicultural supervision: a reaction to Leong and Wagner, Cook, Priest and Fukuyama. *Counselor Education and Supervision*, 34, 159–71.

Bernard, J. M. and Goodyear, R. (1992) *Fundamentals of Clinical Supervision*. Boston: Allyn & Bacon.

Bion, W. R. (1961) *Experiences in Groups*. London: Tavistock.

Bion, W. R. (1973) *Brazilian Lectures 1*. Rio de Janeiro: Imago Editora.

Bion, W. (1974) *Brazilian Lectures, 2*. Rio de Janeiro: Imago Editora.

Blake, R., Avis, W. and Mouton, J. (1966) *Corporate Darwinism*. Houston, Texas: Gulf Publishing.

Bohm, D. (1980) *Wholeness and the Implicate Order*. London: Routledge & Kegan Paul.

Bohm, D. (1987) *Unfolding Meaning*. London: Routledge & Kegan Paul.

Bohm, D. (1989) Meaning and information, in P. Pylkkanen (ed.) *The Search for Meaning*. Northamptonshire: Crucible/Thorsons.

Bohm, D. (ed.) (1994) *Thought as a System*. London, UK: Routledge.

Bond, M. and Holland, S. (1998) *Skills of Clinical Supervision for Nurses*. Buckingham: Open University Press.

Bond, T. (1993) *Standards and Ethics for Counselling*. London, UK: Sage.

Borders, L. D. (1994) *Supervision: Exploring the Effective Components*. Greensboro: University of North Carolina.

Borders, L. D. and Leddick, G.R. (1987) *Handbook of Counseling Supervision*. Alexandria, VA: Association for Counselor Education and Supervision.

Boyd, J. (1978) *Counselor Supervision: Approaches, Preparation, Practices*. Muncie, Indiana: Accelerated Development.

Bramley, W. (1996) *The Supervisory Couple in Broad-Spectrum Psychotherapy*. London: Free Association Books.

Brinkmann, U. and Weerdenburg, O.V. (1999) The Intercultural Development Inventory: a new tool for improving intercultural training? Paper presented at the Sietar Europe Conference, Trieste, Italy.

British Association for Counselling (1987) *How Much Supervision Should You Have?* Rugby: BACP.

British Association for Counselling (1990) *Information Sheet No. 8: Supervision*. Rugby: BACP.

British Association for Counselling (1995) *Code of Ethics and Practice for Supervisors of Counsellors*. Rugby: BACP.

Brown, A. (1984) *Consultation: An Aid to Effective Social Work*. London: Heinemann.

Brown, A. and Bourne, I. (1996) *The Social Work Supervisor*. Buckingham: Open University Press.

Burke, W. R., Goodyear, R. K. and Guzzard, C. R. (1998) Weakenings and repairs in supervisory alliances: multiple case study. *American Journal of Psychotherapy*, 52(4), 450–62.

Butler-Sloss, E. (1988) *Report of the Inquiry in Child Abuse in Cleveland 1987*: HMSO.

Butterworth, C. A. and Faugier, J. (eds) (1992) *Clinical Supervision and Mentorship in Nursing*. London: Chapman and Hall.

Campbell, B. (1988) *Unofficial Secrets: Child Sexual Abuse. The Cleveland Case*. London: Virago.

Capewell, E. (1996a) Staff care, in B. Lindsay and J. Tindall (eds) *Working with Children in Grief and Loss*. Newbury: Centre for Crisis Management and Education.

Capewell, E. (1996b). Handouts of Working with Trauma: Centre for Crisis Management and Education.

Caplan, G. (1970) The Theory and Practice of Mental Health Consultation. London: Tavistock.

Carifio, M. S. and Hess, A. K. (1987) Who is the ideal supervisor? *Professional Psychology: Research and Practice*, 18, 244–50.

Carroll, M. (1987) Privately circulated papers: Roehampton Institute, University of Surrey.

Carroll, M. (1994) Counselling supervision: international perspectives, in L. D. Borders (ed.) *Supervision: Exploring the Effective Components*. Greensboro: University of North Carolina.

Carroll, M. (1995) The stresses of supervising counsellors, in W. Dryden (ed.) *The Stresses of Counselling in Action*. London: Sage.

Carroll, M. (1996) *Counselling Supervision: Theory, Skills and Practice*. London, UK: Cassells.

Carroll, M. and Holloway, E. (1999) *Counselling Supervision in Context*. London, UK: Sage.

Carroll, M. and Tholstrup, M. (eds) (2001) *Integrative Approaches to Supervision*. London: Jessica Kingsley.

Casement, P. (1985) *On Learning from the Patient*. London: Routledge.

Casey, D. (1985) When is a team not a team? *Personnel Management*, 9.

Casey, D. (1993) *Managing Learning in Organizations*. Milton Keynes: Open University Press.

Centre for Supervision and Team Development (1999) *Supervision Workbook* www.cstd.co.uk.

Chen, E. C. and Bernstein, B.L. (2000) Relations of complementarity and supervisory issues to supervisory working alliance: a comparative analysis of two cases. *Journal of Counseling Psychology*, 47(4), 485–97.

Cherniss, C. (1980) *Staff Burnout: Job Stress in the Human Services*. Beverly Hills: Sage.

Cherniss, C. and Egnatios, E. (1978) Clinical supervision in community mental health. *Social Work*, 23(2), 219–23.

Claxton, G. (1984) *Live and Learn: An Introduction to the Psychology of Growth and Change in Everyday Life*. London: Harper & Row.

Clutterbuck, D. and Sweeney, J. (1998). Coaching and mentoring, in *Handbook of Management*. Hampshire: Gower.

Clynes, M. (1989) *Sentics: The Touch of the Emotions*. Dorset: Prism Unity.

Coche, E. (1977) Training of group therapists, in F. W. Kaslow (ed.) *Supervision, Consultation and Staff Training in the Helping Professions*. San Francisco: Jossey-Bass.

Conn, J. D. (1993) Delicate liaisons: the impact of gender differences on the supervisory relationship within social services. *Journal of Social Work Practice* (1), 41–53.

Cook, D. A. (1994) Racial identity in supervision. *Counselor Education and Supervision*, 34, 132–41.

Cook, D. A. and Helms, J.E. (1988) Visible racial/ethnic group supervisees' satisfaction with cross-cultural supervision as predicted by relationship characteristics. *Journal of Counseling Psychology*, 35(3), 268–74.

Cooperrider, D. et al. (2000) *Appreciative Inquiry: Rethinking Human Organization Towards a Positive View of Change*. Champaign, Illinois, USA: Stipes Publishing.

Cooperrider, D. L. and Srivastva, S. (1987) Appreciative inquiry in organizational life, in D. L. Cooperrider and S. Srivastva (eds) *Research in Organizational Change and Development* (Vol. 1). Cleveland Ohio: Journal of Appreciative Inquiry Press, pp. 129–69.

Covey, S. R. (1990) *Principle-Centred Leadership*. New York: Simon & Schuster.

Cushway, D. and Knibbs, J. (2004) Trainees' and supervisors' perception of supervision, in I. Fleming and L. Steen (eds) *Supervision and Clinical Psychology*. Hove: Brunner-Routledge.

Daniels, J. A. and Larson, L.M. (2001) The impact of performance feedback on counseling self-efficacy and counselor anxiety. *Counselor Education and Supervision*, 41(2), 120–31.

Dass, R. and Gorman, P. (1985) *How Can I Help?* London: Rider.

Davies, H. (1987) Interview with Robin Shohet.

De Mello, A. (1985) *One Minute Wisdom*. Anand, India: Gujarat Sahitya Prakash.

Dearnley, B. (1985) A plain man's guide to supervision. *Journal of Social Work Practice*, 2(1), 52–65.

Disney, M. J. and Stephens, A.M. (1994) *Legal Issues in Clinical Supervision*. Alexandria, VA: American Counseling Association.

Doehrman, M. J. (1976) Parallel processes in supervision and psychotherapy. *Bulletin of the Menninger Clinic*, 40(1).

Dryden, W. and Norcross, J.C. (1990) *Electicism and Integration in Counselling and Psychotherapy*: Gale Centre Publications.

Dryden, W. and Thorne, B. (eds) (1991) *Training and Supervision for Counselling in Action*. London: Sage.

Edelwich, J. and Brodsky, A. (1980) *Burn-Out*. New York: Human Sciences.

Ekstein, R. (1969) Concerning the teaching and learning of psychoanalysis. *Journal of the American Psychoanalytic Association*, 17(2), 312–32.

Ekstein, R. and Wallerstein, R. W. (1972) *The Teaching and Learning of Psychotherapy*. New York: International Universities Press.

Eleftheriadou, Z. (1994) *Transcultural Counselling*. London: Central Book Publishing Ltd.

Ellis, M. V. and Dell, D. M. (1986) Dimensionality of supervisor roles: supervisors' perceptions of supervision. *Journal of Counseling Psychology*, 33(3), 282–91.

Ernst, S. and Goddison, L. (1981) *In Our Own Hands: A Book of Self-Help Therapy*. London: The Women's Press.

Faith Regen (2005) *Faith Communities Toolkit*. London: Centre for Excellence in Leadership.

Farris, J. (2002) Some reflections on process, relationship, and personal development in supervision, in B. Campbell and B. Mason, (eds) *Perspectives on Supervision*. London: Karnac Books.

Feltham, C. and Dryden, W. (1994) *Developing Counsellor Supervision*. London: Sage.

Fineman, S. (1985) *Social Work Stress and Intervention*. Aldershot: Gower.

Fink, S. L., Beak, J. and Taddeo, K. (1971) Organizational crisis and change. *Journal of Applied Behavioral Science*, 17(1), 15–37.

Fisher, D. and Torbert, W.R. (1995) *Personal and Organizational Transformations*. London, UK: McGraw-Hill.

Fleming, I. and Steen, L. (eds) (2004) *Supervision and Clinical Psychology*. East Sussex: Brunner-Routledge.

Frankham, H. (1987) Aspects of supervision. Unpublished dissertation, University of Surrey.

Freeman, E. (1985) The importance of feedback in clinical supervision: implications for direct practice. *The Clinical Supervisor*, 3(1), 5–26.

Freitas, G. J. (2002) The impact of psychotherapy supervision on client outcome: a critical examination of two decades of research. *Psychotherapy*, 39(4), 354–67.

French, J. R. P. and Raven, B. (1959) The bases of social power, in D. Cartwright (ed.) *Studies in Social Power*. Ann Arbor, MI: Institute for Social Research.

Freud, S. (1927) The Future of an Illusion (Standard edn 21). London: Hogarth Press.

Friedlander, M. L. and Ward, L. G. (1984) Development and validation of the supervisory styles inventory. *Journal of Counseling Psychology*, 31(4), 541–57.

Friedlander, M. L., Siegel, S. and Brenock, K. (1989) Parallel processes in counseling and supervision: a case study. *Journal of Counseling Psychology*, 36, 149–57.

Fukuyama, M. A. (1994) Critical incidents in multicultural counseling supervision: a phenomenological approach to supervision research. *Counselor Education and Supervision*, 34(2), 142–51.

Galassi, J. P. and Trent, P. J. (1987) A conceptual framework for evaluating supervision effectiveness. *Counselor Education and Supervision*, June, 260–9.

Gallwey, W. T. (1997) *The Inner Game of Tennis*. New York: Random House.

Gardner, L. H. (1980) Racial, ethnic and social class considerations in psychotherapy supervision, in A. K. Hess (ed.) *Psychotherapy Supervision: Theory, Research and Practice*. New York: Wiley.

Garratt, B. (1987) *The Learning Organisation*. London: Fontana/Collins.

Geertz, C. (1973) *The Interpretation of Cultures*. New York: Basic Books.

Gendlin, E. (1978) *Focusing*. New York: Everest House.

Gilbert, M. and Evans, K. (2000) Psychotherapy Supervision *in Context: An Integrative Approach*. Buckingham: Open University Press.

Gitterman, A. and Miller, I. (1977). Supervisors as educators, in F. W. Kaslow (ed.) *Supervision, Consultation and Staff Training in the Helping Professions*. San Francisco: Jossey-Bass.

Glouberman, D. (2002) *The Joy of Burnout*. London: Hodder and Mobius.

Goldberg, C. (1981) The peer supervision group – an examination of its purpose and process: *Group* 5: 27–40.

Golembiewski, R. T. (1976) *Learning and Change in Groups*. London: Penguin.

Grindler, J. and Bandler, R. (1981) *Trance-Formations*. Utah: Real People Press.

Guardian Newspaper (1999). Front and back pages.

Guggenbuhl-Craig, A. (1971) *Power in the Helping Professions*. Dallas: Spring.

Hale, K. K. and Stoltenberg, C. D. (1988) The effects of self-awareness and evaluation apprehension on counselor trainee anxiety. *The Clinical Supervisor*, 6, 46–69.

Hammer, M. R. (1998) A measure of intercultural sensitivity: the intercultural development inventory, in S. M. Fowler and M.G. Mumford (eds) *The Intercultural Sourcebook: Cross-cultural training methods (Vol. 2)*. Yarmouth, ME: The Intercultural Press.

Handy, C. (1976) *Understanding Organizations*. London: Penguin.

Harrison, R. (1995) *The Collected Papers of Roger Harrison*. London: McGraw-Hill.

Hawkins, P. (1979) Staff learning in therapeutic communities, in R. Hinshelwood and N. Manning (eds) *Therapeutic Communities, Reflections and Progress*. London: Routledge & Kegan Paul.

Hawkins, P. (1980) Between Scylla and Charybdis, in E. Jansen (ed.) *The Therapeutic Community Outside of the Hospital*. London: Croom Helm.

Hawkins, P. (1982) Mapping it out. *Community Care*, 17–19.

Hawkins, P. (1985) Humanistic psychotherapy supervision: a conceptual framework. Self and Society: *Journal of Humanistic Psychology*, 13(2), 69–79.

Hawkins, P. (1986) *Living the Learning*. University of Bath.

Hawkins, P. (1988a) A phenomenological psychodrama workshop, in P. Reason (ed.) *Human Inquiry in Action*. London: Sage.

Hawkins, P. (1988b) The social learning approach to day and residential centres, in A. Brown and R. Clough (eds) *Groups and Groupings: Life and Work in Day and Residential Settings*. London: Tavistock.

Hawkins, P. (1991) The spiritual dimension of the learning organisation. *Management Education and Development*, 22(3).

Hawkins, P. (1993) *Shadow Consultancy*: Bath Consultancy Group.

Hawkins, P. (1994a) The changing view of learning, in J. Burgoyne (ed.) *Towards the Learning Company*. London, UK: McGraw-Hill.

Hawkins, P. (1994b) *Taking stock, facing the challenge*. Management Learning Journal, 25(1).

Hawkins, P. (1994c) *Organizational Culture Manual*: Bath Consultancy Group.

Hawkins, P. (1995) Supervision, in M. Jacobs (ed.) *The Care Guide*. London: Mowbrays.

Hawkins, P. (1997) Organizational culture: sailing between evangelism and complexity. *Human Relations*, 50(4).

Hawkins, P. (2005) *The Wise Fool's Guide to Leadership*. London: O Books.

Hawkins, P. (2006) Coaching Supervision, in J. Passmore (ed.) *Excellence in Coaching*. London: Kogan Page.

Hawkins, P. and Chesterman, D. (2006) *Every Teacher Matters*. London: Teacher Support Network.

Hawkins, P. and Smith, N. (2006) *Coaching, Mentoring and Organizational Consultancy: Supervision and Development*. Maidenhead: Open University Press.

Hawkins, P. and Maclean, A. (1991) *Action Learning Guidebook*: Bath Consultancy Group.

Hawkins, P. and Miller, E. (1994) Psychotherapy in and with organizations, in M. Pokorny and P. Clarkson (eds) *Handbook of Psychotherapy*. London: Routledge & Kegan Paul.

Hawkins, P. and Schwenk, G. (2006) Coaching Supervision. CIPD Change Agenda.

Hawkins, P. and Shohet, R. (1989, second edn 2000) Supervision in the Helping Profession. Milton Keynes: Open University Press.

Hawkins, P. and Shohet, R. (1991) Approaches to the supervision of counsellors, in W. Dryden (ed.) *Training and Supervision for Counselling in Action*. London: Sage.

Hawkins, P. and Shohet, R. (1993) A review of the addictive organisation by Schaef and Fassel. *Management Education and Development*, 24(2), 293–6.

Hawthorne, L. (1975) Games supervisors play. *Social Work*, 179–83.

Haynes, R., Corey, G. and Moulton, P. (2003) *Clinical Supervision in the Helping Professions*. CA: Thomson Brooks/Cole.

Herman, N. (1987) *Why Psychotherapy*? London: Free Association Books.

Heron, J. (1974) Reciprocal Counselling. Unpublished Human Potential Research Project. Guildford: University of Surrey.

Heron, J. (1975) Six-Category Intervention Analysis. Guildford: University of Surrey.

Heron, J. (1996) *Co-operative Inquiry: Research into the Human Condition*. London, Sage.

Heron, J. and P. Reason (2001) The Practice of Co-operative Inquiry, in P. Reason and H. Bradbury, *Handbook of Action Research*. London: Sage.

Herskowitz, M. J. (1948) *Man and his Works*. New York: Knopf.

Hess, A. K. (1987) Psychotherapy supervision: Stages, Buber and a theory of relationship. *Professional Psychology: Research and Practice*, 18(3), 251–9.

Hess, A. K. (ed.) (1980) *Psychotherapy Supervision: Theory, Research and Practice*. New York: Wiley.

Hickman, C. R. and Silva, M. A. (1985) *Creating Excellence*. London: Allen & Unwin.

Hillman, J. (1975) *Loose Ends*. Zurich: Spring Publications.

Hillman, J. (1979) *Insearch: Psychology and Religion*. Dallas, Texas: Spring.

Hinshelwood, R. and Manning, N. (1979) *Therapeutic Communities: Reflections and Progress*. London: Routledge & Kegan Paul.

Hofstede, G. (1980) *Culture's Consequences: International Differences in Work-related Values*. Beverly Hills, CA: Sage.

Hogan, R. A. (1964) Issues and approaches in supervision. *Psychotherapy: Theory, Research and Practice*, 1, 139–41.

Holloway, E. L. (1984) Outcome evaluation in supervision research. *The Counseling Psychologist*, 12(4), 167–74.

Holloway, E. L. (1987) Developmental models of supervision: is it development? *Professional Psychology: Research and Practice*, 18(3), 209–16.

Holloway, E. L. (1995) *Clinical Supervision: A Systems Approach*. USA: Sage.

Holloway, E. L., and Carroll, M. (eds) (1999) *Training Counselling Supervisors*. London, UK: Sage.

Holloway, E. L. and Gonzalez-Doupe, P. (2002) The learning alliance of supervision research to practice, in G. S. Tyron (ed.) *Counseling Based on Process Research: Applying What We Know*. Massachusetts: Allyn & Bacon.

Holloway, E. L. and Johnston, R. (1985) Group supervision: widely practised but poorly understood. *Counselor Education and Supervision* (24), 332–40.

Holloway, E. L. and Neufeldt, S. A. (1995) Supervision: its contributions to treatment efficacy. *Journal of Consulting and Clinical Psychology*, 63(2), 207–13.

Honey, P. and Mumford, A. (1992) *The Manual of Learning Styles*. Maidenhead: Peter Honey.

Houston, G. (1985) Group supervision of groupwork. Self and Society: *European Journal of Humanistic Psychology*, XIII(2), 64–6.

Houston, G. (1990) *Supervision and Counselling*. London: Rochester Foundation.

Hughes, L. and Pengelly, P. (1997) *Staff Supervision in a Turbulent Environment*. London: Jessica Kingsley.

Hunt, P. (1986) Supervision. *Marriage Guidance* (Spring), 15–22.

Illich, I. (1973) *Deschooling Society*. London: Penguin.

Inskipp, F. and Proctor, B. (1993) *The Art, Craft & Tasks of Counselling Supervision: Pt. 1: Making the Most of Supervision*. Twickenham, Middlesex: Cascade Publications.

Inskipp, F. and Proctor, B. (1995) *The Art, Craft & Tasks of Counselling Supervision: Pt. 2: Becoming a Supervisor*. Twickenham, Middlesex: Cascade Publications.

Jampolsky, G. (1979) *Love is Letting Go of Fear*. Berkeley, CA: Celestial Arts.

Jampolsky, G. (1999) *Forgiveness: The Greatest Healer of All*. Hillsboro, OR: Beyond Words Publishing.

Jones, M. (1982) *The Process of Change*. London: Routledge & Kegan Paul.

Jourard, S. (1971) *The Transparent Self*. New York: Van Nostrand.

Juch, B. (1983) *Personal Development*. Chichester: Wiley.

Kaberry, S. E. (1995) *Abuse in Supervision*. University of Birmingham.

Kadushin, A. (1968) Games people play in supervision. *Social Work*, 13.

Kadushin, A. (1976 and 1992) *Supervision in Social Work*. New York: Columbia University Press.

Kadushin, A. (1977) *Consultation in Social Work*. New York: Columbia University Press.

Kadushin, A. (1992) *Supervision in Social Work (3rd edn)*. New York: Columbia University Press.

Kagan, N. (1980) Influencing human interaction – eighteen years with IPR, in A. K. Hess (ed.) *Psychotherapy Supervision: Theory, Research and Practice*. New York: Wiley.

Kareem, J. and Littlewood, R. (1992) *Intercultural Therapy: Themes, Interpretations and Practice*. Oxford: Blackwell Science.

Karpman, S. (1968) Fairy tales and script drama analysis (selected articles). *Transactional Analysis Bulletin*, 7(26), 39–43.

Kaslow, F. W. (ed.) (1977) *Supervision, Consultation and Staff Training in the Helping Professions.* San Francisco: Jossey-Bass.

Katzenbach, J. R. and Smith, D. K. (1993) *The Wisdom of Teams: Creating High Performance Organization.* Boston: Harvard Business School Press.

Kelly, G. A. (1955) *The Psychology of Personal Constructs* (Vols 1 and 2). New York: Norton.

Kemshall, A. (1995) Supervision and appraisal in the probation service, in J. Pritchard (ed.) *Good Practice in Supervision.* London: Jessica Kingsley.

Kevlin, F. (1987) Interview with Robin Shohet.

Kevlin, F. (1988) *Peervision. A Comparison of Hierarchial Supervision of Counsellors with Consultation amongst Peers.* University of Surrey, London.

Khan, M. A. (1991) Counselling psychology in a multicultural society. *Counselling Psychology Review*, 6(3), 11–13.

Kluckhohn, F. R. and Stodtbeck, F. L. (1961) *Variations in Value Orientations.* New York: Row, Peterson and Co.

Kolb, D. A., Rubin, I. M. and McIntyre, J. M. (1971) *Organizational Psychology: an Experimental Approach.* New York, NY: Prentice Hall.

Kolb, D. (1984) *Experiential Learning: Experience as the source of Learning and Development.* London: Prentice Hall.

Krause, I. (1998) *Therapy Across Culture*: Sage.

Ladany, N. (2004) Psychotherapy supervision: what lies beneath. *Psychotherapy Research*, 14(1), 1–19.

Ladany, N., Ellis, M. V. and Friedlander, M. L. (1999) The supervisory working alliance, trainee self-efficacy and satisfaction. *Journal of Counseling and Development*, 77, 447–55.

Lago, C. and Thompson, J. (1996) *Race, Culture and Counselling.* Great Britain: Open University Press.

Lambert, M. J. and Arnold, R. C. (1987) Research and the supervisory process. *Professional Psychology: Research and Practice*, 18(3), 217–24.

Langs, R. (1978) *The Listening Process.* New York: Jason Aronson.

Langs, R. (1983) *The Supervisory Experience.* New York: Jason Aronson.

Langs, R. (1985) *Workbook for Psychotherapists.* Emerson, New Jersey: Newconcept Press.

Langs, R. (1994) *Doing Supervision and Being Supervised.* London: Karnac Books.

Leddick, R. and Dye, H. A. (1987) Effective supervision as portrayed by trainee expectations and preferences. *Counselor Education and Supervision*, 27, 139–54.

Leong, F. T. L. and Wagner, N. S. (1994) Cross-cultural counseling supervision: What do we know? What do we need to know? *Counselor Education and Supervision*, 34, 117–131.

Lewin, K. (1952) Defining the field at a given time, in D. Cartwright (ed.) *Field Theory in Social Sciences.* London: Tavistock.

Liddle, B. J. (1986) Resistance to supervision: a response to perceived threat. *Counselor Education and Supervision*, 117–27.

Lievegoed, B. C. J. (1973) *The Developing Organisations.* London: Tavistock.

Lindsay, G. and Clarkson, P. (1999) Ethical dilemmas of psychotherapists. *The Psychologist*, 12(4), 182–5.

Liss, J. (1985) Using mime and re-enactment to supervise body orientated therapy. *Self and Society: Journal of Humanistic Psychology*, XIII(2), 82–5.

Loganbill, C., Hardy, E. and Delworth, U. (1982) Supervision, a conceptual model. *The Counseling Psychologist*, 10(1), 3–42.

Loizos, P. (2002) Misconceiving refugees, in R. K. Papadopoulos (ed.) *Therapeutic Care for Refugees: No Place like Home*. London: Karnac Books.

Marken, M. and Payne, M. (eds) (1988) Enabling and Ensuring: Supervision in practice. Leicester: National Youth Bureau and Council for Education and Training in Youth and Community Work.

Marshall, J. (1982) Job Stressors: Recent Research in a Variety of Occupations, 20th International Congress of Applied Psychology. Edinburgh.

Martin, J. S., Goodyear, R. K. and Newton, F. B. (1987) Clinical supervision: an intensive case study. *Professional Psychology: Research and Practice*, 18(3), 225–35.

Martindale, B., Morner, M., Rodriquez, M. E. C. and Vidit, J. (1997) *Supervision and its Vicissitudes*. London: Karnac Books.

Maslach, C. (1982) Understanding burnout: definitional issues in analysing a complex phenomenon, in W. S. Paine (ed.) *Job Stress and Burnout*. Beverley Hills: Sage.

Matthews, S. and Treacher, A. (2004) Therapy models and supervision in clinical psychology, in I. Fleming and L. Steen, (eds) *Supervision and Clinical Psychology: Theory, Practice and Perspectives*. Hove: Brunner-Routledge.

Mattinson, J. (1975) *The Reflection Process in Casework Supervision*. London: Institute of Marital Studies.

McBride, M. C. and Martin, G. E. (1986) Dual-focus supervision: a nonapprenticeship approach. *Counselor Education and Supervision*, 25(3), 175–82.

McLean, A. (1986) *Access Organization Cultures*: University of Bath.

McLean, A. and Marshall, J. (1988) *Working with Cultures: A Workbook for People in Local Government*. Luton: Local Government Training Board.

Mearns, D. (1991) On being a supervisor, in W. Dryden and B. Thorne (eds) *Training and Supervision for Counselling in Action*. London: Sage.

Menzies, I. E. P. (1970) *The Functions of Social Systems as a Defence Against Anxiety*. London: Tavistock Institute of Human Relations.

Mintz, E. (1983) Gestalt approaches to supervision. *Gestalt Journal*, 6(1), 17–27.

Modood, T., Berthoud, R. et al. (1997) *Ethnic Minorities in Britain: Diversity and Disadvantage*. London: Policy Studies Institute.

Morgan, G. (1986) *Images of Organization*. London: Sage.

Morrison, T. (1993) *Staff Supervision in Social Care: An Action Learning Approach*. London: Longman.

Munson, C. E. (1987) Sex roles and power relationships in supervision. *Professional Psychology: Research and Practice*, 18(3), 236–43.

Nelson, M. L. and Holloway, E. L. (1990) Relation of gender to power and involvement in supervision. *Journal of Counseling Psychology*, 37, 473–81.

O'Toole, L. (1987) *Counselling skills and self-awareness training: their effect on mental well-being and job satisfaction in student nurses*. Guildford: University of Surrey.

Oshry, B. (1996) *Seeing Systems*. San Francisco: Berret Koehler.

Page, S. (1999) *Shadow and the Counsellor*. London: Routledge.

Page, S. and Wosket, V. (1994) *Supervising the Counsellor: A Cyclical Model*. London, UK: Routledge.

Papadopoulos, R. K. (2002) Refugees, home and trauma, in R. K. Papadopoulos (ed.) *Therapeutic Care for Refugees: No Place like Home*. London: Karnac Books.

Papadopoulos, R. K. and Byng-Hall, J. (1997) *Multiple Voices: Narrative in Systemic Family Psychotherapy*. London: Duckworth.

Parker, M. (1990) Supervision Constructs and Supervisory Style and Related to Theoretical Orientation. Guildford: University of Surrey.

Patton, M. J. and Kivlighan, D. M. (1997) Relevance of the supervisory alliance to the counseling alliance and to treatment adherence in counselor training. *Journal of Counseling Psychology*, 44(1), 108–15.

Payne, C. and Scott, T. (1982) *Developing Supervision of Teams in Field and Residential Social Work* (No. 12). London: National Institute for Social Work.

Pederson, B. P. (1997) *Culture-Centred Counselling Interventions*. London: Sage.

Pederson, B. P. (ed.) (1985) *Handbook of Cross-Cultural Counselling and Therapy*. London: Praeger.

Peters, T. J. and Waterman, R. H. (1982) *In Search of Excellence*. New York: Harper & Row.

Peterson, F. K. (1991) *Race and Ethnicity*. New York: Haworth.

Philipson, J. (1982) *Practising Equality: Women, Men and Social Work*. London: CCETSW.

Pines, A. M., Aronson, E. and Kafry, D. (1981) *Burnout: From Tedium to Growth*. New York: The Free Press.

Plant, R. (1987) *Managing Change and Making it Stick*. London: Fontana/Collins.

Ponterotto, J. G. and Zander, T. A. (1984) A multimodal approach to counselor supervision. *Counselor Education and Supervision*, 24, 40–50.

Pope, K. S. and Vasquez, M. J. T. (1991) *Ethics in Psychotherapy and Counseling: A Practical Guide for Psychologists*. San Francisco: Jossey-Bass.

Pritchard, J. (ed.) (1995) *Good Practice in Supervision*. London: Jessica Kingsley.

Proctor, B. (1988a) *Supervision a Working Alliance* (videotape training manual). St Leonards-on-Sea, East Sussex: Alexia Publications.

Proctor, B. (1988b) Supervision: a co-operative exercise in accountability, in M. Marken and M. Payne (eds) *Enabling and Ensuring*. Leicester: Leicester National Youth Bureau and Council for Education and Training in Youth and Community Work.

Proctor, B. (1997) Contracting in supervision, in C. Sills (ed.) *Contracts in Counselling*. London: Sage.

Proctor, B. (2000) *Group Supervision: A Guide to Creative Practice*. London: Sage.

Ramos-Sanchez, L., Esnil, E., Riggs, S., Goodwin, A., Touster, L.O., Wright, L.K., Ratanasiripong, P. and Rodolfa, E. (2002) Negative supervisory events: effects on supervision satisfaction and supervisory alliance. *Professional Psychology: Research and Practice*, 33(2), 197–202.

Reason, P. (1988) *Human Inquiry in Action*. London, UK: Sage.

Reason, P. (1994) *Participation in Human Inquiry*. London, UK: Sage.

Reason, P. and Bradbury, H. (eds) (2001) *Handbook of Action Research*. London: Sage.

Reason, P. and Bradbury, H. (2004) Action Research: Purpose, Vision and Mission. *Action Research* 2(1).

Revans, R. W. (1982) *The Origins and Growth of Action Learning*. London, UK: Chartwell-Bratt, Bromley & Lund.

Richards, M., Payne, C. and Sheppard, A. (1990) *Staff Supervision in Child Protection Work*. London: National Institute for Social Work.

Ridley, C. R. (1995) *Overcoming Unintentional Racism in Counselling and Therapy. A Practioner's Guide to Intentional Intervention*. London: Sage.

Rioch, M. J., Coulter, W. R. and Weinberger, D. M. (1976) *Dialogues for Therapists* (1st edn). San Francisco: Jossey-Bass.

Rogers, C. R. (1957) The necessary and sufficient conditions of therapeutic personality change. *Journal of Counseling Psychology*, 21, 95–103.

Rosinski, P. (2003) *Coaching Across Cultures*. London & Boston: Nicholas Breatey Publishing.

Rowan, J. (1983) *Reality Game: A Guide to Humanistic Counselling and Therapy*. London: Routledge & Kegan Paul.

Ryan, S. (2004) *Vital Practice*. Dorset: Sea Change.

Ryde, J. (1997) *A Step Towards Understanding Culture in Relation to Psychotherapy*. Bath: Bath Centre for Psychotherapy and Counselling.

Ryde, J. (2004) *BCPC Refugee and Asylum Seeker's Project 2004 Snapshot Review*. Bath: Bath Centre for Psychotherapy and Counselling.

Ryde, J. (2005) Exploring White Racial Identity and its Impact on Psychotherapy and the Psychotherapy Professions. University of Bath, PhD thesis.

Sansbury, D. L. (1982) Developmental supervision from a skills perspective. *The Counseling Psychologist*, 10(1), 53–7.

Savickas, M. L., Marquart, C. D. and Supinski, C.R. (1986) Effective supervision in groups. *Counselor Education and Supervision*, 26(1), 17–25.

Scaife, J. (2001) *Supervision in the Mental Health Professions*. Hove: Brunner-Routledge.

Scaife, J., Inskipp, F., Scaife, J., Walsh, S. and Proctor, B. (2001) *Supervision in the Mental Health Professions: A Practitioner's Guide*. East Sussex: Brunner-Routledge.

Schaef, A. W. (1992) *When Society Becomes an Addict*. Northamptonshire: Thorsons.

Schaef, A. W. and Fassel, D. (1990) *The Addictive Organization*. San Francisco: Harper & Row.

Schein, E. H. (1985) *Organizational Culture and Leadership*. San Francisco, LA: Jossey-Bass.

Schon, D. (1983) *The Reflective Practitioner*. New York, NY: Basic Books.

Schroder, M. (1974) *The Shadow Consultant. The Journal of Applied Behavioral Science*, 10(4), 579–94.

Schutz, W. C. (1973) *Elements of Encounter*. Big Sur, CA: Joy Press.

Scott Peck, M. (1978) *The Road Less Travelled*. New York: Simon & Schuster Inc.

Searles, H. F. (1955) The informational value of the supervisor's emotional experience, in *Collected Papers of Schizophrenia and Related Subjects*. London: Hogarth Press.

Searles, H. F. (1975) The patient as therapist to his analyst, in R. Langs (ed.) *Classics in Psychoanalytic Technique*. New York: Jason Aronson.

Self and Society vol. 33, No. 7, April-May 2005.

Senge, P. (1990) *The Fifth Discipline: The Art and Practice of The Learning Organization*. New York: Doubleday.

Shainberg, D. (1983) Teaching therapists to be with their clients, in J. Westwood (ed.) *Awakening the Heart*. Colorado: Shambhala.

Sharpe, M. (ed) (1995) *The Third Eye: Supervision of Analytic Groups*. London: Routledge.

Shearer, A. (1983) Who Saves the Social Workers? *Guardian*, 6 July.

Shipton, G. (1997) *Supervision of Psychotherapy and Counselling: Making a Place to Think*. Buckingham: Open University Press.

Shohet, R. (1985) *Dream Sharing*. Wellingborough: Turnstone Press.

Shohet, R. and Wilmot, J. (1991) The key issue in the supervision of counsellors, in W. Dryden and B. Thorne (eds) *Training and Supervision for Counselling in Action*. London: Sage.

Shohet, R. (2005) Passionate Medicine London: Jessica Kingsley Publishers.

Shohet R. (forthcoming) Passionate Supervision. London: Jessica Kingsley Publishers.

Shulman, L. (1993) Interactional Supervision. Washington DC: NASW Press.

Skovholt, T. M. and Ronnestad, M. H. (1995) The Evolving Professional Self: Stages and Themes in Therapist and Counselor Development. Chichester: Wiley.

Smith, D. (1985) The client as supervisor: the approach of Robert Langs. Self and Society: European Journal of Humanistic Psychology, XIII(2), 92–5.

Spice, C. G. J. and Spice, W. H. (1976) A triadic method of supervision in the training of counselors and counseling supervisors. Counselor Education and Supervision, 15(251–8).

Stevens, A. (1991) Disability Issues: Developing Anti-discriminatory Practice. London: CCETSW.

Stolorow, R. G., Atwood, G. E. and Orange, D. (2002) Worlds of Experience: Interweaving Philosophical and Clinical Dimensions in Psychoanalysis. New York: Basic Books.

Stoltenberg, C. and Delworth, U. (1987) Supervising Counselors and Therapists: A Developmental Approach. San Francisco: Jossey-Bass Wiley.

Subby, R. (1984) Inside the chemically dependent marriage: denial and manipulation, in Co-dependence: An Emerging Issue. Hollywood Beach, Florida: Health Communications.

Sue, D. W. and Sue, D. (1990) Counseling the Culturally Different: Theory and Practice. New York: Wiley.

Symington, N. (1986) The Analytic Experience: Lectures from the Tavistock. London: Free Association Books.

Teitelbaum, S. H. (1990) Supertransference: the role of the supervisor's blind spots. Psychoanalytic Psychology, 7(2), 243–58.

Thompson, J. (1991) Issues of Race and Culture in Counselling Supervision Training Courses. Polytechnic of East London.

Thompson, N. (1993) Anti-Discriminatory Practice. London: BASW/Macmillan.

Tichy, N. M. (1997) The Leadership Engine: How Winning Companies Build Leaders at Every Level. New York: HarperCollins.

Tonnesmann, M. (1979) The Human Encounter in the Helping Professions. Paper presented at the London Fourth Winnicott Conference, London, UK, March.

Trivasse, M. (2003) Counselling through an interpreter. Counselling and Psychotherapy Journal, 14(4), 21–2.

Trompenaars, A. (1994) Riding the Waves of Culture. Burr Ridge, IL: Irwin.

Tuckman, B. (1965) Developmental sequence in small groups. Psychological Bulletin, 63(6), 384–99.

Tudor, K. and Worrall, M. (2004) Freedom to Practice: Person-centred Approaches to Supervision. Ross on Wye: PCCS Books.

Tyler, F. B., Brome, D. R. and Williams, J. E. (1991) Ethnic Validity, Ecology and Psychotherapy: A Psychosocial Competence Model. New York: Plenum Press.

van Ooijen, E. (2003) Clinical Supervision Made Easy: A Practical Guide for the Helping Professions – The 3-Step Method. Oxford: Churchill Livingstone.

van Weerdenburg, O. (1996) Thinking values through and through, in B. Conraths (ed.) Training the Fire Brigade: Preparing for the Unimaginable. Brussels, Belgium: efdm.

Weiler, N. W. and Schoonover, S. C. (2001) Your Soul at Work. Boston: Paulist Press.

Wester, S. R., Vogel, D. L. and Archer, J. (2004) Male restricted emotionality and counseling supervision. Journal of Counseling and Development, 82(1), 91–8.

Whitehead, A. N. and Russell, B. (1910–13) Principia Mathematica. Cambridge: Cambridge University Press.

Whitmore, J. (1992) *Coaching for Performance: A Practical Guide to Growing Your Own Skills.* London: Nicholas Brealey.

Wilmot, J. and Shohet, R. (1985) Paralleling in the supervision process. *Self and Society: European Journal of Humanistic Psychology*, XIII(2), 86–92.

Winnicott, D. W. (1965) *Maturational Processes and the Facilitating Environment.* London, UK: Hogarth Press.

Winnicott, D. W. (1971) *Playing and Reality.* London: Tavistock.

Woodcock, J. (2005) Can work with trauma harm psychotherapists? Paper presented at the Centre for Psychosocial Studies, University of West of England.

Worthington, E. L. (1987) Changes in supervision as counselors and supervisors gain experience: a review. *Professional Psychology: Research and Practice*, 18(3), 189–208.

Yalom, I. (2002) *The Gift of Therapy: An Open Letter to a New Generation of Therapists and Their Patients.* New York: HarperCollins.

Index

about this book
  audiences 6–7
  foci of individual parts 5–6, 219
  structure 5–6
  themes 6–7, 219
accreditation
  standard route for 227–8
  of supervisors 147–8
action agreement 61, 62
action learning 19, 130, 136, 139, 148, 207, 222
action research 76–9
  built in 78–9
active listening 61, 62
The Addictive Organization (Schaef, A.W. and Fassel, D.) 199
addictive organizations 196, 199–201
advantages of
  group supervision 152, 168
  peer supervision 165–6
  team supervision 163
Albott, W. 50
Aldridge, L. 50
'Anti-Discrimination and Oppression in Supervision' (CSTD) 112
anti-discrimination practices 222
anti-oppressive practices 54–5, 151, 216, 222
anxiety
  anxieties of supervise in supervision 37
  management of 50
  multiple transference and 186–7
appraisal 222
appreciative inquiry 203–5
  stimulation of 209, 210
appropriate authority 112–13
appropriateness, skill of 99–100
aradford.co.uk 15
Argyris, C. and Schon, D. 37, 77–8, 194
arrangement
  arrangements for supervision 68
  of supervision needs 34–5
assessment
  of learning needs 125–9
  supervisees' anxieties 38
associations, supervisee's use of 92
asylum seekers 120–23

audit and review in practice development 216
authority
  difficulties with 37
  in group supervision 171–2
  taking appropriate 53–4

back watching in organizations 196, 198
BACP (British Association for Counselling and Psychotherapy)
  criteria for supervisors 227–9
  ground rules for supervision 57
Bandler, R. and Grinder, G. 70
Barrett, R. 204
BCPC (Bath Centre for Psychotherapy and Counselling) 121–3, 201
Beebe, Jaffe et al 77
behaviourist 69, 222
behind the back, response sharing 160
Belbin, M. 164
Bennett, Dr Milton 108
Bernard, J.M. 52
Berne, Eric 53–4
Bion, Wilfred R. 8, 85, 171
blind spots in supervision 69
blocks to appropriate supervision 36–40
Bohm, David 205–6, 207
Bond, M. and Holland, S. 4, 40, 136
Borders, L.D. and Leddick, G.R. 35, 130–31
boundaries
  confidentiality boundaries 65
  in contract formation 64–5
  of supervision, understanding of 51
Boyd, J. 69
brainstorming 87
Bramley, W. 55
Brinkmann, U. and Weerdenburg, O.V. 108
British Association of Counselling and Psychotherapy *see* BACP
Brown, A. 203
Brown, A. and Bourne, I. 4, 29–30, 67, 109, 111
bucket theory of containment and displacement 183–5
bureaucratic efficiency, striving for 196, 197–8
burn-out 222
  apathy and 28

avoidance of 27–9
betrayal and 29
depression and 28
disillusionment and 28
Butler-Sloss, Dame Elizabeth 189–90

Campbell, B. 190
capabilities of supervisors 126–7
capacities of supervisors 126–7, 128
Capewell, E. 30
Carifio, M.S. and Hess, A.K. 50
caring
    caretaking 10
    desire to help, fundamental nature of 14
    expectations in role of 8–9
    exploration of motivations towards 10–11
    healer-patient archetype 11
    healing wish, fundamental nature of 14
    helping roles of supervisors 52–3
    humility in 9–10
    Jungian 'shadow side' and 8–10
    motivations towards 8–14
    needs, meeting helper's own needs 13–14
    non-attachment 9–10
    power
        discrepancy in feelings of 11–12
        potential misuse of 12
    understanding motives, relevance of 11–12
Carroll, M. and Holloway, E. 4, 109, 120
Carroll, Michael 4, 52, 55, 63, 67, 75, 144, 146
case notes, dealing with 67
Casement, Patrick 16–17, 78, 90, 110, 114
Casey, D. 162
catalytic intervention 61, 135–6
cathartic intervention 135–6
change
    defensive retreat from 214
    factors fuelling resistance to 212
    phases of response to 213–14
    political support for change, maximization of 211
    resistances to change, dealing with 210, 212–14
    'top-down' or 'bottom-up' 211
Cherniss, C. and Egnatios, E. 32
Chesterman, D. 30
CIPD (Chartered Institute of People Development) 76
Claxton, Guy 17–18, 131
CLEAR supervision model 61–3
Cleveland sexual abuse case 189–91
clients
    client-centred level in supervisee development 72–3
    client context, focusing on 97

client/supervisee matrix 81–2
client/supervisee relationship, exploration of 83, 88–90, 114, 115–16
    describing clients 85
    focus on what and how they present 82, 84–6, 114–15
    learning from the client 89
    transference by, attending to 89
co-counselling 91, 142, 222
co-dependence 200
co-learning 24
Co-operative Inquiry 77
Coche, E. 50
Code of Ethics and Practice for Supervisors of Counsellors (British Association of Counselling) 55
collusive transactions 53
comparatives, supervisee's use of 92
competences of supervisors 126–7
competition in group supervision 171–2
complexity of supervision 5–6
compulsive pragmatism 20
confidentiality boundaries 65
confrontative interventions 135–6
congruence 26, 50, 93, 127, 222
consultancy supervision 60
containment, bucket theory of 183–5
continuity in supervision learning 215
continuous research 78–9
contract formation
    boundaries 64–5
    case notes, dealing with 67
    clarity in 63
    confidentiality boundaries 65
    contract negotiation 67–8
        CLEAR model 61, 62
    exploratory contract interview, outline for 67–8
    face-to-face work 64
    key areas 63
    meeting arrangements 64
    note taking 66–7
    organizational context 66
    practicalities 64
    professional context 66
    session format 66
    working alliance 65
contracting
    contract (glossary entry) 222
    early stage contracting for group supervision 153
    for group supervision 157
    within group supervision 175–6
    for supervision needs 34–5
Cooperrider, D.L. 15

Cooperrider, D.L. and Srivastva, S. 197
Cooperrider, D.L. et al 207, 210
counselling
   and coaching skills 50
   increase in use of 3–4
counter-transference 90–92, 222
crisis driven organizations 196, 198–9
cross-cultural and transcultural work 105
CSTD (Centre for Supervision and Team
   Development) 112
cultures 222–3
   acknowledgement of cultural difference
      108–9
   awareness in supervision of cultural difference
      109–10, 119
   awareness of organizational cultures 201
   cultural blocks to appropriate supervision 39
   cultural orientations 107–8
   cultural power 111–12
   dealing with cultural assumptions 145, 146
   explanation of 194–5
   lack of cultural neutrality 119–20
   levels of culture 195–6
   organizational culture 194–6, 196–201
   particularist response to culture 105
   perceptions of cultural difference 110
   understanding culture 106

Dass, Ram and Gorman, Paul 8–9
Davies, H. 86
De Mello, A. 220
deaf spots in supervision 69
Dearnley, Barbara 11–12, 96, 131
decision making, process for ethical 55
defensive routines against supervision 36–7
degenerate supervision 196–201
depression 27–8, 89, 115, 121, 186–7, 225
desensitization to triggers 143
development
   developing and resourcing ourselves 16–24
   developmental approach to supervision
      70–75
   developmental function in supervision 57–8,
      59, 60
   of supervision policy 209–16
   of transcultural supervision 119–20
Dialogues for Therapists (Rioch, M.) 170
difference
   acknowledgement of cultural difference 108–
      9
   awareness in supervision cultural difference
      109–10, 119
   perceptions of cultural difference 110
   power and difference 111–13, 123

in relation to seven modes of supervision
   114–18
dimensions of relating 21–3
disadvantages of
   group supervision 152–3, 168–9
   peer supervision 165–6
   team supervision 163
displacement, bucket theory of 183–5
distancing, detachment and 88–9
Doehrman, Margery 94–5
double loop learning 78
double matrix model of supervision process
   80–103
drama therapy 223
dream groups 173
dumb spots in supervision 69
dynamics 223
   of groups
      group supervision 171–3
      peer supervision 170–79
      team supervision 170–79
   of organizational culture, degenerate
      supervision and 196–201

Edelwich, J. and Brodsky, A. 28
Ekstein, R. 69
Ekstein, R. and Wallerstein, R.W. 37, 219–20
Eleftheriadou, Z. 105
Ellis, M.V. and Dell, D.M. 52
Emerson, William 142
emotional stress 27
emotional well-being 21
empathy 223
engagement with others 21–3
estrangement 176–7
ethics
   ambiguities of ethical decisions 146
   creation of ethical sensitivity 146
   ethical principles 54–5
   implementation of ethical decisions 146
   moral actions, formulation of courses of 146
   training in ethical dilemmas 144, 146
ethnic 223
ethnocentric 223
   and ethnorelative development 108–9
evaluation of supervisors 147–8
   by supervisees 35
Evans, K. and Gilbert, M. 119
expectations in role of caring 8–9
experienced route for accreditation 228–9
experiences and expectations of supervisors 49,
   50–51, 52
experiential training of supervisors 130–31
experiments in development of supervision
   policy, initiation of 210, 211–12

exploration
  of dynamics of groups 170–79
  of motivations towards caring 10–11
  and reflection in supervision 61, 62
  of supervision 133
exploratory contract interview, outline for 67–8

face-to-face work 64
Facing the Truth (BBC TV) 220
faith and truth in supervision 220
faith communities, working across 110–11
Faith Communities Toolkit (Faith Regen) 111
fear and negativity in supervision 4–5
fearless compassion 220
feedback
  giving and receiving of 134–5
  in group supervision 176
Fineman, Steve 12, 28, 37, 38, 47, 164, 198
Fink, S.L. et al 213–14
Fleming, I. and Steen, L. 4, 76
flexibility in supervisors 50
focus for good supervision 51–2
force-field analysis 212–13, 223
forgiveness, importance of 219
frameworks for supervising
  choice of 79
  development of 51–2
Freeman, E. 134–5
French, J.R.P. and Raven, B. 112
Freud, Sigmund 84–5
fudge factors 99
The Functioning of Social Systems (Menzies, I.) 197
functions of supervision 4, 57–60

Gallwey, W.T. 17
game 223
Garratt, Bob 211
Geertz, Clifford 195
generative learning in supervision 206–7
Gilbert, M. and Evans, K. 4, 37, 50, 99, 109
Gittermann, A. and Miller, I. 50
Glouberman, D. 28
'good enough' supervision 3
group supervision 151–69
  advantages of 152, 168
  authority in 171–2
  behind the back, response sharing 160
  climate setting for 157–8
  competition in 171–2
  contracting for 157
  contracting within 175–6
  course in group and team supervision 138–9
  disadvantages of 152–3, 168–9
  dream groups 173
  dynamics of groups 171–3

early stage contracting for 153
  estrangement 176–7
  exploration of dynamics of groups 170–79
  feedback 176
  group dynamic, acknowledgement of 161–2
  group stages 170–71
  limiting mind-sets, challenges for 174–5
  peer supervision 164–8
  practicum groups 160–61
  response sharing, example of 159–60
  sculpting the group 177–8
  self-disclosure, setting climate for 157–8
  seven-eyed supervision, process model of 87
  sharing responses 159–60
  structuring the group 158
  styles and foci 154–6
  supervisors 129, 138
  tag supervision 161
  team reviews, facilitation of 173–9
  team supervision 162–4
  techniques for 158–61
  therapeutic engagement during, pitfall of 173
  wider context, exploration of 178–9
  see also peer supervision; team supervision
The Guardian 217
Guggenbuhl-Craig, A. 8, 10, 11
guided fantasy 223

Handy, Charles 196, 198
Harrison, R. 196
Hawkins, P. and Chesterman, D. 15, 21
Hawkins, P. and MacLean, A. 194
Hawkins, P. and Schwenk, G. 76
Hawkins, P. and Shohet, R. 199
Hawkins, P. and Smith, N. 4, 21, 54, 57, 61, 130,
  160–61, 174–5, 220
Hawkins, Peter 15, 17, 26, 28, 52, 60, 72, 73, 78,
  81, 106, 124, 136, 195, 201, 202
Hawthorne, L. 37, 53
healer-patient archetype 11
healing wish, fundamental nature of 14
helping *see* caring
Heron, J. and Reason, P. 77
Heron, John 77, 88, 91, 135, 142
Herskovitz, M.J. 106, 194
Hess, A.K. 50, 52, 57, 69, 74, 134–5
Hillman, James 13, 29, 39
Hippocrates 55
Hofstede, G. and Stodtbeck, F.L. 107
Hogan, R.A. 71
Holloway, E.L. 4, 52
Holloway, E.L. and Carroll, M. 4, 67, 105, 119,
  120
Holloway, E.L. and Neufeldt, S.A. 76
Honey, P. and Mumford, A. 19

hopelessness, coping with senses of 122–3
Houston, Gaie 165–6
Hughes, L. and Pengelly, P. 4
humanistic psychology 223
humanistic psychotherapy 165
humility in
  caring 9–10
  supervisors 50
humour in supervisors 50
Hunt, Pat 34, 99, 221

individual autonomy, danger of 147
individual power in supervision 111–12
informal supervision arrangements 68
informative interventions 135–6
inner space, provision of 23–4
Inskipp, F. and Proctor, B. 4, 34, 35, 67–8, 81,
  109, 111, 154
institutional autonomy, danger of 147–8
inter-personal process recall 140–41
interactivity
  seven-eyed supervision, process model of 99
  in supervisor/supervisee development stages
  74–5
Intercultural Sensitivity 108–9
intergroup 223
internal dialogues 85–6
interpretation 223
interruptions
  'tuning out' 143–4
  unconscious receptors and 95–6
interventions
  intervention categories 87–8
  intervention skills
    seven-eyed supervision, process model of
    87–8
    supervisors 127–8, 135–6
  of supervisee, exploration of 83, 86–8, 114,
  115
intrapsychic 223
introjection 223
isolated practitioners 38–9

Jampolsky, G. 218–19
Jones, M. 208
Jourard, S. 157
Juch, B. 19
Jungian 'shadow side' 8–10

Kadushin, A. 37, 51, 57, 112, 113, 137, 206
Kagan, N. 43, 86, 140–41, 143–4
Karpman, S. 113
Katzenbach, J.R. and Smith, D.K. 162–3
Kelly, G.A. 92
Kevlin, Frank 92

knowledge
  of discipline supervised 50
  of supervisors 127
Kolb, D.A. 77
Kolb, D.A. et al 19
Krishnamurti, Jiddu 205
Kuhn, Thomas 69–70

Ladany, Nick 76
Ladany, Nick et al 76
Langs, Robert 89–90
leadership and supervision 184
learning
  addictive organizations 196, 199–201
  appreciative inquiry 203–5
  back watching in organizations 196, 198
  bureaucratic efficiency, striving for 196,
    197–8
  from the client 89
  co-dependence 200
  co-learners 24
  compulsive pragmatism in 20
  creativity in 7
  crisis driven organizations 196, 198–9
  degenerate supervision and organizational
    culture 196–201
  developing and resourcing ourselves 16–24
  dimensions of relating 21–3
  double loop learning 78
  dynamics of organizational culture,
    degenerate supervision and 196–201
  emotional well-being 21
  engagement with others, increasing capacity
    for 21–3
  generative learning in supervision 206–7
  group approaches to 24
  inner space, provision of 23–4
  learning culture, organizational context of
    supervision 193–208
  learning developmental culture, creation of
    202–3
  learning organization 205–6
  learning patterns 20
  learning style, clarity in and expansion of
    18–20
  love of 16–18
  navel-gazing in 20
  paralysis by analysis 20
  pathways to 207
  personal pathology, hunt for 196–7
  personal practices, renewal and 23–4
  physical well-being 23
  post-mortemization in 20
  problem-centred supervision 197
  process for supervisors 126

pseudo-therapeutic supervision 197
PTSD (post-traumatic stress disorder), learning
     to deal with 29–30
relating with others, increasing capacity for
     21–3
resourcing system, mapping of personal 25
self-renewal and 15–24
self-renewing cultures for 205–6
shifting the cultural pattern 201
single loop learning 78
spiritual practices, renewal and 23–4
supervision and 205–6
totalitarianism in 20
vulnerability, learning and toleration of
     17–18
work effectiveness and 16, 17
see also burn-out; culture; stress
Learning Cycle 77
On Learning From the Patient (Casement, P.) 90
Leddick, R. and Dye, H.A. 50
legitimate power 112
Leong, F.T.L. and Wagner, N.S. 119
Lewin, Kurt 212–13
libido 223
limiting mind-sets, challenges for 174–5
Loganbill, C. et al 57, 72
Loizos, P. 120
love of learning 16–18

McLean, A. and Marshall, J. 194
major themes within microcosm of minute or
     two, training in identification of 142–3
management
  of evaluation and accreditation 147–8
  managerial supervision 60
  manipulation of power games 54
  skills of supervisors 127
Mao Tse-tung 184
mapping
  maps and models of supervision 56–79
  of personal resourcing system 25
  of supervision 136
Marchant, Harold 131
Marken, M. and Payne, M. 131
Maslach, C. 28
Maslow, Abraham 86–7
Mathews, S. and Treacher, A. 102
Mattinson, J. 83, 96
maximize 223
mental stress 27
Menzies, Isobel 197
metaphor in supervision 69–70
metavision 223
Modood, T. and Berthhoud, R. 111
moral actions, formulation of courses of 146

Morrison, Tony 93, 215
motivations
  understanding motives, relevance of 11–12
motivations towards caring 8–14
multi-perspectival view 50
multicultural 223
multifunctional role of supervisors 52
multiple therapeutic agencies, client
     involvement with 185–6
multiple transference 186–7

navel-gazing in learning 20
Neuro Linguistic Programming 70
non-attachment 9–10
non-judgmental attention, training in 142
non-verbal behaviour, sensitivity to 142
note taking 66–7
nursing triad 3, 224

oedipus theory 224
ongoing development, commitment to 128–9
ongoing learning, development of 210, 215
openness
  to inquiry, transcultural work and 105–6
  to learning in supervisors 50, 131–2
  in supervision 217–21
organizational blocks to appropriate supervision
     39–40
  overcoming blocks 40–42
organizational context of contract formation 66
organizational learning 224
Oshry, B. 184
O'Toole, L. 75
outcome-based studies 76

Page, S. 9
Page, S. and Wosket, V. 4, 17, 54, 61, 63, 64–5,
     67
pain and hurt, dealing with 217–18
Papadopoulos, R.K. 120
parallel processing 224
  awareness of 143
  seven-eyed supervision, process model of
     93–5
paralysis by analysis 20
particularist response to culture 105
Passionate Supervision (Shohet, R.) 205
pathways to learning 207
patience in supervisors 50
Payne, C. and Scott, T. 68, 162
peer supervision
  advantages of 165–6
  disadvantages of 165–6
  dynamics of groups 170–79
  formation of peer supervision groups 167–8

group supervision 164–8
  humanistic psychotherapy and 165
  organization of peer supervision meetings 168
  traps of 165–6
persecutor/victim/rescuer triangles 190–91
personal construct theory 224
personal inhibition towards supervision 36–7
personal pathology, hunt for 196–7
personal power in supervision 112
personal practices, renewal and 23–4
phenomenology 224
physical stress 27
physical well-being 23
Pines, A.M. et al 28
Pitman, Liz 214–15
Plant, R. 212
policy and practice in organizations 209–16
political support for change, maximization of 211
post-mortemization in learning 20
power
  abdication of power games 54
  appropriate handling of 50
  cultural power 111–12
  difference and 111–13, 123
  discrepancy in feelings of 11–12
  individual power in supervision 111–12
  legitimate power 112
  manipulation of power games 54
  personal power in supervision 112
  potential misuse of 12
  power relationships 112
  role power 111–12, 113
  taking appropriate 53–4
Power in the Helping Professions (Guggenbuhl-Craig, A.) 10
practical blocks to appropriate supervision 38–9
practicalities in contract formation 64
practice in supervision, dearth of literature 4
practicum groups 160–61
prejudiced feelings 123–4
prescriptive interventions 135–6
problem-centred supervision 197
process 224
  see also seven-eyed supervision, process model of
process-centred level in supervisee development 73
process-in-context-centred level in supervisee development 73–4
process models of supervision 61
Proctor, B. and Inskipp, F. 156
Proctor, Brigid 35, 49, 50, 57, 58–9, 138
projection 224
pseudo-therapeutic supervision 197

psyche 224
psychoanalytic 224
psychodynamic 224
psychotherapy, increase in use of 3–4
PTSD (post-traumatic stress disorder), learning to deal with
  learning 29–30

qualitative function 57, 58, 59, 60
qualities for effective supervision 50–52

race 224
racism 224
rapport with supervisee, achievement of 70
Reason, P. and Bradbury, H. 77, 120
reasons for becoming supervisors 47–9
reflective practice 3, 33
refugees 120–23
relationships 114, 194, 202
  collegial relationships 174
  importance of quality in 220–21
  power relationships 112
  relating with others, increasing capacity for 21–3
  relationship building for supervisors 131
  roles and relationships 178
  social relationships 206
  supervision relationships 113, 144, 167, 173–4
  triangular relationships 138
reliability, assumption of reliability in supervisees 49
reluctant supervisors 48
resources 25, 33, 230–32
resourcing function 57, 58, 59, 60
response sharing, example of 159–60
responsibilities 52, 60
  blueprint of 138
  feelings and 189
  rights and 214
  for supervisees 34, 48, 137
restimulation 224
Revans, R.W. 19
review
  of actions in supervision 61, 62–3
  audit and review in practice development 216
  of developmental approach 74–5
  team reviews, facilitation of 173–9
Rioch, Margaret 170
Rioch, Margaret et al 5, 171–2, 220
Rogerian 224
Rogers, C.R. 50
role conflicts 38, 53–4
role-play 225
role power 111–12, 113

roles of supervisors 52–3
Rose, Geraldine 40–42
Rosinski, P. 107
Rowan, J. 69
Ryan, S. 18
Ryde, Judy 104–5, 107, 121–3, 144

Scaife, J. 4
Scaife, J. and Walsch, S. 173–4
Scaife, J. et al 93
scapegoat 225
Schaef, Ann Wilson 199
Schaef, A.W. and Fassel, Diane 199–201
Schein, E.H. 195
Schutz, W.C. 74, 171
sculpting 177–8, 225
Searles, Harold F. 14, 83, 93
Self and Society: Journal of Humanistic Psychology
204
self-assessment questionnaire 127–9
self-centred level in supervisee development 71
self-disclosure, setting climate for 157–8
self-judgment, protectiveness and 36–7
self-renewal and learning 15–24, 205–6
self-supervision 5, 42–3, 218–19
Senge, P. 15
senior organizational supervisors 129
sensitivity to wider contexts 50
session format in contract formation 66
seven-eyed supervision, process model of 140,
155, 193
  appropriateness, skill of 99–100
  associations, supervisee's use of 92
  brainstorming 87
  choice of focus, factors influencing 101
  client context, focusing on 97
  client focus, what and how they present 82,
  84–6, 114–15
  client/supervisee relationship, exploration of
  83, 88–90, 114, 115–16
  client's transference, attending to 89
  comparatives, supervisee's use of 92
  counter-transference 90–92
  critiques of model 101–2
  describing clients 85
  difference in relation to seven modes 114–18
  distancing, detachment and 88–9
  fixed notions on how work should go 85
  fudge factors 99
  group supervision 87
  hierarchic nature of model 101
  integration of processes 98–100
  integrative nature of 102
  interactivity 99
  internal dialogues, becoming aware of 85–6

interruptions, unconscious receptors and
95–6
intervention categories 87–8
intervention skills 87–8
interventions of supervisee, exploration of 83,
86–8, 114, 115
learning from the patient 89
linking model to development perspective
100–101
listening to the relationship 88–9
modes and foci in 82–4, 84–8
parallel processing 93–5
process model of 80–103
spontaneous association 92
strategies of supervisee, exploration of 83, 86–
8, 114, 115
supervisee/client relationship, focusing on
context of 97
supervisee focus, responses to work with
clients 83, 90–93, 114, 116
supervisee interventions in professional
context, focusing on 97
supervision styles, three types of 99
supervisor, focusing on context of 98
supervisor/client relationship 96
supervisor focus on own processes 83, 95–6,
114, 117–18
supervisors' feelings towards supervisees 95–6
supervisory relationship, focus on 83, 93–5,
114, 116–17
theoretical perspectives, making use of 86
timing, skill of 99–100
unconscious communications from the client
89–90
wider context focus as work happens 84, 96–
8, 102, 114, 118
wider world of supervisee, focusing on 98
sexual abuse, dealing with 187–9
shadow 225
Shainberg, D. 84–6
sharing responses 159–60
Shohet, R. and Wilmot, J. 65
Shohet, Robin 4, 8
single loop learning 78
sociodrama 225
Spice, C.G.J. and Spice, W.H. 130–31
spiritual practices, renewal and 23–4
spiritualityatwork.org 15
splitting 225
  multiple transference and 186–7
spontaneous association 92
standard route for accreditation 227–8
Stolorow, R.G. et al 77
Stoltenberg, C. and Delworth, U. 4, 71, 72, 73,
74–5, 100

stress 225
  accommodation to 221
  avoidance of 26–7
  behavioural stress 27
  flows of 184
  management of 30
  positive aspects of 26
  reflective practice and 3
  sharing of 26–7
  symptoms of 26, 27
Subby, R. 200
Sue, D.W. and Sue, D. 107
supervisees
  interventions in professional context,
    focusing on 97
  supervisee/client relationship, focusing on
    context of 97
  supervisee focus, responses to work with
    clients 83, 90–93, 114, 116
  supervisor/supervisee matrix 81–2
  see also supervision; supervisors
supervision 225
  action agreement 61, 62
  action research 76–9
  active listening 61, 62
  anxieties and multiple transference 186–7
  anxieties of suprevisee in 37
  application of developmental approach 75
  appreciative inquiry, stimulation of 209, 210
  appropriate authority, learning to exercise
    112–13
  arrangement of supervision needs 34–5
  arrangements for 68
  assessment, supervisees anxieties 38
  of asylum seekers 120–23
  audit and review in practice development 216
  authority, difficulties with 37
  BACP ground rules for 57
  blind spots 69
  blocks to receipt of appropriate 36–40
  bucket theory of containment and
    displacement 183–5
  built in action research 78–9
  catalytic intervention 61
  CLEAR supervision model 61–3
  Cleveland sexual abuse case 189–91
  client-centred level in supervisee development
    72–3
  client/supervisee matrix 81–2
  Co-operative Inquiry 77
  complexity of 5–6
  consultancy supervision 60
  containment, bucket theory of 183–5
  continuity in supervision learning 215
  continuous research 78–9

contract negotiation (CLEAR model) 61, 62
contracting for supervision needs 34–5
costs of lack of, demonstration of 210–11
cross-cultural and transcultural work 105
cultural blocks to appropriate 39
cultural neutrality, awareness of lack of
  119–20
cultural orientations 107–8
cultural power 111–12
deaf spots 69
defensive routines against 36–7
definition of 57
depression 186–7
development of supervision policy 209–16
development of transcultural supervision
  119–20
developmental approach to 70–75
developmental function 57–8, 59, 60
displacement, bucket theory of 183–5
double matrix model of supervision process
  80–103
dumb spots 69
effectiveness as supervisee 32
elements in supervision situation 81–2
ethnocentric to ethnorelative development
  108–9
evaluation of supervisors by supervisees 35
experiments in development of supervision
  policy, initiation of 210, 211–12
exploration and reflection 61, 62
exploratory contract interview, outline for
  67–8
factors fuelling resistance to change 212
faith and truth in 220
faith communities, working across 110–11
fear and negativity in 4–5
fearless compassion 220
force-field analysis 212–13
forgiveness, importance of 219
framework choice 79
functions of 4, 57–60
'good enough' 3
hopelessness, coping with senses of 122–3
identification of needs in 40–42
illustrations of different functions 58–9
individual power 111–12
informal supervision arrangements 68
interactions in supervisor/supervisee
  development stages 74–5
Intercultural Sensitivity 108–9
interest in development of supervision policy,
  stimulation of 209, 210–11
isolated practitioners 38–9
leadership and 184
learning and 205–6

Learning Cycle 77
legitimate power 112
managerial supervision 60
maps and models of 56–79
metaphor in 69–70
multiple therapeutic agencies, client
    involvement with 185–6
multiple transference 186–7
ongoing learning, development of 210, 215
openness in 217–21
openness to inquiry, transcultural work and
    105–6
organizational blocks to appropriate 39–40
outcome-based studies 76
overcoming blocks to receipt of appropriate
    40–42
pain and hurt, dealing with 217–18
particularist response to culture 105
persecutor/victim/rescuer triangles 190–91
personal inhibition towards 36–7
personal power 112
policy and practice in organizations 209–16
political support for change, maximization of
    211
power and difference 111–13, 123
practical blocks to appropriate 38–9
practice in, dearth of literature 4
prejudiced feelings 123–4
previous experience, influence on current 36
primary foci of supervision 59
proactivity towards support and 33
process-centred level in supervisee
    development 73
process-in-context-centred level in supervisee
    development 73–4
process models of 61
qualitative function 57, 58, 59, 60
rapport with supervisee, achievement of 70
reflection of supervision needs 33
reflective practice and 3
of refugees 120–23
relationships, importance of quality in 220–
    21
resistances to change, dealing with 210, 212–
    14
resourcing function 57, 58, 59, 60
resourcing oneself through 33
responsibilities for supervisees 34
review of actions 61, 62–3
review of developmental approach 74–5
role conflicts 38, 53–4
role power 111–12, 113
self-centred level in supervisee development
    71
self-judgment, protectiveness and 36–7

self-supervision 42–3, 218–19
sexual abuse, dealing with 187–9
splitting, multiple transference and 186–7
stages in development of supervision policy
    209–16
statement of policy on supervision 214
stress, accommodation to 221
stress, flows of 184
sulutary story on transcultural supervision
    124
supervisee/supervisor matrix 81–2
supervision research 76
supervisor/supervisee relationship 36
supervisory styles 69–70
support, difficulty in receiving 39
taking responsibility for supervision needs
    34–5, 40–42
theoretical framework for 56–79
training supervision 60
transcendentalist response to culture 105
transcultural abilities, improvement in 119–
    20
transcultural effectiveness, stages towards
    108–9
transcultural supervision 104–24
tutorial supervision 60
types of supervision 60–61
understanding culture 106
universalist response to culture 105
vertical supervision 60–61
see also contract formation; group supervision;
    seven-eyed supervision, process model of
supervisors
abdication of power games 54
accreditation 147–8
advanced supervision course 140–44
ambiguities of ethical decisions 146
anxiety management 50
assessment of learning needs 125–9
assumption of reliability in supervisees 49
authority, taking appropriate 53–4
BACP criteria for 227–9
becoming a supervisor 47–55
boundaries of supervision, understanding of
    51
capabilities 126–7
capacities 126–7, 128
catalytic interventions 135–6
cathartic interventions 135–6
challenge and scope of 48
collusive transactions 53
commitment to ongoing development 128–9
competences 126–7
confrontative interventions 135–6
counselling and coaching skills 50

cultural assumptions, dealing with 145, 146
decision making, process for ethical 55
desensitization to triggers 143
ethical decisions, implementation of 146
ethical dilemmas, training in 144, 146
ethical principles 54–5
ethical sensitivity, creation of 146
evaluation 147–8
experienced route for accreditation 228–9
experiences and expectations 49, 50–51, 52
experiential training 130–31
exploration of supervision 133
feedback, giving and receiving 134–5
flexibility in 50
focus for good supervision 51–2
framework for supervising, development of
    51–2
group and team supervision, course in 138–9
group supervision 129, 138
helping roles 52–3
hidden motives for becoming 48–9
humility in 50
humour in 50
individual autonomy, danger of 147
informative interventions 135–6
institutional autonomy, danger of 147–8
inter-personal process recall, use of 140–41
interruptions, 'tuning out' 143–4
intervention skills 127–8, 135–6
knowledge 127
knowledge of discipline supervised 50
learning process for 126
major themes within microcosm of minute or
    two, training in identification of 142–3
management of evaluation and accreditation
    147–8
management skills 127
manipulation of power games 54
mapping supervision 136
moral actions, formulation of courses of 146
multi-perspectival view in 50
multifunctional role of 52
new supervisors, core supervision for 132–6
non-judgmental attention, training in 142
non-verbal behaviour, sensitivity to 142
openness to learning 50, 131–2
parallel process, awareness of 143
patience in 50
prerequisites for effectiveness as 49, 50–52
prescriptive interventions 135–6
qualities required in effective 50–52
reasons for becoming 47–9
relationship building 131
reluctant supervisors 48
responsibilities blueprint 138

roles of 52–3
self-assessment questionnaire for 127–9
senior organizational supervisors 129
sensitivity to wider contexts 50
standard route for accreditation 227–8
starting out 49
student and practice supervisors, core
    supervision for 137–8
student responsibilities 137–8
sub-roles of 52
supervisory feedback skills 133–5
supervisory responsibilities 137–8
teaching group supervision skills 138–9
therapeutic supervision courses 139–40
training and development, key principles 130
training and development of 125–48
training courses, setting up of 129–32
transcultural abilities 50
transcultural supervision, training in 144–6
trigger tape questions 143
types of training courses for 132
unconscious reactivity, notice of 143
video, use of 140–42
symbiotic 225
Symington, N. 8

tag supervision 161
team supervision
    advantages of 163
    disadvantages of 163
    dynamics of groups 170–79
    effective team characteristics 163
    group selection 164
    group supervision 162–4
    team as entity needing supervision 164
    team characteristics 162–3
    working group, characteristics of 162
theoretical framework for supervision 56–79
theoretical perspectives, making use of 86
therapeutic community 225
therapeutic engagement 173
therapeutic supervision courses 139–40
therapeutic triad 225
timing, skill of 99–100
Tonnesmann, Dr Margaret 221
totalitarianism in learning 20
training
    and development, key principles 130
    and development of supervisors 125–48
    setting up of courses for supervisors 129–32
    training supervision 60
transactional analysis 225–6
transcendentalist response to culture 105
transcultural abilities 50, 119–20
transcultural competence 226

transcultural effectiveness, stages towards 108–9
transcultural supervision 104–24
  training in 144–6
transference 226
trigger tape questions 143
Trivasse, M. 120
Trompenaars, A. 107
Tuckman, B. 171
Tudor, K. and Worrall, M. 101, 140–41
tutorial supervision 60
Tutu, Archbishop Desmond 220
Tyler, F.B. et al 105
types of supervision 60–61
types of training courses for supervisors 132

unconscious 226
  unconscious communications from the client
    89–90
  unconscious reactivity, notice of 143
Understanding Organizations (Handy, C.) 198
United States 4
universalist response to culture 105

van Ooijen, E. 20
vertical supervision 60–61
video, use of 140–42
vulnerability, learning and toleration of 17–18

Weerdenburg, Oscar van 108–9
Weerdenburg, O.v. and Brinkmann, U. 108
Whitehead, A.N. and Russell, B. 101
wider context
  exploration in group supervision 178–9
  focus as work happens 84, 96–8, 102, 114, 118
  wider world of supervisee, focusing on 98
Wilmot, Joan 94
Wilmot, Joan and Shohet, Robin 94
Winnicott, Donald W. 3, 217, 221
Woodcock, J. 121
work effectiveness and learning 16, 17
working alliance in contract formation 65
working group, characteristics of 162
worklifesupport.com 15
Worrall, M. and Tudor, K. 142–3
Worthington, E.L. 71